ELECTRONIC MARKETING AND THE CONSUMER

editor
ROBERT A. PETERSON

ELECTRONIC MARKETING AND THE CONSUMER

SAGE Publications
International Educational and Professional Publisher
Thousand Oaks   London   New Delhi

For information:

SAGE Publications, Inc.
2455 Teller Road
Thousand Oaks, California 91320
E-mail: order@sagepub.com

SAGE Publications Ltd.
6 Bonhill Street
London EC2A 4PU
United Kingdom

SAGE Publications India Pvt. Ltd.
M-32 Market
Greater Kailash I
New Delhi 110 048 India

Printed in the United States of America

Library of Congress Cataloging-in-Publication Data

Main entry under title:

Electronic marketing and the consumer / editor, Robert A. Peterson.
p.   cm.
Includes bibliographical references and index.
ISBN 0-7619-1069-7 (acid-free paper). — ISBN 0-7619-1070-0 (pbk.: acid-free paper)
1. Internet marketing. 2. Broadcast advertising. 3. Twenty-first century—Forecasts. I. Peterson, Robert A. (Robert Allen), 1944–
HF5415.1265.E395   1997
656.8'4—dc21   97-4753

This book is printed on acid-free paper.

97 98 99 00 01 02 03 10 9 8 7 6 5 4

Production Editor: Sherrise Purdum

Contents

List of Tables and Figures

TABLES

FIGURES

Foreword

In the late 40s and 50s, when I first became involved in the use of radio and
television for soliciting mail orders, even the leading direct marketers such as
Sears Roebuck and Montgomery Ward never paid much attention to a medium
that they believed offered little revenue potential. This was in spite of the fact
that, even in the early days of radio mail-order advertising, it was not unusual for
a radio station such as WCKY in Cincinnati, KXLO in St. Louis, WLW in New
Orleans, or one of several stations on the Mexican border (such as XENT or
XERF) to deliver as many as 7,000 mail orders in a single day.

At the very dawn of television, when major advertisers would not even
consider the medium viable because of the limited number of sets in use, many
stations relied on electronic mail-order advertisers clients for their cash flow and
to help limit losses. Even more significant losses were experienced by early
cable program originators such as Ted Turner, who found great resistance from
general advertisers when cable was able to deliver only about two percent of the
TV homes and had not achieved a five percent penetration in any major
marketing area. It was not unusual during this period for electronic mail-order
advertisers to pay in advance to help cable pioneers meet their payrolls.

I use the term "mail order" instead of "direct marketing" because that's
really how the electronic media functioned. Their forte was a direct solicitation of
a sale for a product or a service, which in most cases was then delivered through
the U.S. mail.

Today, creative marketers visualize the importance that radio, television,
cable, and computer networks will bring to the marketing world of the twenty-
first century. These individuals also visualize the future success of proprietary
products, as well as business-to-business marketing, accomplished through three-
dimensional video presentations and fiber optic communication networks.

There is no doubt that the Communication Revolution will reverse many
of the trends of the Industrial Revolution. People will no longer need to live in

heavily populated areas. Education will be delivered to small clusters of students or even totally through at-home study. People will be able to shop Harrod's of London, the Bazaar of Turkey, and the flea markets of Africa or Asia as casually as they now shop their local malls. Many of the new concepts and technologies will originate or be structured in the halls of ivy and will be championed by future generations of students.

For such reasons symposia such as one the that resulted in this book are so important. Not only do they bring academics and practitioners together to speculate about the future, they also facilitate the transfer of knowledge to today's students, who in turn will create the future. Likewise, this book is important because it will stimulate students' thinking about electronic marketing, both as it is employed today and as it will be employed in the future.

Alvin Eicoff
A. Eicoff & Company

Preface

Electronic Marketing and the Consumer derives its title from a symposium held at The University of Texas at Austin. This symposium brought together a diverse group marketing academics and business practitioners from across the United States. The academic participants came from numerous public and private educational institutions, whereas the business participants came from firms ranging from sole proprietorships to *Fortune 50* companies. In addition, the symposium attracted representatives from both nonprofit and governmental organizations. In all, nearly one hundred people actively participated in the symposium.

The symposium's mission was straightforward: to obtain up-to-date insights on applying and evaluating "electronic marketing" in the context of marketing to consumers. Electronic marketing was viewed broadly as consisting of marketing that is accomplished or facilitated by any number of devices, techniques, tools, technologies, or systems that rely on electrical impulses. The intent of the symposium, and consequently this book, was to establish a better understanding of how electronic marketing affects consumers as well as the overall discipline of marketing. Many electronic marketing applications, such as broadcast fax, telemarketing, and EDI, are relatively developed and understood in the context of business-to-business marketing. However, there is a gap in knowledge regarding the application of electronic marketing to consumers. The purpose of the symposium and the book was to fill this gap.

As might be expected, because of the breadth of electronic marketing, only selected aspects could be covered in the symposium. Specifically, the symposium consisted of plenary sessions followed by lively give-and-take discussions. For virtually every opinion or conclusion offered, a counter opinion or conclusion was set forth. It is an understatement to say that interaction among symposium participants was both extensive and intensive.

There were three types of plenary sessions, "foundation" sessions wherein particular aspects of an electronic marketing topic were overviewed, "application" sessions wherein practitioners related how their firms actually applied electronic marketing, and "research" sessions wherein the results of empirical studies involving electronic marketing were reported. Sessions addressed such marketing topics as database marketing, television retailing, and on-line shopping. Other topics included likely manifestations of consumer behavior in the next few years and technical and social issues relating to consumer surveillance and privacy on the Internet. In addition to the plenary sessions, several "break-out" sessions allowed groups of symposium participants to discuss in depth the implications of the information presented and make predictions regarding consumer-focused electronic marketing in the future.

Although completely capturing the essence of the symposium would be impossible, this book tries valiantly to do so. Nine of the eleven chapters (Chapters 2 through 10) communicate the material presenters transmitted to audience members at the symposium. Chapter 1 provides a context for the material covered in the book and attempts to circumscribe the domain of electronic marketing and to stimulate thinking about one particular electronic marketing medium, the Internet. The final chapter, which resulted from the symposium's break-out sessions, attempts to coalesce several predictions made at the symposium regarding electronic marketing. The book also attempts to convey both the excitement and the promise of electronic marketing, as well as its challenges and implications.

According to Molenaar (1996, p. 23), the 1990s ushered in five new marketing strategies: lean marketing, turbo marketing, customized marketing, relationship marketing, and integrated marketing communications. Currently electronic marketing appears to be leading to a sixth marketing strategy: performance-based marketing. A common thread across electronic marketing applications, broadly speaking, is that the applications provide a mechanism for making marketing accountable by directly linking resources expended on an activity to revenues and profits generated by the activity. As such, electronic marketing is leading to changes in how firms will conceptualize and execute marketing in the future.

Electronic marketing, as well as the technologies that have enabled the concept of electronic marketing, has implications going far beyond those suggested by the concept of performance-based marketing. Electronic marketing and its underlying technologies both determine and reflect changes that are occurring in society and in economic systems. These changes are creating contradictory trends that are both amorphous and concrete, unique and interdependent, so much so that it is almost impossible to discursively separate them. Consider just the following two trends that have been fomented by electronic marketing and its underlying technologies. The first is the trend toward "marketing virtuality"—virtual companies, virtual distribution channels, and virtual stores. The second is the trend in consumer behavior. Given their "empowerment" through electronic marketing, consumers are increasingly displaying a tendency to be more proactive, assertive, and unpredictable in their shopping, buying, and consuming behaviors. They are also becoming less brand and firm loyal.

Next, consider in turn the influence of the following on electronic marketing (and consumers). Due in part to technological advances and structural changes in the (global) economy, lifetime employment with a single company is probably a relic of the past. Companies are moving as rapidly as possible toward shorter and shorter term contracts for their workers in attempts to increase efficiency and flexibility and minimize overhead. Workers in such situations are increasingly under contract with two or more companies simultaneously and will increasingly work from their homes or in temporary quarters leased by their employers. The implications of such employment arrangements are multifold. At a minimum, pension plans and health care will have to be reformulated and linked to an individual, not to an employer. Not only will people work out of their homes, many of them in electronic marketing applications, but these homes will be geographically distant from their employers. One may work for a (virtual) corporation based in the Netherlands, but be physically situated in Peru. This, in turn, has major implications for cities. Indeed, as McRae (1994, p. 176) speculated, "the glue holding a city together will increasingly become cultural and social, rather than economic," such that cities that have "developed a high intellectual and cultural base will prosper at the expense of those which have not."

This book exists because of the assistance of a number of organizations and individuals. The IC^2 Institute and the Graduate School of Business at The University of Texas at Austin cosponsored the symposium. Consequently, special thanks are due to Dr. Robert S. Sullivan, director of the IC^2 Institute, and Dr. Robert G. May, dean of the Graduate School of Business, for supporting the symposium. Although numerous individuals deserve thanks, without the assistance of Galen Bollinger, Bobby Duncan, and Linda Teague, this book would never have been completed in a timely fashion. Last, but not least, great appreciation is due Alvin Eicoff, an electronic marketing pioneer and the person who not only originated the idea for the symposium but also provided the resources to ensure that it took place. Thanks, Al.

Robert A. Peterson
The University of Texas at Austin

1

Electronic Marketing:
Visions, Definitions, and Implications

Robert A. Peterson

Thirty years ago, in an article published in the *Harvard Business Review*, Doody and Davidson (1967) articulated their vision of what currently might be termed "electronic shopping." Paraphrasing Doody and Davidson, think about Susan Brown sitting down at a desk in her kitchen at approximately 11:15 on a Thursday night. Above her desk is a "tiny color television screen" mounted on the kitchen wall. She is about to do her weekly shopping.

To begin her shopping session, "Susan lifts the protective cover from the Direct-Shop console on the desk and presses a set of buttons that connects her directly with the Customer Communications Department of Citywide Distribution Center, Incorporated" (p. 4). With a series of keystrokes, "[I]mages of many kinds of merchandise appear on the screen, some fleetingly and some held several seconds for her examination" (p. 5). When Susan finishes her shopping, she presses a tally button on the console and a recap of her order appears on the television screen. The recap itemizes her purchases and provides a total price. After examining the order, Susan makes another keystroke that confirms and clears the order, thus authorizing Citywide "to begin processing the order and clearing payment from her checkless banking account" (p. 5).

Doody and Davidson's vision is as intuitively appealing now as it was when articulated. The vision incorporated a comprehensive, yet flexible, distribution system for grocery products, drugs, and sundries. It used a central distribution facility and electronic funds transfer to control costs. It simplified consumer shopping by allowing routine processing of frequently purchased goods. Automated order filling and next-day delivery were standard features.

In addition to presenting their vision of electronic shopping, Doody and Davidson addressed numerous implications of the vision, including disintermediation and changes in the role of advertising and packaging. This remarkably prescient vision brings to mind recent endeavors of companies such as Peapod, Streamline, and ShoppingLink. At the same time, though, the vision was a bit deficient in the sense that the timing was optimistic: Doody and

Davidson believed that their vision of electronic shopping would be operational
in the 1970s.

A STARTING POINT

What, one might ask, is the purpose of the Doody and Davidson anecdote?
Given the themes of this book, "electronic marketing" and "the consumer," the
purpose of the anecdote is threefold. First, it is simply to introduce the notion of
electronic marketing with an example that is inherently interesting and
simultaneously informative, and at least moderately provocative. In other words,
the intent is to attract a reader's attention and entice him or her to continue
reading. The second purpose is less obvious; it is to illustrate two tendencies
that seem to characterize discussions of electronic marketing—the tendency to
always be future oriented and the tendency to be optimistic regarding the
implementation of electronic marketing techniques and activities. The third
purpose is to establish a starting point for discussing what electronic marketing
"is" and what it "is not." Stated somewhat differently, the Doody and Davidson
anecdote provides a context for the material to be presented in this book. If a
reader has made it this far, the first purpose has been accomplished. The other
two require some elaboration.

Visions and Predictions

Even today, thirty years after Doody and Davidson's vision, discussions of
electronic marketing tend to be both future oriented and optimistic. For example,
Burger (1996) predicted that by the year 2000 sales of goods and services through
electronic marketing would reach $230 billion (up from an estimated $3.4
billion in 1996)—a figure that appears to be very optimistic. In 1980,
Schneiderman (p. 60) predicted that by 1990 "American consumers will be
buying fully one-half of all general merchandise without setting foot in a retail
store," a forecast that, although intriguing, has yet to be realized and perhaps
never will be. This optimism, though, is no different from most visions of the
future that focus on relatively esoteric phenomena. Apart from those
prognosticators who seek notoriety by specializing in "gloom and doom"
predictions, exceptions to this observation of optimism are rare. Consider the
literally thousands of "predictions" contained in the widely cited *The Book of
Predictions* (Wallechinsky, Wallace, and Wallace 1981). Most are either
explicitly or implicitly positive. The pessimistic view of science and technology
that Bertrand Russell (1924) set forth in *ICARUS or the Future of Science* is
notable only because it was so negative.

In the same vein, visions of the future often tend to be influenced by either
the intended audience or the purpose for which they have been developed.

Klopfenstein (1989), analyzing 29 forecasts of the home video market, that "[n]ot surprisingly, the audience to which the report is directed has bearing on its content. Few studies were pessimistic.... Many of the reports ... painted a very rosy picture of the home video market. An optimistic bias in such reports seems almost inherent" (p. 23).

Eight decades ago, Steinmetz (1915) correctly predicted the existence of electric automobiles, temperature-controlled homes (i.e., homes with centralized electrical heating and air conditioning), wireless telephones (cell telephones), and cooking by electricity on the kitchen table (microwave ovens). Despite these successful predictions, most of Steinmetz's predictions were incorrect. (Similar to most incorrect predictions, Steinmetz's faulty forecasts seem to have been forgotten.) Incidentally, notwithstanding the fact that Steinmetz worked for the electricity-generating industry, most of his predictions that related to a "better life" for consumers were predicated on the use of electricity.

As an aside, Doody and Davidson should be commended for the specificity of their vision and especially for their boldness in providing a temporal boundary on it. Most visions of the future appear to be so ambiguous, abstract, or even obtuse that they are subject to multiple interpretations and rarely can be shown to be false. Consider a prediction that Kahn and Wiener (1967), perhaps the foremost futurists of their day, made at the same time that Doody and Davidson were articulating their vision. Kahn and Wiener (also) predicted that "automated grocery and department stores" were likely to exist by the year 2000. Although concise and perhaps intuitive, what exactly does this prediction imply? Does the prediction imply that there will be completely automated grocery and department stores in which customers order through computers and robots fill, ship, and deliver the order, as per the Doody and Davidson vision? Or does it simply imply that grocery and department stores will be using scanning devices at checkout counters? At this time, Kahn and Wiener's prediction is either completely correct, completely incorrect, or both correct and incorrect. In their defense, however, Kahn and Wiener did predict several innovations that, in retrospect, were right on target and either reflected or incorporated electronic marketing techniques. A few of these predictions are presented in Table 1.1; readers are encouraged to interpret the predictions liberally.

Electronic Shopping Revisited

Writing in the *Harvard Business Review* a decade after Doody and Davidson published their vision, McNair and May (1978) acknowledged that Doody and Davidson were perhaps a bit optimistic with respect to when their vision would occur. However, although they disagreed with Doody and Davidson's timing, they agreed completely with the vision. In particular, McNair and May stated that "some authorities expect that by early in the twenty-first century, almost all food and other basic household needs will be acquired through the use of in-home television computer systems, and shopping choices will be made after viewing assortments, selections, prices, and brands on the television screen, together with programming of the household's customary wants, needs, customs, and habits" (p. 81).

Table 1.1. Technical Innovations Very Likely 1967–2000

Inexpensive design and procurement of "one of a kind" items through use of computerized analysis and automated production [mass customization!]

Extensive and intensive centralization (or automatic interconnection) of current and past personal and business information in high-speed data processors [databases/legacy systems!]

Automated universal (real time) credit, audit and banking systems [ATMs!]

Simple inexpensive home video recording and playing

Inexpensive high-capacity, worldwide, regional, and local (home and business) communication (perhaps using satellites, lasers, and light pipes) [fiber optics!]

Practical home and business use of "wired" video communication for both telephone and TV (possibly including retrieval of taped material from libraries or other sources) and rapid transmission and reception of facsimiles (possibly including news, library material, commercial announcements, instantaneous mail delivery, other printouts, and so on)

Pervasive business use of computers for the storage, processing, and retrieval of information

Shared time (public and interconnected?) computers generally available to home and business on a metered basis

Other widespread use of computers for intellectual and professional assistance (translation, teaching, literature search, medical diagnosis, traffic control, crime detection, computation, design, analysis and to some degree as intellectual collaborator generally)

Personal "pagers" (perhaps even two-way pocket phones) and other personal electronic equipment for communication, computing, and data processing [cell phones!]

Direct broadcasts from satellites to home receivers

Inexpensive (less than $20), long lasting, very small battery operated TV receivers

Home computers to "run" household and communicate with outside world

Inexpensive (less than one cent a page), rapid high-quality black and white reproduction; followed by color and high-detailed photography reproduction— perhaps for home as well as office use

Conference TV (both closed circuit and public communication system)

Source: Adapted from Kahn and Wiener (1967), *The Year 2000,* New York, NY: The Macmillan Company, pp. 52–56.

McNair and May then proceeded to present a more concrete notion of what they termed teleshopping than did Doody and Davidson. In particular, McNair and May thought teleshopping would be accomplished by "television scanning of store shelves, a kind of TV catalog located in existing supermarkets" that would allow consumers to "interact with the TV catalog to obtain additional desired information, or to delete unwanted data" (p. 86). Analogous to Doody and Davidson, McNair and May discussed factors that would facilitate the implementation of their version of teleshopping, as well as some of the potential implications. With respect to these implications, McNair and May believed that "electronic distribution might have capital cost advantages [because] it could use less expensive real estate" and "the amount of inventory needed to meet consumer demand would be significantly lowered as a result of the decline in the number of outlets [required]" (p. 88).

Rosenberg and Hirschman (1980), also writing in the *Harvard Business Review,* attempted to refine the notion of electronic shopping even further. Specifically, although Rosenberg and Hirschman believed that distribution would be fully automated and that payment would be made through electronic funds transfer, they proffered an "in-home display catalog" operating through a form of telecommunications. Like Doody and Davidson, and McNair and May, Rosenberg and Hirschman believed that electronic shopping would irreversibly transform traditional or conventional retailing. As one might expect, this belief is relatively widespread. Even Isaac Asimov, a leading science fiction writer and noted futurist, had an opinion on the subject of electronic shopping. In 1977, Asimov (1977, p. 53) wrote that

> The year 2025 will see the "drive-in market," a kind of computerized convenience store. The customer will call the store by using his own computer, and make his grocery list. The order will automatically be picked off the shelves of a computerized warehouse, packed, and ready for pickup by car, or whatever mechanized vehicle we'll be driving in during the next century. Only liquids will not be packaged this way.

Whether Asimov drew upon the vision of Doody and Davidson will never be known. Likewise, whether Doody and Davidson themselves drew upon Bellamy's (1888) vision of an automated product distribution system in the year 2000 will also never be known.

A Lack of Predictability

Before leaving the topic of visions relating to electronic shopping, we should reflect on one particular aspect of electronic marketing: the fact that electronic marketing is, at its essence, based on advances made in electronic circuitry and related technologies, especially digitization. In the context of electronic marketing, a technological advance represents what might be termed a market discontinuity—a "shift in any of the market forces or their interrelationships that cannot be predicted by a continuation of historical trends and that, if it occurs, can dramatically affect the performance of a firm or an industry" (Mahajan and Wind 1989, p. 187). For example, the integrated circuit is a market discontinuity; it has effected and will continue to effect changes in marketing strategy, marketing tactics, and marketing operations that are simply not foreseeable.

No prediction, vision, or forecast to date has accurately charted either the occurrence of those technological advances that currently "drive" electronic marketing or the speed with which they have occurred. Given the quantum leaps that have taken place in technology (and the consequent decreasing product life cycles), it should not be surprising that predictions regarding electronic marketing have been faulty. Moreover, it should not be surprising that, notwithstanding media hype, to date most attempts to apply electronic marketing have resulted in less than resounding success. Analogous to the success of new products in general, it would seem that the success of various electronically dependent marketing activities is influenced more by consumer acceptance than by the characteristics of the underlying technology per se. (Consumer acceptance, in turn, is influenced by consumer expectations.) Similar to the introduction of "vaporware," many "electronic technologies" are introduced by creating unrealistic—and unobtainable—consumer expectations before the technologies have been perfected. Not meeting consumer expectations virtually guarantees lack of acceptance. All of this cumulates in a simple conclusion: no one can predict what the future holds for electronic marketing, especially given the increasingly assertive and unpredictable behavior of consumers (Molenaar 1996, p. 102ff).

This is particularly true for perhaps that most pervasive "electronic technology" yet—the Internet. Even such well-regarded marketing visionaries as Hyde, Steidtmann, and Sweeney (1990) failed to acknowledge the existence of the Internet and foresee its potential impacts on the practice of marketing in their widely circulated forecast at the beginning of the decade. Similarly, in a major investigation conducted for the Direct Marketing Association on the implications of technology on direct marketing, Deloitte & Touche (1990) never addressed the Internet and World Wide Web, even though they have become the focal point of direct marketing in less than three years. As recently as 1995, the Web browser Mosaic was deemed "the on-line world's killer app" in a Standard and Poor's Industrial Survey ("Computers" 1995). By the beginning of 1996, Mosaic had disappeared from the marketer's lexicon.

WHAT IS ELECTRONIC MARKETING?

So far in this discussion, the definition of "electronic marketing" has been purposefully ignored. What is electronic marketing? Although literally hundreds of references to electronic marketing have appeared in both the popular press and the academic literature in the past couple of years (a *Business Periodicals Index* subject search yielded 108 different search subcategories for the term "electronic marketing"), no agreed-upon definition currently exists. Some pundits (e.g., Kiley 1995) view electronic marketing relatively narrowly as "selling on-line or via the Internet." Others (e.g., Hoge 1993) view it more broadly as including television, radio, telephones, multimedia kiosks, video catalogs, and so forth.

Even a cursory reading of business or marketing dictionaries (e.g., Williamson 1994; Bennett 1995) reveals that most do not yet contain a definition of electronic marketing. This is due in part to the recency of the term, together with the likelihood that no one has yet perceived a need to define it precisely. Definitions that do exist appear to be somewhat inconsistent.

Consider the following representative dictionary excerpts. Rosenberg .(1995, p. 107) defined electronic marketing as "utilizing electronically generated consumer purchase information in marketing and sales promotion activities; used in supermarkets and other stores where information is received by having customers use computer-readable cards, such as bar codes, that log data on their product purchases." Rosenberg also distinguished between electronic marketing and electronic direct marketing. Specifically, he defined "electronic direct marketing" as "an interactive unit that unites the ideas of direct marketing with television, radio, and/or the telephone" (p. 107). Koschnick (1995) did not directly define electronic marketing but did, however, define "electronic shopping" as "the use of electronic devices to complete purchases remotely through interactive video systems, computer networks, or telephones" (p. 173). He thought that to be effective, "electronic marketing must be based on widely affordable, standardized, or specifically modifiable products; on information (when there is not necessarily a physical product); and on limited services (such as travel or event reservations). For electronic marketing to work, customers must have some preconceived ideas of what they want to buy" (p. 173). Similarly, Baker (1995) did not refer directly to electronic marketing. However, like Koschnick, he defined "electronic shopping" as a subset of home shopping, with offering systems that include videotext services, shopping channels, and interactive cable television systems. Not only are such definitions inconsistent, they are ambiguous and probably too narrow in scope, especially if the term "electronic marketing" is considered literally.

Even so, despite this definitional lacuna, we will not attempt to precisely define electronic marketing here. Doing so is neither necessary nor constructive for our purposes. It is, however, instructive to consider what currently constitutes electronic marketing. Marketing (per se) is typically defined as "a social and managerial process by which individuals and groups obtain what they need and want through creating, offering, and exchanging products of value with others" (Kotler 1997, p. 9). When modifying marketing, the word "electronic" implies the use of electronic devices, appliances, tools, technologies, techniques, and/or systems in marketing. Thus, if electronic marketing is in fact marketing that is accomplished or facilitated through the application of electronic devices, appliances, tools, techniques, technologies, and/or systems, then much of what passes for marketing today can be called "electronic marketing."

In particular, electronic marketing is considered here as marketing that is accomplished or facilitated by

- Radio
- Television (both one-way and two-way transmissions)
- Computers and computer-based technologies (including databases)
- Telephone and telephone-based technologies
- Facsimile machines
- Videography (including that found on shopping carts)
- CD-ROM technologies
- Interactive kiosks
- ETMs (electronic ticket machines)
- Pagers
- Optical scanners
- Smart cards

The above list is obviously only illustrative. No claim is made that this list of facilitating devices or technologies is either mutually exclusive or exhaustive. Indeed, it should be apparent that no comprehensive "list" can ever be developed. The devices and technologies constitute a hodge-podge; they are being physically combined and modified continuously, and new devices and technologies are being added weekly.

Commonalities

Apart from falling under the general rubric of being electronically based and facilitating the process of marketing to consumers, the devices and technologies listed possess certain other commonalities. For example, by definition, all require an electrical current or impulse to function, and all rely on the electronic transmission of data. Each, in its own way, reflects and incorporates some form of "advanced" technology, most of which is or probably will soon be based on digitization and integrated circuits. Virtually none were developed with the intention of facilitating marketing, especially to consumers. Rather, most were developed without any thought to marketing at all or to consumers per se. In fact, most of them—including facsimile machines, pagers, television, and computers—were developed for either business use or for the military.

Further, businesses and consumers use most of the devices independently of their role as facilitators of the marketing process (although many require the cooperation or even direct interaction of marketers and consumers when employed in a marketing context). Finally, most of these devices or technologies are inherently linked through computers, and there is a rapid coalescing of computer and communication technologies in electronic marketing activities.

From a marketing perspective, what the devices and technologies have in common is that they allow marketers to measure the results of marketing activities and hold the activities accountable. When electronic marketing is considered in the context of television, for example, it is thought of with regard to direct response advertising, television-based shopping, and infomercials. Image advertising is not considered as being in the realm of electronic marketing. Consequently, electronic marketing is frequently co-aligned with the more common term, "direct marketing."

Of the existing electronic devices and technologies, the Internet and its World Wide Web (WWW) probably receive the most attention in the news media. Even so, their influence, from a financial as well as a marketing perspective, is currently minimal with respect to consumer marketing. Even such common appliances as facsimile machines (e.g., broadcast fax) and telephones (inbound and outbound telemarketing) have many times the impact of the Internet or the World Wide Web as marketing facilitators. Likewise, computers are being used much more effectively by marketers managing the personal selling function (e.g., Moriarty and Swartz 1989; Schwartz 1996) than by consumers proactively involved in the marketing process through the Internet or World Wide Web. Despite its present status, the Internet/WWW is intriguing enough that it will be discussed later.

Electronic versus Interactive

In many regards, electronic marketing appears to be a term like interactive marketing. Neither term has been rigorously defined, and both are relatively ambiguous. Yet, both are widely used terms whose respective meanings appear to be generally understood. Technically, the two terms differ in that *electronic marketing* is a general *method* of marketing (through the use of electronic devices or electronically based technologies), whereas *interactive marketing* is a general *approach* to marketing (creating a situation or mechanism through which a marketer and a consumer can interact, usually in "real time"). As such, direct selling exemplifies one type of interactive marketing that is not necessarily electronically based. Usually, though, interactive marketing uses some form of electronic marketing to achieve its purpose. Moreover, the two terms are frequently used interchangeably, even though they are technically not the same. See, for example, Forrest and Mizerski (1996) for illustrations of their interchangeability.

Clearer communication might result from simply eliminating the use of both terms unless they are placed in a very specific context or employing more precise terminology. Or perhaps a new, more descriptive term should be coined that combines and supersedes them. To illustrate the coining of a new term in the context of direct marketing, A. T. Kearney (1995) defined "new media" as

> Any electronic, interactive communications media that allow the user to request or receive delivery of information, entertainment, marketing materials, products, and services.

From an applications or operations perspective, cataloging the respective characteristics of electronic and interactive marketing may be necessary so that they can be applied without confusion. Given the rapidity with which changes are occurring in the scope and nature of both, however, today's definitions and distinctions might be outmoded tomorrow.

IMPLICATIONS OF ELECTRONIC MARKETING

It is possible to become enamored and even overwhelmed by the devices and technologies used in electronic marketing and miss what is arguably electronic marketing's most important contribution to business: making marketing more accountable. Succinctly stated, electronic marketing has been instrumental in creating what might be termed "performance-based marketing." Although this point was made previously, it is worth repeating because of its importance. Electronic marketing has also enabled the practical application of relationship marketing, micro marketing (or targeted marketing), mass customization, and so forth, but these contributions pale in comparison with the impact electronic marketing has had on strategic thinking at the business unit level. Partly because of the manner in which electronic marketing is—and can be—applied, marketing strategies of all kinds now incorporate quantifiable success criteria and action plans whose results are measurable. Resources must link directly to revenues and profitability. It is not an exaggeration to state that electronic marketing has been instrumental in changing the fundamental business paradigm.

One of the side effects of accountability is that it has fostered new business partnerships in which the participants share risks and rewards. Consider the following illustration. Not that long ago, television stations would simply rent time to firms wishing to air direct response advertisements or informercials. Now, because of the desire for accountability, together with the means of measuring results due to electronic marketing, television stations frequently forgo a portion or all of the "rent" to share in the rewards of a successful advertisement or infomerical. In return for sharing the risk, rendering payment a function of performance, a television station gets to share in the rewards of its partner's marketing program. By entering into a partnership, both firms limit their risk exposure in return for a portion of the reward.

Impact of the Internet

Although the rubric of electronic marketing encompasses numerous devices and technologies, one technology has so captivated both the public's and businesses' attention that it has become almost synonymous with the term electronic marketing. This is the Internet and its World Wide Web. The subject of *electronic commerce* (on the Internet) has engendered a level of interest perhaps unprecedented in the history of business (see Hoffman and Novak [1996] for some interesting insights on "Internet marketing"). Without question, the interest level has increased more rapidly and widely than any phenomenon in memory. It is perhaps not too hyperbolic to state that interest has spread with the speed of an epidemic. As Fox (1995) so lucidly noted, however, no one can accurately predict what the impact of the Internet will be on business and even on life in general as close as one year in the future or as distant as a decade. The Internet may be more influential in cost reduction (i.e., as a viable alternative to commercial electronic data interchange networks) than in revenue generation (i.e., as a repository of virtual stores for businesses). Consumers may use it for entertainment, in their work, or as a delivery medium for products, services, or information (Miller 1996).

Six ways to make money on the Internet currently exist: (1) marketing existing products or services, (2) selling advertising space, (3) charging fees for accessible content (e.g., on a Web site), (4) charging fees for on-line transactions or links, (5) providing technical services, or (6) writing books or presenting lectures on using the Internet. Experience to date suggests that only the latter has been consistently profitable, albeit at rather low levels. Internet-related business success is currently more hope and hype than reality. Witness such book titles as *How to Make a Fortune on the Information Superhighway: Everyone's Guerrilla Guide to Marketing on the Internet and Other On-line Services* (Canter and Siegal 1994) and *Selling on the Internet: How to Open An Electronic Storefront and Have Millions of Customers Come to You* (Gonyea and Gonyea 1996) as illustrative of the hope and hype. This, though, is likely to change. What has already changed, however, are mindsets and behaviors. What will change are cultures and world views.

The Internet and Taxes. In virtually the blink of an eye, the Internet has given new meaning to the terms "international business" and "global presence." In the last decade, individuals as well as firms of all sizes and from nearly all countries have attempted to internationalize their businesses and create what might be termed a global presence. The more successful firms have traditionally been the larger ones, those with the financial resources and personnel to physically establish a presence in a variety of countries. The idea of selling products on the Internet with a server located in one country, computer processing in other countries, and distribution emanating from yet other countries is unprecedented. When the product is software distributed directly from the Internet or the service is prestored advice, a question arises as to what is in fact the "home country" or what is the primary business location of a firm. What if a server is located on a satellite in space or in the middle of an ocean? What laws apply in "Cyberland?" Which government entities can levy and collect sales or franchise taxes and which ones cannot?

Just as catalog marketers offering their wares in a variety of states have created legal battles about who should pay and who should collect sales taxes, marketing over the Internet has created a global taxing nightmare for firms, consumers, and governments alike (e.g., Glicklich, Goldberg, and Levine 1996). Given the need of governments for revenues at all levels, one can easily foresee gigantic battles being waged over taxes that relate to marketing over the Internet. One might speculate that eventually every user of the Internet will be charged some sort of "access fee" by some governmental body, analogous to a fee charged for a driving license or a toll road, or the creation of a universal taxing agency (in addition to usage-based fees paid to providers to support the Internet's infrastructure). Indeed, it is not too farfetched to speculate that Internet-based marketing may result in a global, unified cooperative taxation effort involving all countries.

The Internet and Competition.   Although the war over Internet taxing will be obvious, Internet marketing may possibly result in another, more subtle type of warfare: price competition. Marketers now promoting their wares on the Internet do not seem disposed to compete on price. Yet such a competitive basis seems inevitable. To the extent that (1) an offering is a branded product derived from the same source and possesses standard features, (2) the major characteristic distinguishing retailers—location—is no longer operative, and (3) firm resources (including tradition and image) are no longer as relevant as they are in conventional retailing, the Internet environment is conducive to pure competition (see, for example, Benjamin and Wigand 1995).

Consider the marketplace environment of the Internet. Travel time and cost have been virtually eliminated for the buyer. Both buyers (consumers) and vendors (marketers) have nearly perfect information on goods and services being marketed. Entering and exiting the marketplace are relatively easy for both buyers and sellers. Buyers will have a "substantial" number of vendors to choose from, and vendors will have a greatly expanded market that is not geographically based. As English (1990, p. 12) observed, "electronic parity will be much easier to achieve than physical parity."

Competitive pressures will lead to average price levels that are lower than those that currently exist, as well as to more homogeneous prices, for a large proportion of products sold over the Internet. Moreover, this competition will not be limited to the Internet but will "spill over" into traditional retailing settings as well. For example, one can now get a price quote on the Internet for a particular make and model of automobile, then take that quote to a local dealer and use it as leverage in negotiating a price with the dealer. Consequently, retail margins must shrink and firms must become extremely efficient simply to survive. Service and support will be the primary competitive tools for Internet-based firms.

Table 1.2 contains prices for a Spyder™ paintball gun obtained by browsing different Web sites. The table reveals that prices differ substantially for an identical product. (The Arctic price was based on the October 1996 kroner-dollar exchange rate; the firm has a Swedish Internet address.) For comparison, the price of a Spyder™ paintball gun at a local fixed-location retailer at the time of the Web browsing was $225. Readers are encouraged to price this product at these Web sites and others at their convenience. It is predicted that (1) the average price will have decreased (on October 19, 1996, it was $177.22); (2) the price range ($139.95–$240.00) will have narrowed considerably from that displayed in the table; and (3) many of the firms listed in the table will no longer be marketing Spyder™ paintball guns on the Web.

Table 1.2. World Wide Web Prices for Spyder™ Paintball Gun on October 19, 1996

Company	Price
Arctic Paintball	$240.00
Coast to Coast	139.95
Command Post	199.95
HORC	194.95
Olympic	175.99
On the Go	162.50
Paintball Headquarters	169.95
Paintball Mania	182.95
Paintball On-Line	176.53
Paintball Paradise	159.00
Planet Sports	159.99
Skan-line	164.85

Spyder™ is distributed by Kingman International Corp. (Walnut, California).

The movement toward pure competition will be accelerated by "intelligent agents"—robotic software that consumers will use to continuously "shop" the Internet searching for good deals. These agents will be countered by vendors' own intelligent agents that track consumers' shopping patterns in an attempt to customize product offerings for them.

In sum, the effect of the Internet on business is likely to be enormous. New business paradigms will be required, and new firms will arise to take advantage of the paradigm shifts (existing firms that try to adapt their current business approach to the Internet, or the Internet to their business, will probably experience limited success). Consumers and businesses alike will increasingly band together into buying groups to leverage their purchasing power. Both marketing concepts and their execution will be affected markedly by the Internet. "Purchasing" may be replaced with "leasing," "pay-per-use pricing," or metering, especially for such things as software and music. To counter nearly perfect price information on the Internet, price bundling for products will become commonplace, and the number of "configured" products will increase tremendously. As Internet sites proliferate, network marketing (multilevel marketing) concepts will be used to gain distribution, and partnerships among Internet site operators will occur as attempts are made to increase traffic. Brand names will become more important, and firms will act aggressively to protect their intellectual property and the equity that brands have acquired (e.g., the recent federal antidilution statute will be increasingly invoked to protect firms' trademarks). Entire industries, such as gambling and (real-time, real-person) interactive gaming, will extend their presence on the Internet (especially if there is a fusion of computer, telecommunications, and television technologies.)

The Internet and Communication

An even more subtle impact of the Internet will be its influence on the manner in which individuals interact on a person-to-person basis and on the people with whom they interact. Indeed, Lanham (1993) has argued that the Internet (electronic communications) will bring back an ancient emphasis on interaction, individuality, and open debate. However, not every individual will access the Internet for reasons that include lack of interest, financial barriers, "technophobia," and the like, reasons that have been well articulated in the literature. Moreover, not everybody will shop on the Internet for reasons that also have been amply discussed in the literature, including the need of some consumers to interact with live salespeople and retail clerks (see, for example, Forman and Sriram 1991).

At the same time, though, currently one of the most popular features of the Internet is the "chat room." Chat rooms allow individuals, who are literally scattered all over the globe, to communicate and have what might be termed "conversations." These conversations take place through keystrokes that create verbal interactions, but in the future these interactions most likely will be oral and even visual. Although these chat room conversations can expand a participant's horizons greatly (e.g., geographically, culturally, and so forth), they are still sterile, artificial, and lack the ambiance of true face-to-face interactions. In fact, many of the chat room participants are paid conversationalists (by an on-line service or cybermall) who have been enlisted to encourage conversations. Moreover, many of the chat room participants are not as they portray themselves conversationally. As an aside, it is interesting to compare the role of the cybermall in stimulating "conversations" with the role of the Agora, the original marketplace in Greece (e.g., Fleischman 1993), in stimulating conversations. The parallels are striking.

On the basis of current trends in chat room behavior, especially among teenagers and young adults, in the future the Internet most likely will directly impact communication and interaction skills. Although it will increase both the number and type of people one can potentially communicate with, the Internet will probably also facilitate a decline in oral communication and grammatical skills. There will be fewer opportunities to develop nonverbal communication skills and, given the "short-form" English used on the Internet together with the proclivity for "symbolic bytes," chat room conversations may ultimately lead to a lessening of reading skills and even a decline in comprehensive thinking ability.

FINAL THOUGHTS

The Internet is representative of other electronic marketing devices in that it is likely to exacerbate a trend that is now just beginning to be recognized in more developed countries. That trend is the increase in stress and pressure people feel because of the need to respond quickly to masses of instantaneously transmitted information, even though the available time to do so is less and less. In brief, electronic marketing is contributing to stress induced by information overload.

One of the most cited consequences of electronic devices and technologies mentioned in this chapter is the quantity of information that is now routinely being generated and the increased speed with which that information is delivered. Databases create massive amounts of information that is available for decision makers. One frequently is exposed to claims that new technologies have increased both the amount and timeliness of decision-relevant data by factors of 100 or more. Decision makers in turn are pressured to make decisions very quickly. The telephone, e-mail, facsimile machines, and even express mail delivery have replaced surface mail communication and interpersonal communication in many situations. Although this increased communication speed has been touted as increasing decision-making effectiveness, making decisions more "real time" and improving response capability, it is also creating information overload with the simultaneous pressure to make decisions and/or respond instantaneously. At the same time, humans are constrained by a 24-hour day and other demanding activities and responsibilities. In the long run, stress induced by electronic marketing devices and technologies may (unfortunately) be their most impactful legacy.

Just as the distribution of wealth is producing two groups of consumers—those who have it and those who do not—the computer, the most ubiquitous electronic device *and* technology, will lead to two groups of consumers: those who have computers and access to the Internet and those who do not. (Note that in 1995 more computers than television sets were sold for the first time.) Consumers who have computers will be able to enjoy (and profit from) the fruits of technology as it relates to their work and leisure activities. Those who do not will increasingly struggle to be efficient and effective in all of their activities.

Despite the potential problems that the Internet poses, its implications for electronic marketing are virtually without limit. Technology will not be a roadblock; today's technology-related worries will create tomorrow's opportunities. For example, current landline telephone capacity constraints will most likely lead to wireless solutions that are as yet to be conceived.

Traditional shopping involves five senses. The World Wide Web can now accommodate two of them, vision and hearing. However, it is only a matter of time until the Web allows smelling and tasting (utilizing technology similar to that employed in color printing). When that occurs, virtual reality will have truly arrived.

2

Consumer Behavior
in the Future

Jagdish N. Sheth and Rajendra S. Sisodia

In the not-too-distant future, rapid advances in technology, escalating global competition, and rising consumer expectations for quality, speed of response, and customization will require companies to substantially rethink their business models. One thing is clear: the future will be substantially different from the present. Society went through dramatic change and upheaval as a result of the transition from the agricultural age to the industrial age; the transition to the information age will be accompanied by even greater change. That transition is well underway, but still remains in its early stages.

The emerging consensus about the future of today's various information industries is that they will converge because they are all increasingly based on digital electronic technology. The vision revolves around the presence of an interactive broadband digital "highway" terminating in very high resolution multimedia display terminals in consumers' homes and workplaces. The viewer would be in control of content scheduling and selection; information would not, for the most part, be "broadcast" (except for live events); rather, it would be stored in digital "video servers" to be viewed or downloaded on demand. For a detailed discussion of some of the characteristics of future "information malls," see Sheth and Sisodia (1993).

Today's World Wide Web (WWW) represents a crude approximation of the capabilities and functionality that are expected to be widely deployed by the middle of the next decade. It is serving as a very large test bed for companies and as a "training platform" for consumers to learn new modalities of interaction and consumption.

From the perspective of consumers, the primary impact of the deployment of such an infrastructure will be to ease the often severe time and place constraints that are currently placed on them. No longer will goods and services be offered primarily at the convenience of the seller; "anytime, anywhere" purchasing as well as consumption will become commonplace.

These impacts will become more acute as communication bandwidths rise exponentially and terminal equipment becomes simultaneously more powerful, sophisticated, easier to use, affordable, and portable (smarter, easier, cheaper and smaller). Once the appropriate hardware is in place and the telecommunications infrastructure has been established, an enormous range of services can be exchanged at nominal incremental cost, such as location-independent shopping and banking, computer-mediated education, and training, professional consultations, and various informational, entertainment, and leisure services. This combination of technologies is likely to become quite widespread in the United States by the year 2005, and in other advanced countries by 2010.

Changing consumer behavior will make it necessary for the marketing function to change dramatically as well. In fact, we believe that the marketing function will be at the center of change; marketing will become increasingly decentralized and fully integrated into business operations. Marketing and its institutions have a great deal to lose as well as many opportunities to make dramatic gains. We believe that successful marketing in this new environment will involve "monocasting" or "pointcasting" of communications, "mass customization" of all marketing mix elements, a high degree of customer involvement and control, and far greater integration between marketing and operations. There will be more efficient utilization of marketing resources, reduced customer alienation resulting from misapplied marketing stimuli, increased pressure to deliver greater value, and intense jostling for the loyalties of "desirable" customers. In this chapter, we present a framework for analyzing the types of changes we expect to see emerge in the future, speculate about the impacts of these changes on consumer behavior, and suggest how the marketing function will have to respond.

FORCES DRIVING CHANGES IN CONSUMER BEHAVIOR

Two major forces influence consumer behavior, evolving technology, and changing lifestyles and demographics. These are respectively described below.

Supply Side: Technology Evolution

Undoubtedly, the pace of technological evolution in recent years is having and will continue to have a great impact on the lives of consumers. Rudy Puryear, a senior information technology strategist at Andersen Consulting, describes the new age as the "age of less." Technology allows consumers to go shopping without going to the store (storeless); travel without a ticket (ticketless); work without going to an office (officeless), and so on. Three aspects of technology are of particular significance.

Production Technology. Breakthroughs in production technology, such as CAD-CAM, flexible manufacturing systems, and just-in-time production are affecting competitive marketing in a number of ways. For example, they are redefining the limits of quality, greatly increasing the level of affordability for many products, enabling a higher level of customization, and providing customers with a great deal of variety. Other significant technologies in this arena include photorealistic visualization, groupware (e.g., conferencing systems across design functions and across design, manufacturing and sales), virtual reality, design-for-manufacturability-and-assembly databases, component performance history databases, and 3-D physical modeling technologies such as stereolithography.

Distribution Technology. Recent innovations in distribution technology include (1) computer-assisted logistics (CALS), (2) the refinement of scanner and other product identification and tracking technologies, (3) electronic data interchange (EDI), (4) point-of-sale (POS) terminals linked to vendors, (5) expert systems, (6) satellite-based locational systems, (7) automated retail and warehouse ordering, and (8) flow-through logistics. Benefits include (1) reduced damages, (2) reduced supplier and distributor wholesale inventories, (3) warehousing, transportation, administrative, and manufacturing efficiencies, (4) reduced "forward buying," (5) better market coverage, (6) fewer stockouts and distress sales, (7) more refined target marketing, and (8) faster response to market trends.

Technologies for Personal Use. Technologies having the fastest gains in price–performance are those intended for personal rather than institutional use. Personal information devices have been riding and will continue to ride a steep experience curve based on the unique "economics of electronics." One of the fundamental properties of such technologies is their inverse economies of scale; the smaller the unit, the greater the price–performance. This is due to the fact that smaller units can be produced in mass quantities with very low (sometimes near-zero) variable costs. Large units, on the other hand, tend to be produced in small volumes and retain a significant proportion of variable costs. Thus, today's personal computers offer far more by way of "MIPS per dollar" than do today's mainframes or supercomputers; video games and other lower end consumer devices tend to offer even better price–performance than that.

Consumers will rely heavily on these technologies, while producers will rely on a mix of personal and institutionally oriented technologies. As the power and pervasiveness of the technologies at their command grow, consumers will be in the hitherto unique and unaccustomed position of controlling a far greater share of the information and communication flow between the buyer and seller than ever before. In other words, consumers can and will have more information about product providers in most cases than providers will have about consumers;

far from being passive "targets" of marketing activity, consumers will dictate the timing and modality of communications, and they will determine the time and place of any resulting transaction.

Demand Side: Lifestyle and Demographic Changes

Broad demographic shifts are underway that are causing gradual but major changes in society. These macro-level changes have a major impact on individual consumer behavior.

Negative Growth Birth Rates and Rising Median Age in Developed Countries. The birth rate in the United States has been falling for more than two decades. The decline in the birth rate began in 1965, when the arrival of "the pill" caused the fertility rate to fall by 30 percent in one year. The legalization of abortion a decade later caused another precipitous drop.

Wolfe (1996) described this phenomenon as "deyouthing—an historically unprecedented event going relatively unnoticed." During the 1990s, the number of adults under the age of 35 will decline by 8.3 million. This transition is having a major effect on consumption patterns. For example, as a result of deyouthing, the housing industry has shrunk dramatically; new housing starts have declined from 1.8 million per year in the 1970s to less than a million currently.

Other developed nations are experiencing even more severe effects from this trend because they tend to have much lower levels of immigration than the United States (more than 90 percent of the population growth in the United States between 1990 and 2050 will be due to immigration). Populations in most developed countries are actually shrinking. The trends for Japan are especially ominous. Between 1990 and 2030 alone, the number of Japanese under the age of 50 will decrease by some 24 million people, a net 26 percent loss of population. Birth rates in less developed countries by and large continue above the replacement level, although the overall trend is downward.

The differences in median ages across countries can be quite dramatic. The median age of adults in the United States is now 43 and will reach 50 in less than two decades. According to Wolfe (1996), the "psychological center of gravity" (PCG) is a five-year window around this median age of adults, or 38 to 48. He suggests that this PCG defines the primary tendencies of a culture; for the United States, this suggests that middle-age values and perspectives will increasingly come to dominate the national psyche. In particular, older consumers tend to respond more favorably to relationship marketing approaches than do younger consumers.

More Women in Workforce. Full-time working women now re-present 56 percent of all women and will represent 65 percent by the year 2000.

This has put tremendous pressure on the "traditional" family. The old model was that women would stop working when they decided to have kids. The new model is that most women MUST work if they want to have kids.

As a result of the loss of its anchor (i.e., a full-time homemaker), the family as a unit of social and consumption analysis is becoming obsolete. As single-person or dual-career households proliferate, the need to define a separate existence or space will result in highly individualistic lifestyles and behaviors, even within family units. We will increasingly have to look at individual behavior; family members exhibit more of a roommate lifestyle. This will increase the need for personalized attention to each household.

Also as a result of this trend, most households are now relatively time poor and money rich; any time marketers impose a time or place constraint, the market will react negatively. Time in particular will become the most precious commodity. As activities compete for time, consumers will redesign tasks that consume too much time and embrace time-saving and time-shifting technologies. They will demand hassle-free ("get it right the first time") service on demand.

Cooking in the home is quickly becoming a dying art; nobody does it anymore (almost). A third of our meals are eaten out now; this will rise to two-thirds. Of this remaining two-thirds, 50 percent are not cooked by us at all. The kitchen is increasingly the communication center of the house rather than the food center.

The increased numbers and visibility of women in the workplace have led to a gradual blurring of gender distinctions. For men, jewelry, cosmetics, personal care items, and plastic surgery are all growth markets.

Lifestyle, Income, and Ethnic Diversity. By 2000, only 55 percent of the U.S. population will be WASPs. Hispanics are the fastest growing group and will be the largest minority by that time. African Americans will remain at 12 percent, whereas the percentage of Asians will grow. California and Texas will become white-minority states.

As a result of the changing ethnic make-up of U.S. society, several changes are underway. In many sectors, neglected ethnic markets are becoming lead markets; for example, salsa and other Mexican sauces now sell more than ketchup. The local grocery store is now a world bazaar, something that requires extraordinary logistic systems. Increasing cultural diversity is leading to a clash of value systems: the Protestant work ethic versus other values. There are also increasing linguistic problems, especially in schools and the workplace.

Although we will still have a sizable middle class, there will be a sharp dichotomy between the rich and poor. A large percentage of the population will be affluent, and a sizable group will be below the official poverty level. The middle class will decline from 60 percent of the population in 1950 to 30 percent in 2000. The affluent class will go from 10 percent to 30 percent. As a result of such polarization, we will see simultaneous growth at the extremes: more and more premium products, and more economical ones as well. Products will also have to become more customized. Price ranges in product categories are getting ever wider; for example, in 1960 soups ranged from 19 cents to 59 cents per serving, whereas in 1990 they ranged from 39 cents to $4.00.

Other Demand-side Shifts

Numerous other demand-side shifts are taking place that will have enormous influence. Among them, five stand out.

Increase in Regional Differences. The population shift to the Sunbelt and to small towns, with their respective differences in climate, value structure, and even occupation, will widen the cultural differences in parts of the country. The United States is apt to more closely resemble Europe, where regions vary significantly in growth, employment, language, and consumption values.

Increased Stress. The blurring of traditional family roles, the increase in autonomy, older age, and the need to manage time all point toward a society that will have higher levels of stress, both at home and work. Stress, in turn, will generate productivity issues and behavioral problems, such as drug and alcohol abuse.

Greater Concern for Privacy. People will become more aware of their lack of privacy and potential loss of individual rights. As the social norms of a previously homogeneous society give way to pluralistic and diverse values, the legal rights of individuals will be emphasized.

Emphasis on Safety and Security. Concern for personal and public safety will rise sharply, partly because of the aging population and partly because of income redistribution. Additionally, as more people live alone, they will feel more vulnerable. Law enforcement will remain a major social issue.

Entrepreneurial Spirit. Opportunities created by exploding new technologies and the rise in niche markets will encourage personal entrepreneurship. As a result, small businesses will continue as the dominant component of societal change in terms of new business formation, employment growth, political power, regulatory policy, and personal wealth.

THE IMPACT ON CONSUMER BEHAVIOR

Already we can see that human behavior is changing rapidly as a result of the latest technological revolution; changes in marketplace behavior will naturally follow. As people start to change the way they work, communicate, and spend their leisure time, they will undoubtedly exert strong pressure on companies to change the way they do business with them. Accustomed to always being within electronic reach of their family and colleagues, they will chafe at marketers who demand adherence to rigidly defined modes of commerce. Used to instantaneous response to their requirements for information and entertainment, they will scarcely tolerate delays of weeks or months to receive a desired product. Being able to optimize their lifestyle factors more and more, they will shun clothing retailers who fail to meet their size or color requirements a third of the time. Capable of "doing more with less" with constantly improving technology, they will resent the high costs (primarily in time and effort) of acquiring the goods and services they need.

Clearly, future consumers will be dramatically different from past or even present consumers. They will be more demanding, more time-driven, more information intensive, and highly individualistic.

A combination of a ubiquitous broadband digital communications network and high-definition display terminals will further accelerate changes in consumer behavior. With targeted, interactive digital media in the future, advertisers will be able to "mass customize" their messages as well as allow for user interaction and input. Consumers are already migrating to direct marketing systems in huge numbers. With the deployment of advanced technologies, this trend will accelerate. When consumers can "walk" down a virtual grocery shopping aisle on their HDTV set and click on the products they want, huge numbers are bound to respond. This can be taken a step further; virtual reality linked to a broadband pipe creates "telepresence," so that users can actually "travel" to other places and experience different things.

Such elements of virtual reality will help, but will not be a prerequisite. One-way home shopping via television is already a large business; with much higher resolutions and more interactivity, it will take over a larger share of retailing's current domain. While enhancing convenience, such systems will also lead buyers to make more informed purchases. For one thing, buyers will gain immediate access to a variety of independent buying services, providing distributed expertise on demand. Because of interactive advertising, buyers will be much more active in seeking even marketer-provided information.

From Time-bound and Location-bound Marketing to Time-free and Location-free Marketing

Commerce today, for the most part, tends to be time and location bound. That is, transactions are constrained to occur at particular times and/or at particular locations. If the consumer is unable to transact at those times or those locations, the transaction either will not occur at all, or will occur between the consumer and another supplier. Even if the transaction does occur, that is, the consumer is able to comply with the time and place requirements set by the supplier, it will often force undesirable trade-offs on the consumer. In other words, the consumer may have no choice, and hence complies, but is left with a latent sense of dissatisfaction. Most consumers have numerous ways to spend that same time, and the location constraint imposes an additional burden on the time, effort, and expense of making oneself physically available to make the transaction.

As anyone who has lived through the past two decades can attest, time and place constraints are slowly giving way, under the pressure of increasingly hectic consumer lifestyles, heightened competition, and myriad enabling technologies. Behavioral barriers to the adoption of alternative modes of interacting, be they based on ingrained habits or perceived risks, have become increasingly porous.

We believe that this forward momentum will result in a positive feedback loop that will accelerate the rate of consumer migration toward alternative modes of transacting. Although no positive feedback loop can persist forever, we believe that a period of rapid, even explosive, growth lies ahead in this arena. It will subside only as a large majority of consumers have been converted to the new model of commerce. (See Figure 2.1.)

Figure 2.1. Past and Future Modes of Marketing

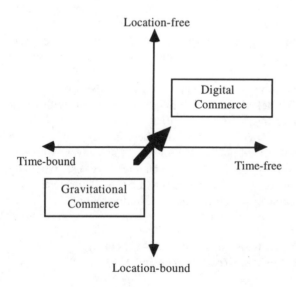

We are, then, in the midst of a sea-change from gravitational commerce, demarcated by its time and location constraints upon customers, to an era of digital commerce, which will be almost entirely free of those constraints. The future will see anytime, anywhere procurement coupled with anytime, anywhere consumption; more and more products and services will be purchased and consumed anytime, anywhere. Consumers will receive advertising and other forms of information "on demand."

The crucial importance of increased time and place utility is nowhere more evident than in the banking industry. Banks face a massive dislocation in the near future, as their vast and expensive time- and location-bound distribution networks (branches) become rapidly obsolete. Ironically, some banks are still building branches, while others are moving proactively to reconfigure their branch networks. For example, Wells Fargo announced in the fall of 1995 that it planned to move 72 percent of its existing branch network into in-store (supermarket) locations. Since in-store branches require only 20 to 25 percent of the cost of conventional branches, this represents a substantial cost saving, as well as a way to expand market coverage in terms of time as well as geography. The more major shift, of course, is the move toward home or remote banking. This trend, still in its early infancy, will take time and place utilities to much higher levels.

With regard to supermarket retailing, the impact of increased emphasis on time and place utilities will be even greater. Already, supermarkets can offer electronic ordering and home-delivery services for relatively low start-up costs. A recent survey indicates that more than 25 percent of supermarket chains offer home delivery, potentially reaching more than 40 percent of the population. A significant barrier to broader adoption of home shopping is the delivery charge, which runs from $7 to $10 an order. Survey research by Management Horizons shows significant consumer resistance to any delivery charge (*Supermarket News* 1996).

What is needed is a business model that is optimized for home shopping, rather than one in which the service is added on as an ancillary to traditional retailing. An analysis by Management Horizons indicates substantial savings can be made in operating a delivery depot compared to operating a supermarket. On a typical $100 order, home delivery will cost a typical supermarket operator an extra $10 to process, pick, check out, and deliver from the supermarket. A delivery depot can process and deliver the same order for about $10 to $12 less in total cost than the supermarket can.

To summarize, the future success of marketers will depend on their ability to deliver total customer convenience. This includes hassle-free search (advertising-on-demand), hassle-free acquisition (home delivery), hassle-free consumption (e.g., products with built-in expert systems to enable maximal value extraction), and hassle-free disposal.

EMERGING TRENDS IN CONSUMER BEHAVIOR

We foresee eight major trends in consumer behavior. These trends are listed in Figure 2.2; each is briefly discussed.

Figure 2.2. Emerging Trends in Consumer Behavior

Disintermediation and Reintermediation

Current marketing practice depends heavily on the presence of multiple intermediaries between the producer and consumer. These intermediaries primarily add time and place utilities to the functional utility "engineered" into the offering by the producer. They provide broader and more convenient access to products for a wider range of customers.

In addition to serving as essential conduits for getting products to the market, intermediaries have also served as informational conduits. Producers typically have little or no direct contact with end-user customers and must rely almost entirely on intermediaries for information pertaining to those customers. Likewise, intermediaries often play a role in directing and filtering information from producers that is intended for end users.

Building an adequate distribution channel is usually the biggest hurdle that a new entrant must face in establishing a foothold in a market; this is usually the slowest and most expensive part of the marketing mix to implement. Distribution channels add huge cost elements. For example, they may include multiple warehouses at the factory, wholesaler, retailer, and even consumer level.

As has already been well documented, the electronic world changes all that. Companies small and large are able to achieve a high level of accessibility almost immediately. Establishing a two-way information flow directly with end users is readily possible. The automation of numerous administrative tasks enables the company to serve huge numbers of customers efficiently and effectively. Innovations such as demand-driven marketing can dramatically lower systemwide inventory levels.

As a result, more and more companies are finding it possible to deal directly with more and more of their customers. In the process, they are putting enormous pressures on their intermediary (e.g., wholesaling and retailing) partners. This trend toward disintermediation is still in its early phases, and massive dislocations will occur as a result of it.

The trend will also cause major growth in the support services needed by companies that deal directly with larger numbers of customers. For example, growth in small package shipping will likely far exceed that in bulk shipments or the building of warehouse space.

Another consequence of this trend may well be what we call reintermediation. By this we mean that new categories of intermediaries will emerge to capture the value-creating opportunities that will undoubtedly be spawned by the confluence of new ways of interacting between consumers and producers. As with traditional intermediaries, these too will thrive on the basis of economic transfer principles; intermediaries that deliver greater value at lower cost will prosper.

Examples of new types of intermediaries may include rating services, automated ordering services, services based on consolidating numerous small orders from numerous consumers into more economically viable quantities, and so forth. Market specialists could emerge who would orchestrate the offerings of numerous suppliers around the specialized needs of a single customer.

Personalization: From Aggregation to Disaggregation and Reaggregation

The emergence of a relatively homogeneous mass market earlier in this century led to the development of various mass marketing approaches that continue to define and dominate the marketing function today. For some time now, we have recognized that the mass market is splintering (even atomizing) into ever smaller segments. Talk has even arisen in recent years of a so-called segment of one, and Stan Davis came up with the powerful oxymoron of "mass customization" as the way in which we will have to increasingly operate in the future.

Although we certainly agree with the broad premise of this argument, we believe some important caveats apply. First, customers are not always looking for customized products; they may be perfectly content in many cases with a well-designed standardized product. However, mass customization applies to more than the product; it should encompass all the appropriate elements of the marketing mix. Thus, the price, advertising message, and/or the distribution mode may be customized, even if the product is not.

Second, new forms of aggregation of demand will undoubtedly occur. In the past, these were driven entirely by producers. In the future, it will become increasingly facile for the aggregation to be driven by customers. For example, customers who individually purchase small quantities of a product will find it very easy to pool their purchases to enjoy better terms.

Shopping on Demand

As discussed earlier, consumer behavior in the future will increasingly feature shopping on demand and consumers will cease to be held hostage to the time and place constraints historically imposed on them by businesses. Shopping on demand will include anytime, anywhere procurement as well as anytime, anywhere consumption.

Consumers as Co-producers

In many facets of consumption, consumers will take on increasingly active roles. For example, they will become directly involved in designing and customizing the products they purchase. They will take over some of the support and service functions that are normally performed by companies; this trend is akin to the one toward self-service in retailing. For example, FedEx now allows its customers to track their own packages via the Internet, bypassing the customer service department altogether.

From Insourcing to Outsourcing. Somewhat paradoxically, we believe that as consumers take more control over certain commercial relationships, they will also relinquish a measure of control in other areas. This is not as contradictory as it might first appear; after all, consumers have a limited amount of time and effort that they are willing to expend, necessitating trade-offs. As a result of escalating time pressures and growing economic resources, consumers will begin to outsource household functions much more over time. The argument here is very similar to the one that drives outsourcing in the business context; specialist vendors will be used to deliver far better price-performance value than consumers can create in-house. In other words, the make-versus-buy question will increasingly be resolved in favor of buy. Many services (such as lawn care, house cleaning, and child care) are already outsourced to a significant degree. Many new areas will be added in the future. For example, household product needs may be outsourced to such firms as Proctor and Gamble, and in-home dining may be outsourced to restaurants that will deliver prepared food daily to the consumer's home.

Greater Value Consciousness

Although they have benefited in many ways as well, consumers have paid the price for marketing's extraordinary lack of productivity in the past. High advertising budgets, the proliferation of brands, runaway sales promotions, uneconomic levels of inventory build-up—all of these activities added costs way out of proportion to the value they created (which was, in many cases, negative).

As marketing reforms, customer expectations for value received will soar. Consumers will demand and receive more value in exchange for the four primary resources at their disposal: money, time, effort, and space.

Money. Consumers will expect to pay less for most products. They will willingly pay more, provided that the additional value offered exceeds the incremental price. Because of their recent experience with major product categories such as computers and consumer electronics, consumers have come to expect as a given the proposition that products get better and cheaper over time. We believe (and many economists concur) that an era of negative inflation will characterize many more product categories.

Time. For many consumers, especially those in two-income households, time is a more valuable currency than money. Many consumers will gladly make a trade-off, paying a higher price if they can save time in the process. Marketers must be extremely wary of placing heavy time demands on consumers.

Effort. As life gets ever more complex in so many dimensions, consumers are looking for convenience and simplicity wherever they can find it.

Space. Given a choice, consumers would rather not be forced to warehouse large quantities of products in their basements in order to benefit from lower prices. Heavy users should get the advantages of scale economy; however, they should not have to swallow huge lumps of inventory in order to do so.

Value buying will become paramount, as consumers become more value-conscious than ever. They will be better educated about offerings. Given the efficiency with which information will be shared between customers and between customers and companies, it will be almost impossible for companies to survive without delivering peak value. In contrast with the past, consumers will respond far more to innovation-based differentiation than to image-based differentiation.

Barriers to consumption will increasingly disappear as a result of the adoption of value-based marketing, more creative pricing approaches (leasing, metering), the separation of form from function, and the removal of artificial constraints. Given the right value equation, the limits to consumption will be revealed as being far less than were believed possible. It is now commonplace for households to have numerous radios, telephones, calculators, and even computers. Many consumers own three or more watches.

Greater competitive pressures on pricing, coupled with an enhanced ability to easily locate the best price, will be a fact of life in the new world. The impact of this will be threefold. First, successful manufacturers will increasingly seek to control their prices at retail to minimize what they view as destructive intrabrand price competition. Second, the primary drivers of profitability will be mostly on the cost side; companies with highly efficient production and marketing systems will prosper. Third, strong customer relationships will give companies an opportunity to broaden those relationships through the provision of an ever-expanding array of products and services. In essence, we believe that many successful producers of a product will become retailers of a multitude of other products for the same customer.

Blurring Between Consumer and Business Markets

The lines between the home and the workplace are rapidly blurring. More and more people work at least part-time in their homes, and a growing number of people undertake some of their personal tasks at the office. As this trend continues, many consumer decisions will become more like business decisions. Many technology applications traditionally seen as home based will be important to businesses as well. For example, video shopping has great potential in a business environment; an automobile mechanic will be able to see a picture before ordering a part. To see how to make repairs the worker has not done in a long time, he or she will be able to view a video clip.

This movement of home-based services to business and vice versa can already be observed. Typical home-bound applications such as television and VCRs are now "trickling up" into business applications. Telephone answering machines trickled up to businesses as voice mail. Business applications such as e-mail, the Internet, EDI, and accounting software are trickling down into the home market. Dual-purpose applications include video shopping, distance learning, travel planning, news on demand, legal/financial advice, information services/on-line databases, and so forth. Some applications will remain geared to the business or consumer market, although even here analogous applications may be developed.

Power Shift from Marketers to Consumers

Inevitably, increased competition and greater access to more powerful information tools will put greater power in the hands of savvy consumers. As a result, it is possible that buyers will increasingly be viewed as marketers and sellers as prospects in the marketplace. In any event, consumers will no longer be targets of marketing activity; they will be knowledgeable and demanding drivers of it.

Marketers will have to show far greater respect for consumers, who have increasingly become immune to marketing hype. Instead, they will demand content-rich information and demonstrable product innovations. Transactions will occur in the context of a complex relationship revolving around lifestyle issues. Customer managers will be charged explicitly with identifying, retaining, and growing profitable customer relationships.

Market activity will be driven almost entirely by buyer demand; marketing management will essentially become demand management: the task of influencing the level, timing, and composition of demand in a way that will help the organization achieve its objectives. Customer knowledge will truly become the cornerpiece of effective marketing, and that knowledge will become a highly valued corporate resource. By linking directly into production systems, consumers will effectively become producers; they will engage in self-service, self-design, and self-ordering and provisioning.

Consumers will be highly information-technology literate; they will therefore not be impressed by the mere use of such technology. They will be highly efficient at information searching and processing. Consumers can already conduct product research on-line, log onto bulletin boards and interact with other consumers, and provide and receive helpful hints about the product, its use, and acquisition. In this environment, "information invitations" may become common; companies will have to seek permission to present their case to consumers by inducing interest, unlike the message clutter that is rampant today.

As communication between marketers and customers becomes increasingly interactive, relationship marketing will become the rule rather than the exception. Buyers and sellers will interact in real time. Just-in-time marketing will replace the traditional just-in-case marketing. Time and place constraints on purchasing (and even consumption of many products and services) will become obsolete. The nearly instant gratification of customer needs will be common; thus, lead times of all kinds (e.g., for product development or between order placement and shipment) will have to shrink dramatically.

The Automation of Consumption

Consumers' time poverty and an abundance of information technology will lead to a greatly increased level of automated transactions with marketers. Akin to automatic replenishment as practiced in the business-to-business marketing arena today, such arrangements will become increasingly commonplace in the future. They may happen directly between consumers and manufacturers for larger purchases, and through intermediaries for smaller purchases. As discussed elsewhere, suppliers of large items or major services will have the opportunity to become the supplier of choice for an ever-widening array of goods and services (the concept of customer equity).

Other related concepts from the business marketing arena that will rapidly find analogs in the consumer marketing arena include vendor-managed inventory, supply chain management, electronic data interchange, customized pricing, and various forms of risk sharing (such as the revenue-sharing formulas offered by manufacturers of some infrastructure equipment such as telecommunications gear).

One important development will be that savvy consumers will increasingly demand that corporations share the benefits of cost cutting with them. Just as Wal-Mart demands that P&G lower its costs and then share the benefits with it, so too will customers with a high lifetime value demand and receive similar consideration. Smart companies will do this without being forced; they will proactively invest resources in those relationships with the greatest long-term value. Currently, investment in customers usually stops after they have become customers; spending on customer retention activity is much less than on acquisition. Further, loyal customers tend to subsidize those who are less loyal, as well as the acquisition of new ones. Overall, the economics of customer acquisition and retention will require and will receive much more understanding and attention than they do currently.

The Concept of a Personal Marketplace. The Personal Marketplace (PM) is a hypothetical mechanism to make effective use of the vast amounts of consumer and transaction data generated today. It is a repository where participating companies prepare and market custom-tailored offerings directly to a consumer. These are categorized by product and/or service, as specified by the consumer. By selecting a particular category, the consumer alerts companies that he or she is a potential customer, and offers begin to flow in. The customer voluntarily provides as much customizing information as needed. Participating companies agree not to sell the data they collect outside the PM, and not to use it to market in any other channel.

THE IMPACT OF CHANGING CONSUMER BEHAVIOR ON MARKETING

As we (Sheth and Sisodia 1995a,b) previously pointed out, the marketing function is in the midst of a serious and escalating productivity crisis. For several decades the marketing function has consumed an ever-growing share of corporate expenditures while failing to deliver increased customer loyalty or greater profitability. The marketing tools and tactics that worked well in decades past are increasingly relics of an era that is rapidly fading.

Our discussion of changing consumer behavior suggests that the root cause of marketing's problems is behavioral. In other words, marketing today largely operates under the modalities of industrial-age commerce, while consumer behavior has changed and will continue to change rapidly and dramatically. Industrial-age marketing, coupled with information-age consumer behavior, creates a misalignment that renders much of what marketing does ineffectual and sometimes damaging.

It is not surprising, then, that marketing today is incredibly inefficient. For example, in 1996, $159 billion was spent on advertising in the United States alone, plus a nearly equal amount on sales promotions. This amounts to $1,250 per person per year, or $5,000 per year per four-member household. The advertising dollars buy an average of 1,600 exposures per day per person; only two percent of those result in positive recall.

Even direct marketing is highly inefficient; there are 254,000,000 Americans, but four billion names for rent. Direct marketing is regarded as successful when it is 98 percent wrong. It is viable only because trees continue to be cheap, and postal rates are still relatively low.

In addition to being inefficient, marketing is too often ineffective as well. Customer dissatisfaction runs high in many industries, and brand loyalty continues to erode. Most customers have become conditioned to being opportunistic and short-term oriented.

A full-blown productivity crisis now exists in marketing. Consequently, we can expect to see major budget cuts in marketing in coming years, as companies search for greater operating efficiency.

Interactive broadband communication systems have the potential to make the marketing function far more productive, mainly because they directly target the areas of communications and selling, which is where the bulk of marketing resources are expended. Both outbound communications (e.g., advertising, sales promotion, and personal selling) and inbound communications (e.g., ordering and customer service) will be impacted.

With such systems, companies will be able to integrate advertising, sales promotion, personal selling, and physical distribution to a far greater extent than is now possible. They will be able to achieve maximal market coverage with a relatively small amount of inventory, dramatically reducing costs in the process. Marketing efforts will be tailored for and targeted directly at the most responsive segments of the market. Companies will close the loop by making it almost effortless for customers to interact with them and with each other.

Firefly: Harnessing the Power of Word-of-mouth Marketing

An interesting example of how marketing can leverage emerging networking technology is a new service called Firefly. Firefly is one of the first commercial services to attempt to harness the power of peer recommendations or word-of-mouth marketing (Judge 1996). It (http://firefly.com) works by building detailed psychographic profiles of members, based on their answers to scores of questions. On the basis of this information, Firefly then identifies the individual's "psychographic neighbors" (other individuals who appear to have similar predispositions) and recommends products and services on the basis of what others have reported liking. The information is also used to pinpoint advertising messages to individuals. Although currently limited to music and movies, Firefly is planning to add mutual funds, restaurants, and books.

Going beyond facilitating transactions, Firefly also enables user-to-user communications, with communities based on shared interests. Corporate users of the service so far include Merrill Lynch, MCI, Dun & Bradstreet, Reuters, Yahoo, and ZD Net.

Importantly, Firefly has aggressively sought to maintain user privacy; it does not require users to provide real names and addresses unless they choose to. The company has gone so far as to hire Coopers & Lybrand to conduct audits twice a year to ensure that it is adequately safeguarding user privacy. Firefly's privacy policies have earned it plaudits from the Electronic Frontier Foundation, an entity that advocates privacy for Internet users.

How Marketing Must Respond

Paradoxically, marketing must simultaneously get smaller and bigger in the future. At the most successful marketing companies, there will be fewer full-time marketers than there are today. At the same time, the role of marketing will grow. Marketing will exert functional control over operations, customer service, and pricing to a far greater extent than it currently does. Many more employees will be considered part-time marketers. Marketing will evolve into the truly integrating business function it was always intended to be.

The ongoing information and communications revolution presents a once-in-a-lifetime opportunity for marketing to radically define its base operating models and configure them for maximum efficiency and effectiveness. Because this future is approaching at a much faster rate than previously envisioned, marketers must begin now to understand its dimensions and invest in developing the core capabilities that will be needed to succeed in the future. Marketing will have to do the following.

Become More Technology Savvy. Marketing will have to develop a deep understanding of the drivers and trajectories of computing and communications technology. It will have to develop just-in-time capabilities in areas such as pricing and provisioning. Companies will have to learn to leverage visually interactive communications and refine on-line transaction processing systems. They will have to invest in sophisticated logistical capabilities aimed at serving individual consumers. They will have to become adept users and developers of expert systems and other forms of artificial intelligence technologies, such as voice recognition systems and intelligent agents. All of this will require a massive investment in the information technology platforms that are used in marketing.

Learn How to Retain Customer Loyalty. Consumer behavior in the future, coupled with slow market growth rates, will make customer retention an even more important driver of profitability. Marketing's primary focus on customer acquisition will thus have to change to one based on relationship management.

Learn How to Become the Quarterback. Marketing's ability to quarterback cross-functional teams organized around customer needs will be key in the future. This will require two levels of integration. First, the marketing function will have to integrate its own activities, which are performed today in semiautonomous "silos." Second, the marketing function will have to be linked and integrated with other business functions.

Practice Interactive, One-to-one Marketing. The ability to undertake direct, interactive marketing will be a critical element in future marketing success. This goes far beyond database marketing as currently practiced. The most important element will be to develop virtual empathy with consumers on a one-to-one basis. One-to-one interactions may take several forms: person-to-person (marketer interacts with customer), person-to-system (marketer interacts with customer's "agent"), system-to-person (marketer's "agent" interacts with customer), and system-to-system (marketer's agent interacts with customer's agent). All of these forms of interaction will be necessary in the future.

Agent Technology and Household Management Computers

Increasingly, company-consumer interaction will in fact be computer-computer interaction, as computers at either end take on the personalities of sellers and buyers. Although this may seem far-fetched today, consider the extent to which this is already widespread in the following commercial applications:

- Smart robots are used by travel agents to ferret out the best fares by using a variety of creative approaches.
- Numerous expert systems are being used by companies in areas ranging from the approval of credit applications to the fine tuning of blast furnaces to the prediction of photocopier failures.
- Automated trading systems (program trading) have been used by brokerage firms on Wall Street for many years.

With the blurring of boundaries between the workplace and the home (already there is talk of "home at work" along with "work at home"), we believe it is only a matter of time and appropriate marketing before such innovations are deployed in the mass market, where they will have a much greater impact.

Consider the possibility of a household management computer (HMC). An HMC could operate during off hours at night searching the globe for goods and services needed for the household. Although the search is based on specifications used in the past, these could be modified according to what the HMC may learn in the market. The HMC could operate in one of three ways. For commodities such as oil and heating, the HMC can make purchase decisions, place orders, schedule delivery, and authorize payment without further intervention by the consumer. For somewhat more complex decisions such as which styles of dress shirt to buy, the HMC may collect and store information. The consumer can review that information at a later time and make decisions. The information is verbally presented to the user, and verbal responses are also received by the computer. For more complex decisions requiring large amounts of information and significant financial outlays, the HMC gathers information, requests the delivery of electronic samples and other product information, and presents a recommendation on the basis of agreed-upon criteria.[1]

One possible innovation in the future might be "feel sites." These are locations where consumers can go to try on clothes, taste food, or sit on furniture before returning to the Internet to finalize a purchase decision.[2]

MARKETING'S STRANDED ASSETS

A "stranded asset" is a sunk cost that may no longer provide economic value. For example, in the electric utility industry, many nuclear plants have become stranded assets; they were built at enormous cost but are no longer competitive with more efficient ways of generating electricity. Companies have little choice but to write off such assets and invest in newer ones (or to simply stop producing internally and rely on purchases from the market).

We believe that marketing has built up numerous potentially stranded assets. More and more, these relics of a fast-fading era will have to be replaced. If they are not replaced, they will represent a severe drag on the competitiveness of the firms that continue to own them. Examples of stranded assets include the following:

- Retailing space—banks and supermarkets will be increasingly replaced by home-based retailing; in the last decade, the average time spent at malls by consumers has declined dramatically, from 7 hours a month to only 2 1/2 hours.
- Warehousing space—manufacturers, wholesalers, retailers, consumers; replaced by virtual warehouses.
- Office space—there will be more space-independent working.
- Inflexible manufacturing plants—for example, GM has some plants that are capable of making only one particular type of pick-up truck.
- Outbound telemarketing setups—these have proven to be extraordinarily efficient at alienating large numbers of customers.

Certain capabilities will be in short supply and will thus be at a premium. Examples include small-order-size delivery systems (agile logistics), picking systems, and order-fulfillment experts.

CONCLUSION

Wehling (1996, p. 170), senior vice president of advertising at Proctor and Gamble, recently noted that

> Over the long term, marketers who remain unprepared for the sea-change we're about to experience won't survive. Marketers who understand the implications and get ahead of the curve will not only survive, they'll thrive. They'll emerge more competitive than ever and they'll build relationships with consumers that are deeper and more enduring than any we can create today.

A marketing revolution is only just beginning. We are now climbing onto a technological treadmill; companies that are not already on board may not be able to make up for lost ground. New entrants will base their business model on the starkly different economics of the information age. Consequently, these new entrants will create numerous stranded assets among traditional marketers.

The world is changing in major ways that few of us have begun to fathom. In particular, the world in which marketing exists is getting reshaped with great speed. The microprocessor forever changed the world of computing and nearly destroyed IBM. IBM was forced to change dramatically simply to survive. Analogous to IBM, marketing will die if it does not change.

There will undoubtedly be winners and losers in this process, as well as leaders and laggards. Those marketers who move proactively now to redefine the function and rewrite its value equations will position themselves for a bright future. If it is managed right, marketing may lose the battle but win the war. If it is not managed right, operations or customer services may drive the corporation—to the ultimate detriment of customers as well as shareholders.

NOTES

1. Dwayne McCollum, MBA student, George Mason University.
2. Carol Diggs, MBA student, George Mason University.

3

Television IS the Store: Direct Response Television

August E. Grant

Of all the forms of electronic marketing, no other is as pervasive as television retailing. Although the various forms of television, including broadcast television and cable, are seen primarily as a means of advertising products for sale in other retail channels, television has become an important retail outlet in its own right. In effect, instead of telling people to go to the store, *television is the store.*

This chapter explores the various forms of television retailing and how they differ from traditional and other electronic retailing outlets. In some respects, the comparatively low-tech combination of television shopping channels and toll-free telephone numbers is a far cry from on-line shopping services that provide almost limitless choice and interactivity. At the same time, some aspects of television retailing, such as order fulfillment, are directly comparable to any form of electronic marketing.

The most important difference is the pervasive nature of television retailing. More than 99 percent of all households in the United States have television sets, and virtually all of these at some point relay direct response television commercials, television shopping channels, or infomercials. For comparison, consider that, as of mid-1996, computers with modems were in less than a quarter of all households, and even fewer households subscribed to on-line services and Internet access providers.

Another key difference between television retailing and other forms of electronic marketing is the fact that television retailing is about a decade older, providing lessons in such marketing conditions as growth patterns and shakeouts, which are important to consider in evaluating all forms of electronic marketing.

OVERVIEW

The television industry has long enjoyed an important role in the retail process. Advertising provided the earliest means of economic support for television, which borrowed notions of sponsorship and spot availability from the radio industry. As the medium grew and prospered, new sponsorship arrangements proliferated and the importance of the medium to retailers increased, making television one of the more important advertising media.

An inevitable development of this evolution was television retailing—the idea that the television industry could actually replace the retail outlet and that consumers would purchase products directly after viewing them. The first step in modern television retailing was the development of direct response television (DRTV) advertising, short, one- to five-minute commercial announcements that included a telephone number so that viewers could directly order the item for sale. The demise of commercial limitations on broadcast television and the growth of the cable television industry introduced two long-form television retailing formats: television shopping channels and infomercials.

The television shopping industry was born largely by chance, and its success prompted many to reconsider the manner in which television could be used to sell products. One result was the proliferation of the infomercial—complete programs designed to sell a specific product or service to viewers.

This chapter will explore all three types of television retailing: television shopping networks, infomercials, and direct response advertising. Collectively these three make up a $4 billion television retailing industry. Because television shopping networks account for about three-quarters of the total, they will be studied in more detail. (See Figure 3.1 for a comparison of the three.) The chapter begins with a brief history and then analyzes the economics, audience characteristics, regulatory factors, and technological issues relating to television retailing. The chapter concludes with some projections on the future of television retailing.

At this point it is important to note that a television retailing system is much more complicated than the creation of the television programming or announcement itself. Before any announcement is broadcast, items for sale must be chosen and priced and time must be scheduled. For infomercials and direct response announcements, this involves negotiating the purchase of air time from specific television stations or cable channels. For television shopping, this involves deciding exactly when the product will be featured (and how that product will fit into the flow of products to be offered that hour or day).

As the announcements are broadcast, sales must be monitored to determine when to switch to another product. For infomercials, this involves tracking sales by market for each announcement over days, weeks, or even months. For television shopping, the process is accelerated, because the program producer continuously monitors the number of phone calls and orders to determine when to move on to the next product. As each order is placed, payment information must be obtained and then immediately verified from credit card companies to ensure that the customer has the credit to pay for the product. Finally, after orders are placed, they must be fulfilled. Shipping has to be coordinated from widely distributed warehouses, and getting the product to the customer as quickly as possible is the primary concern.

Figure 3.1. Estimated 1995 Revenues from Direct Response Television

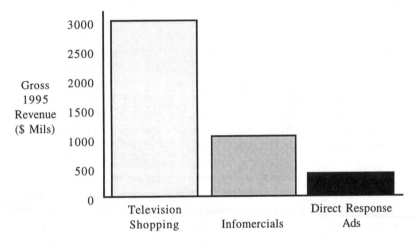

Credit verification, warehousing, and fulfillment are relatively mundane compared to the glitter of the television broadcast itself, but they can be the most important elements in building repeat business for a television retailer. Furthermore, these elements are common to virtually every form of electronic marketing, allowing a number of lessons from television retailing to be applied to other forms of electronic marketing.

Television Shopping Networks

Cable Television. The most common form of television retailing is the television shopping network, sometimes known as "home shopping" because the pioneer in the field was Home Shopping Network (HSN). HSN and Quality, Value, and Convenience Network (QVC) quickly became the leading networks when the industry was born in the early 1980s. Dozens of other networks have come and gone since then, with smaller networks such as ValueVision fighting for a share of the lucrative market. The typical merchandise mixes for HSN and QVC are shown in Table 3.1.

Table 3.1. Television Shopping Merchandise Mix

QVC Network		Home Shopping Network	
Jewelry	35%	Jewelry	42%
Home/Lifestyle	35%	Hardgoods	34%
Apparel Accessories	20%	Softgoods	14%
Other	10%	Cosmetics	10%

Source: NIMA International.

The primary distribution medium for television shopping networks is cable television. Most cable television systems devote a small number of channels (usually one to three) to full-time television shopping services. These cable systems enjoy a percentage of the revenues from sales in their area, usually around five percent. This commission makes television shopping extremely attractive to cable television systems, which would otherwise have to pay for programming to fill those channels.

Broadcast Television. Because more than a third of all households in the United States do not subscribe to cable television, television shopping networks realized that they could extend the reach of their services through broadcast television stations. (As discussed in the history section, the use of broadcast stations was not new to TV shopping pioneers.) HSN attempted to fill this market void by purchasing low-rated UHF (ultra-high frequency—channels 14–69) television stations in major markets to carry a new, broadcast-only service, HSN2. Eventually, HSN operated one of the largest television station groups in the nation (spun off in 1992 as Silver King Communications, Inc.) and created a separate full-time programming channel to serve these stations and a handful of other affiliates.

The success of HSN2 in large markets led HSN to examine smaller markets for similar opportunities. Since full-time television stations were not available in most markets, HSN created a third service, HSN Spree, to deliver television shopping programming on a part-time basis, usually overnight (between 1:00 A.M. and 6:00 A.M.). Although Spree was ultimately merged with HSN's other two services in 1995, its success spawned a group of imitators.

These overnight shopping services were attractive to broadcasters for the same reason shopping channels were attractive to cable television operators. They provided programming to fill a "hole" in a schedule and generated some revenue where the station was previously losing money because audiences were too small to sell advertising in those time slots.

The revenue potential of television shopping services also led many broadcasters and television shopping networks to experiment with individual television shopping programs that would fit into the remainder of a program schedule. As discussed later in this chapter, these programs were very successful in merchandise sales, but fundamental differences in the economics of television shopping and advertiser-supported television programming have rendered these forms incompatible in most parts of a television schedule.

Infomercials.   Although mainstream television shopping companies were not successful with short-form television shopping programming, a number of entrepreneurs realized the potential for using program-length commercial announcements to promote and sell their products. Today, infomercials are a staple of both broadcast and cable television, and television programmers are scheduling large blocks of time for sale to infomercial companies.

On broadcast stations, infomercials provide broadcasters with a guaranteed revenue source for times that are not attractive for advertising sales, such as late night or Sunday mornings. Infomercials generate revenue for a time slot in which the broadcaster would otherwise suffer a certain loss from buying a program that contained little or no advertising. Infomercials are similarly used to fill time on cable television networks, but the smaller audiences available from cable channels makes cable time slots less desirable than those available from over-the-air broadcasters.

Direct Response Advertisements.   The final category of television retailing is the direct response television advertisement. Although the DRTV industry is small compared with other types of television retailing, it still accounts for about half a billion dollars a year in revenue—almost as much as the entire radio network industry.

The economics of DRTV advertisements are a little different from those of other forms of television retailing. Most programmers who air DRTV ads are paid on the basis of the number of responses generated from the advertisement, leading some to refer to them as "per-inquiry" advertising. The typical return to a station or cable channel is about a third of what an ordinary commercial announcement would cost for the same time slot. DRTV ads are therefore scheduled to fill unsold commercial time, because a smaller amount of revenue is better than none at all.

BRIEF HISTORY

During the earliest days of the television industry, advertisers were involved in every aspect of the medium, producing and owning their own programs to attract an audience to their commercial messages. Advertising messages were integrated into program content (and occasionally into the title of the program, such as *The Texaco Star Theatre*).

As the medium evolved and production costs increased, it became more economical for networks or stations to produce programs themselves and sell time in those programs to a number of separate advertisers instead of to a single sponsor. Ultimately, advertising content was almost completely divorced from program content, and broadcasters established limitations (through the National Association of Broadcasters' Television Code) on the number of minutes of advertising allowed on a station per hour.

Although some early sponsor-produced television programming may have resembled infomercials, modern television retailing did not emerge until the 1970s, when direct response television advertising was first used. This author has not been able to ascertain when the first direct response television advertisement was aired, but large-scale use of DRTV advertising was certainly in place by the 1970s, when marketers developed it to take advantage of toll-free long-distance telephone service. This service allowed orders from widely dispersed locations to be processed at a central location.

One problem with the widespread use of DRTV advertising in the 1970s was that many in the broadcast television industry held it in low regard, partly because DRTV spots produced less revenue for a station than did commercial advertising spots. Another factor may have been some resistance to change by those in the industry who were used to thinking of advertising sales as their only source of revenue. A final factor was the products themselves and the incredible pitches made for items that consumers didn't know they really needed. The Ginsu knife not only propelled growth of the industry, but it became part of our national culture. And who can forget Ron Popeil's Pocket Fisherman?

DRTV took on a more prominent role with the development of nationally delivered cable television channels. When Ted Turner's Atlanta television station WTCG (which later was renamed WTBS) joined HBO on Satcom 1 in 1975, Turner knew he had found a means of vastly increasing the audience for his then low-rated television station. The problem was that national television advertisers were used to buying only from television networks, using Nielsen ratings to ascertain the audience size and appropriate spot rate. Turner had no ratings to report and little credibility with national advertising agencies. DRTV advertising became a staple of the network, enabling Turner to take advantage of the national audiences for his programming.[1]

Perhaps the most important feature of DRTV ads in the 1970s and 1980s were that they gave broadcasters a direct stake in the effectiveness of their commercial advertising. Eventually, broadcasters also realized the major advantage of DRTV ads in providing revenue for time that had gone unsold. (Some argue that no product is as perishable as a commercial spot; once the "avail"—the time available for the spot—has passed, there is no way to recover the potential revenue that has been lost.)

Demise of the NAB Code in 1982

Even though advertising was the lifeblood of the television (and radio) industry, it was seen by many as an inconvenience and an interruption in program flow. The idea of a program-length commercial was inconceivable, primarily because such a thing was prohibited by the National Association of Broadcaster's Television Code.

The NAB created the code to set standards for the industry, and the code was adopted by virtually all commercial television stations. A key provision of the code was a strict limit on the amount of commercial advertising that could be aired during an hour of programming—18 minutes.

In 1982, the U.S. Justice Department forced broadcasters to abandon the code, claiming that it violated antitrust law because it placed an anticompetitive limit on the availability of commercial advertising, thus forcing advertisers to pay higher prices.

At the time, few people realized that the Justice Department decision was the key event that allowed the creation of the television retailing industry. Although the industry would have certainly started at some point in time, the specific forms that television shopping and infomercials were to take were a direct result of the Justice Department action.

1982—Birth of Home Shopping Network

Television shopping, as known today, was born by accident in Clearwater, Florida. Lowell "Bud" Paxson and Roy Speer owned a struggling AM radio station in the area. In 1977, an advertiser who couldn't pay a bill for commercial time offered the station a large number of can openers. The station accepted the trade, selling the can openers on the air. The station's success in selling the can openers prompted Paxson and Speer to look for other items to sell on the air. Sales were strong enough to start a daily program featuring housewares and gift items, but listeners frequently complained about not being able to see the products they were buying. Then, in July 1982, someone had the idea of buying time on the local cable television system (Vision Cable) so that listeners could see what they were buying, and sales began to take off (Skumanich 1995). Figure 3.2 displays the growth in television shopping revenues from 1984 through 1996.

Within months, Paxson and Speer had formed the Home Shopping Network, using extraordinarily simple pitches and video production to market a variety of marked-down and close-out products. HSN's first national exposure resulted from leasing time on a nationally delivered cable television network, the Modern Satellite Network.

Figure 3.2. TV Shopping Revenue Growth

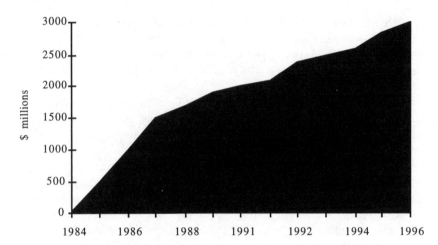

In a few short months, HSN increased from two hours to four hours a day, then more. On July 1, 1985, HSN commenced full-time national programming, delivering around-the-clock television shopping nationwide.

HSN's gross sales reflected the latent demand for such a service, growing from $19 million in 1985 to $582 million in 1987 and leveling off just above $1 billion in the early 1990s. The rapid growth led to a public offering for HSN stock in 1986. Shares initially offered at $18 each were bid to twice that amount the first day and ultimately reached $90 each. Two stock splits followed (two-for-one and three-for-one) as investors attempted to ride HSN's wave of popularity.

But almost as quickly as the stock climbed, it started to fall. The company started experiencing problems in keeping up with the growth. An expensive, high-capacity telephone system that was supposed to propel HSN's sales didn't perform as promised, resulting in litigation between HSN and the vendor. Attempts at diversification of the company into mail-order pharmaceuticals and banking services were not successful. And, perhaps most important, the sales growth leveled off almost as quickly as it began. As a result, the stock price plummeted, eventually reaching $3 a share. Ironically, adjusted for the six-for-one stock splits, the stock was selling for the same $18 price as the initial offering.

Other Shopping Networks Born

As HSN rode the roller coaster of success, other retailers attempted to copy its success. One of the first entrants was the Cable Value Network (CVN), started as a division of the Close Out Merchandise Bureau (COMB), a company specializing in sales of surplus merchandise, the type of product that had become the mainstay of HSN. At about the same time, QVC was created as a higher quality option to the bargain-basement networks. One of the things that distinguished QVC from the competition was its alliance with Sears, which provided access to Sears merchandise and brand names such as Kenmore.

Other channels sprang up to take advantage of special niches. J.C. Penney made a major investment in the Hollywood-based Shop Television Network, the first television shopping channel to prominently feature celebrity pitches. Home electronics entrepreneur Eddie Antar started Crazy Eddie's World of Home Electronics, patterned after his stores of the same name. Other niche channels included The Fashion Channel and The Travel Channel. Mainstream cable channels also attempted to climb on the bandwagon, with the Financial News Network devoting its evening and late-night hours to its Tele-Shop service.

These new channels served an important role in the cable television industry by providing programming to fill cable systems that were expanding from 24 or 36 channels to 54 channels or more. However, almost as quickly as the channels began to appear, they began to disappear. Other emerging cable networks began vying with the shopping networks for available channel space, and cable operators were more concerned with adding programming that would attract new subscribers. Mergers reduced the number of channels as QVC merged with CVN and then acquired the J.C. Penney Shopping Channel (formerly the Shop Television Network) and The Fashion Channel. Also, a number of channels simply failed to make enough sales to continue business because the growth curve had flattened out when HSN and QVC controlled most of the market.

One notable failure during this period was an experimental electronic catalog service from J.C. Penney known as "Telaction." The telaction system was a virtual electronic catalog that allowed viewers to use their telephone to request pictures and descriptions of specific items that could then be directly ordered. To allow hundreds of households to simultaneously see the specific product of interest to them, the system used a centralized video disc player that fed images and sound to video storage devices that served a cluster of homes. The end result was an on-line, electronic catalog that, to the consumer, appeared to use a cable channel and the telephone. After brief experimentation with the system, it was scrapped. As discussed later in this chapter, viewers preferred the folksy presentation of the Home Shopping Network to the shopping on demand of Telaction (Helliwell 1987).

Shopping Craze Led to Syndicated Shopping Programs

As television shopping sales raced passed $1 billion per year and approached the $2 billion mark, the growing television retail industry attracted the attention of mainstream television stations and syndication companies eager to take advantage of the multibillion dollar market. Lorimar television, best known for producing the then top-rated network television program, *Dallas*, entered the market with celebrity-driven VTV—Value Television. MCA entertainment formed a partnership with HSN to produce the Home Shopping Game Show. Each of these shows achieved something that many people deemed impossible just a year earlier—daytime clearances on major television stations in almost every television market in the country. Part of the appeal to stations was that they received a commission from program distributors.

Product sales from these programs were not disappointing. For example, VTV sold 120 $1,000 fur coats during a single segment of one program. On the other hand, program ratings were disappointing. The extra revenues from commissions made up for some of the loss from lower advertising rates resulting from the low ratings, but they weren't enough to compensate for the fact that the syndicated shopping programs also pulled down the ratings of programs they immediately preceded or followed.[2] As a result, these and similar programs were quickly canceled.

Next Evolutionary Step: The Infomercial Format

Although syndicated shopping shows failed the ratings test, they proved television's ability to directly sell products to consumers. Entrepreneurs, including some DRTV companies, realized the potential of using the pitch style of DRTV announcements in long-form programming to provide consumers with more information, testimonials, and product demonstrations than were possible in the comparatively brief DRTV spots.

The result was the infomercial, a program designed to sell a single product or service. Infomercials adopted an informal, chatty style that combined features of a television talk show and a television shopping channel in a format that was, to many, as interesting as most talk shows, with the extra dimension of viewer involvement through the purchase of the product being promoted.

Most broadcast and cable television programmers allocated time for sale to infomercial providers, but others resisted, arguing that many infomercials used deceptive formats designed to mislead viewers into believing that scripted testimonials were objective news broadcasts. The early infomercial period was also marked by a score of get-rich-quick schemes, some of which resulted in federal prosecution of the infomercial producers and distributors.

The infomercial industry took a major step forward with the formation of the National Infomercial Marketing Association in 1990, which was later renamed NIMA International. NIMA set standards for infomercials and earned the nascent industry more respectability in the broadcast community.

The infomercial industry generated almost a billion dollars in revenue in 1995. Today, broadcasters reserve time slots with special rate cards for infomercials, and infomercial companies continuously monitor the success of individual infomercials on specific stations to ensure the maximum return for the investment in air time and production cost.

Unlike other advertisers, infomercial producers are not concerned with ratings. Their measures of performance include the cost per order or cost per lead, as well as the ratio of sales to media cost. As a result, infomercial producers continually monitor the performance of individual broadcasts on each station, because sales can be tied directly to a specific airing (Williams 1995).

Recent Developments

Television Shopping. From 1993 to 1995, a number of new, well-financed television shopping services were announced. QVC, led by Barry Diller, launched an upscale shopping channel, Q2. Macy's, with the introduction of the TV Macy's channel, attempted to enter the business with the help of veteran TV producer Don Hewitt. Also, Time-Warner attempted to develop its own television shopping channel, Catalog One.

To date, none of these new efforts has had a major impact upon the industry. The primary problem for all new services is the availability of "shelf space" on cable television systems. Cable operators had long since filled their systems, and new channels had to fight existing channels for carriage. Most cable systems already carried the two primary television shopping services, HSN and QVC, and chose programming that would increase the value of their service to subscribers rather than risk losing commissions from existing channels to the new shopping channels.

The only major television shopping service to make major inroads during this time was ValueVision, which used a combination of investment from cable operators and a network of owned television stations to become the third largest television shopping service. In 1995 its revenues were $89 million.

HSN continued to evolve, as both Paxson and Speer left the company. In 1995, HSN's three separate services (HSN1 for cable television, HSN2 for broadcast television, and HSN Spree for limited overnight airing on broadcast stations) were combined into a single program feed. HSN also attempted to enter the burgeoning on-line retailing market with HSN Interactive.

Since 1990, the most prominent figure in television shopping has been Barry Diller, the former Paramount executive who became the "father" of the Fox Television Network. In 1992, Diller left Fox to explore new opportunities. Impressed with the promise of television shopping, he began negotiations with QVC. A few months later he became chief executive officer and part owner of QVC, where he used his Hollywood connections to increase the celebrity appearances on the channel. Under his direction, QVC partnered with Tribune Entertainment to produce and distribute Joan River's *Can We Shop?* [3]

Diller's tenure at QVC propelled the network to record revenues, but it was marked by three notable failures. First was the inability of the upscale Q2 network to make substantial inroads. Second was an unsuccessful hostile takeover of Paramount, in which QVC battled and lost to Viacom for control of the entertainment conglomerate. That failure led to a proposed merger with CBS in 1995, with Diller poised to become CEO of the newly merged company. Ultimately, the deal was vetoed by Comcast, which owned a controlling interest in QVC, and Diller left the company.

Soon thereafter Diller turned his sights to Silver King Communications, the HSN spin-off that controls HSN's broadcast television station group. In a complicated series of deals, Silver King proposed taking control of HSN (Harris 1995). As of late 1996, the deal was not yet complete, but speculation abounded in the trade press regarding Diller's intentions. For example, some have speculated that Diller will strengthen HSN's focus on cable delivery, freeing the 12 Silver King television stations to start a new network (Colman 1996).

Infomercials.   The establishment of infomercial standards under NIMA International has led to a period of stability in the infomercial industry. NIMA International reported that 1995 product sales from infomercials totaled $1.15 billion, a 15 percent increase over 1994. According to NIMA, 275 infomercial programs were produced in 1996, with 10,000 separate airings each week at a cost of $550 million for the air time. The most common price of a product sold via infomercials is $29.95 (*NIMA Fact Book* 1996).

Lowell "Bud" Paxson is now hoping to bring the same charm to infomercials that he did to television shopping through a network of television stations airing only infomercials. Paxson built the Infomall TV Network around a network of television stations he purchased with the fortune he created at HSN. The fledgling network is on target to own stations in 20 of the top 30 markets in the United States by the end of 1996 (Gimein 1996).

ANALYSIS OF TELEVISION RETAILING LANDSCAPE

The history of the three forms of television retailing provides a number of lessons regarding the comparative role of television retailing in the television industry. This section offers some observations regarding economics, audience characteristics, regulation, and the role of technology in television retailing.

Economics

The history of television retailing indicates sharp differences between the economics of DRTV efforts and traditional, advertiser-supported television. An understanding of these basic economic differences is essential in order to know how each form of television retailing competes and coexists with traditional television programming.

Cable Television. Most of the revenue for a cable television system comes from subscription fees; advertising revenues, installation, and other fees provide only a small percentage of overall revenues. Commissions from television shopping channels are one of the smallest sources of revenues for cable operators. As a result, when faced with a choice of adding a new shopping channel or adding a channel that will make the service popular to new subscribers, almost all cable operators will add the channel that broadens the appeal of the system.

At least three types of exceptions to this rule are likely. The first is when a system has excess channel capacity, as the cable television industry experienced in the early and mid-1980s. As discussed later in this chapter, another wave of channel expansion may be imminent, offering new opportunities for television retailing entrepreneurs.

The second exception is partial or complete ownership of the television shopping channel by a company that owns a large number of local cable systems (multiple system operator—MSO). In such cases, the parent company stands to benefit at a number of levels from carrying the shopping channel on its own systems. Almost all of the reach of QVC's Q2 network was related to partial ownership of QVC by cable MSOs.

Although the third exception has not yet occurred, it could arise in the next few years. Since passage of the 1992 Cable Act, cable operators have had to negotiate with broadcasters for carriage of broadcast stations on cable systems. Many broadcasters have chosen to start cable channels and require carriage of these channels as a condition of carrying their broadcast stations. Examples include ABC's ESPN2, NBC's CNBC, and Scripps-Howards' Home and Garden Channel. As of mid-1996, pressure to carry these channels has prevented many cable systems from carrying other new channels, including new shopping channels. However, it is conceivable that a broadcaster could someday request (or demand) carriage of a shopping channel as a provision of carrying a broadcast channel.

Broadcast Television. The primary difference in economics of broadcast television from those of cable television is that broadcast TV relies almost exclusively on advertising revenue. For this analysis, the primary feature of advertising revenue is the indirect flow of money from viewers to the medium. In essence, viewers "pay" for television programming as part of the cost of advertised products.

Two features of this indirect flow should be noted. Advertising rates are typically based on past program performance, adding another degree of separation between consumption of television programming and financial support. Also, the marginal cost of adding viewers to a program is zero (assuming that viewers already own television sets). One implication of this second factor is that a direct pricing mechanism is much more efficient for a program designed to reach a small, defined audience, but the indirect pricing mechanism is more efficient for programming targeted to a mass audience (Grant 1993).

Virtually all forms of television retailing provide for a direct flow of money from viewers to the program producers, and thus require a significantly smaller audience to produce the same amount of revenue than that generated by the indirect pricing mechanism. This is one of the reasons that both broadcast and cable television shopping services are able to earn comparatively large revenues even though their audiences are a fraction of those for most other types of programming.

The problem is that, although the small audiences earned by television retailing are sufficient to support the programming, they cannot be readily integrated into a schedule with advertiser-supported programming. Audience flow is a primary factor in television programming, with each program inheriting the audience of the preceding program. Placing an infomercial or television shopping program on a schedule therefore handicaps both the following program (the aforementioned "lead-in" effect) and the preceding program (the aforementioned "lead-out" effect).

When isolated on a single channel that provides only television shopping programming or infomercials, the audience flow is not a problem. However, the impact of one of these programs within a schedule of advertiser-supported programming is so strong that profits from television retailing are not large enough to make up for losses in advertising revenue.

The result is that the only time slots available on most broadcast outlets are those which already have extremely low viewing levels, or those for which there is no demand for advertising time (the two are often the same): late night and assorted weekend time slots.

Infomercials.   In addition to the broadcast concerns noted above, infomercials are affected by a separate set of economic factors. The first of these is the law of supply and demand, which has caused upward pressure on the cost of attractive time slots as the infomercial industry has grown. The lucrative nature of the infomercial and the sheer number of companies in the business promise a continuing competitive market for the limited number of time slots available for infomercials. On the other hand, the increase in what infomercial distributors are willing to pay for air time, combined with the increasing stability of the industry, has increased the number of stations willing to accept infomercials and the number of available time slots. This increase in the number of available time slots has, in turn, moderated the increase in the cost of air time.

A second important economic characteristic of infomercials is the immediate and direct response they provide marketers. This near-perfect marketing feedback allows an infomercial company to continuously alter schedules and buys to maximize revenues.

Direct Response. As discussed earlier, direct response advertisements typically generate between one-third and one-half of the revenue expected from a traditional advertising spot in the same time slot. In preparing this chapter, no research emerged addressing this factor. One possible explanation is that the traditional advertisement enjoys a synergy with other appearances of the same message over time (most advertisers acknowledge that at least three exposures to an advertising message are needed before it has an effect on consumers) and can be effective over long periods of time. (Consumers may act on information received in a commercial hours, days, or even months after seeing the commercial.) Direct response television advertisements, on the other hand, require an immediate response, giving little or no opportunity for delayed effects or follow-up (the exception being when a consumer sees the same DRTV message repeatedly).

The Capacity Cycle. Analysis of the growth of all forms of television retailing suggests the existence of a "capacity cycle." When new capacity is introduced in either broadcasting (new television stations) or cable (expanded channel capacity), a surplus of air time is available. Direct response television in all its forms offers a means of filling the air time while advertising support grows. Ultimately, advertising increases to fill the available air time, minimizing time available for direct response television.

Audience Characteristics

One of the biggest misconceptions facing television retailing is the nature of the audiences. Extensive research over the past few years has provided television retailers with an accurate picture of their customers, but the media and the general public have been slower to realize the nature of the customers for television shopping, infomercials, and DRTV.

Additional research is needed into the role played by television retailing as an enabling technology for mobility-impaired people. Anecdotal accounts suggest that all forms of television retailing, and television shopping in particular, may be more important to this audience than to any other.

Television Shopping. According to a 1993 study commissioned by Deloitte and Touche, 48 percent of all TV shoppers are between the ages of 25 and 44. Minorities are disproportionately represented among regular TV shoppers, as 20 percent are African American (versus 14 percent in the U.S. population), 17 percent are Hispanic (versus eight percent in the U.S. population), and 55 percent are white (versus 72 percent in the U.S. population). The distribution of income among TV shoppers is skewed toward both the lowest and highest income categories, with middle-income consumers less likely to buy. Finally, TV shoppers watch about half an hour more television per day than the average viewer and are more likely to make purchases from catalogs and direct mail (Braun 1993).

One of the biggest problems for new television shopping services has been overestimating the demand by consumers for their services. The practice of describing a channel or service and asking potential customers whether they are likely to buy will tend to inflate the prospects for a new service. A better approach is to measure past behavior. The single best predictor of whether consumers will buy from any form of television retailing is whether they have previously bought from that type of service. The next best predictor might be whether the consumer has purchased products from another type of television retailing. Finally, research consistently demonstrates that catalog shoppers are more likely to be customers of television shopping (Braun 1993; Meadows, Handy, and Grant 1996), so catalog purchasing should be an important behavioral predictor.

Buyers from Infomercials. NIMA International profiled infomercial customers, reporting that most were married women between the ages of 26 and 45 with household incomes of between $20,000 and $50,000. The vast majority—92 percent—indicated that they were either satisfied or very satisfied with their purchases, and 27 percent indicated repeat buying from the same company. The study indicated that repeat viewing was a major factor in infomercial purchases: almost three-quarters of the respondents reported watching an infomercial two or more times before ordering the product, and 15 percent reported watching the same infomercial five times or more before purchasing (Levin 1993).

Parasocial Interaction. One of the most important variables in understanding the relationship between consumers and any form of television retailing is parasocial interaction (Horton and Wohl 1956), the relationship that viewers develop with television personalities. The Grant et al. (1991) model of television shopper behavior (see Figure 3.3) demonstrated that strong parasocial relationships led to increased viewing, which in turn led to an increase in the number of purchases from television shopping programs.

The most tangible evidence of the importance of the parasocial relationship between viewers and television shopping hosts is the success of celebrities as hosts of infomercials and television shopping segments. The Grant et al. (1991) research also demonstrated that some of the strongest relationships were not with celebrities but with regular hosts of the television shopping programs. Regular viewers spend more time with these hosts than with many of their closest friends, and the result is a continuing psychological need to interact with these hosts, both by watching and by making purchases from the service.

Watchers versus Buyers. Because such a small percentage of the population regularly uses each type of television retailing service, most consumer studies related to television retailing use samples drawn from people who have made purchases. A recent study (Meadows, Handy, and Grant 1996) of television shoppers drawn from a sample of the general public explored the phenomenon of "watchers," people who watch television shopping programs but have never made a purchase. The group of watchers (12 percent of the sample) was as large as the group of buyers (11 percent) (the other 77 percent did not watch or buy from any television shopping service). The presence of such a large audience for television retail programming suggests that these programs may fulfill goals other than making purchases. Another possibility is that these audience members are "buyers in training" who will eventually make a purchase. In any case, future consumer studies should pay more attention to the watchers and the potential they represent for television retail services. (For a discussion of the implications of watchers, see Grant, Meadows, and Handy 1996.)

Figure 3.3. Model of Television Shopping Relationships

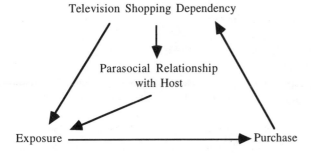

Television Shopping Dependency

Parasocial Relationship with Host

Exposure   Purchase

Source: Adapted from Grant, Gurthrie, and Ball-Rokeach (1991).

Regulatory Considerations

The increasing size of the television retailing industry has led to a number of government inquiries and a measure of regulation. The most notable action in this regard is the continuing refusal of the Justice Department to allow any type of merger between the two television shopping giants: HSN and QVC.

The Federal Communications Commission took a significant step to protect the television shopping industry in 1994. One provision of the Cable Communication and Consumer Protection Act of 1992 was that all television broadcasters could choose whether to demand carriage by local cable systems ("must carry") or force the cable operator to negotiate for permission to carry the channel. Virtually all broadcast television stations carrying television shopping programming full-time opted for must-carry status, forcing some cable operators to drop existing services to make room for the broadcast shopping channels.

Cable operators objected, claiming that the law was not intended to force carriage of television shopping programming. Ultimately, the FCC sided with the broadcasters under the rationale that because the stations had met every test needed to meet the requirements for holding a broadcast television license, they could not differentiate between shopping stations and any other broadcast stations.

State governments have also become concerned with various aspects of television retailing. The state of New York took action against HSN for allegedly misleading customers about original retail prices for product sold. Another concern on the state level is the collection of sales tax on purchases from television retailers.

By far the most important regulatory factor affecting television retailing was the Justice Department move to eliminate the NAB code and its limitations on the amount of commercial advertising allowed in an hour of programming. This action was the critical decision that opened the door for the creation of the television retailing industry.

Technological Considerations

One of the enabling factors behind television retailing is the set of technologies that make television retailing possible. Although dozens of experiments have been conducted with elaborate interactive systems to enable viewers to buy what they see on television, the medium of choice for viewer response is the ordinary telephone.

In fact, the failure of sophisticated technological means of providing television retail services highlights the fact that social and structural factors are much more important than technological factors for any type of television retailing. A good example is offered by the failure of J.C. Penney's Telaction service (discussed earlier) at the same time that the folksy Home Shopping Network was growing tremendously. Telaction was an electronic catalog designed for instrumental use, allowing a user to find and order a specific piece of merchandise. Viewers, however, never knew what specific items would be offered on HSN but tuned in for the "show" and made purchases as a means of interacting with the program. The lesson for those proposing advanced technology to enhance television retailing is that they need to fully understand consumers and their viewing and buying motivations to make sure that they are compatible with any technological system proposed.

Technology and Cable Television. The key cable television technology implicated in television retailing is expansion of the number of channels of programming on cable systems. Although early cable systems were limited to 12 channels, starting in the 1970s cable operators experimented with adding channels, increasing typical capacity to 24, 36, and then 54 channels on a system.

At each level, the cable operator experienced a problem with finding programming to fill the new channels. However, after a period of time the industry would adjust with cable programmers providing more program services to fill the available channel space.

Operators of prospective television shopping services would do well to follow this cycle of "shelf space availability" to time their entry into the market. The primary reason for the failure of shopping services proposed between 1993 and 1995 (as well as the slow growth or failure of other new cable television channels) was a lack of available channel space on cable television systems. However, the expansion of fiber optic technology in cable television systems should significantly increase the number of channels available on most cable television systems, offering an opportunity for additional television shopping channels.

Broadcast TV—Multiplexing. Broadcast television stations have been limited to offering a single program at a time. However, with the imminent introduction of digital broadcast systems, broadcasters may have the option of increasing the number of programs they offer simultaneously over a single channel. Digital broadcast technology was developed to allow broadcasters to transmit high-quality signals known as "high-definition television," but broadcasters have realized that they could use the digital systems to broadcast up to five "standard definition" signals instead of one high-definition signal (Seel 1996). Broadcasters could conceivably use one or more of these channels to offer television retailing services.

Even if broadcasters choose not to use their channel space to offer television retailing services, the flexibility of digital broadcast technology should allow inventive entrepreneurs to explore numerous new television retailing services. Only time will tell what new services technology will allow.

Telephone Technologies. As discussed earlier, the simple telephone network is the most important technology for television retailing. While the customer's end of the phone call is quite simple, the telephone response systems needed for television retail operations are among the most sophisticated in the world. These telephone response systems must handle literally hundreds of simultaneous calls, because almost every lost call is a lost sale.

Automatic telephone response systems are increasing in importance to television shopping networks, automating the order-taking process, one of the most personnel-intensive aspects of the industry. Callers can select whether to speak to an operator or use their touch-tone phone to key in order and payment information.

PEERING OVER THE HORIZON

As of mid-1996, television retailing was at an important crossroad. Infomercial sales were down from the previous year, and television shopping sales were continuing to enjoy only moderate growth. However, a variety of forces are converging in the electronic media industries to offer new opportunities and challenges for television retailers.

The introduction of new technologies will introduce a host of new opportunities for television retailing services. Cable television will be challenged by new multichannel distribution services, including direct broadcast satellites, wireless cable (MMDS), and distribution of video over telephone networks. Each of these distribution systems represents new opportunities for television retailers.

Other forms of electronic retailing will also become a major consideration for television retailers. On-line shopping, electronic catalogs, and new television distribution services will both help and hinder television retailers.

Helps

- New multichannel distribution services will mean additional channel space will be available for shopping channels. Some of this channel space may be used for existing channels, but opportunities will also exist for new channels.
- Additional capacity on cable television systems and other competing multichannel distribution services should lead to an increase in the number of specialized shopping channels.
- One of the key factors behind the success of television shopping was serendipity—and the ability of entrepreneurs to recognize when they had stumbled upon a winning format. Serendipity will continue to be an important factor in the success of certain newcomers.
- New forms of television retailing and broader audience exposure to all forms of television retailing may eventually result in a greater proportion of the audience utilizing all of the forms.
- Advertisers will continue to learn the benefits of television retailing, especially those of infomercials.

Hindrances

- The proliferation of targeted services offering a specific type of product or accommodating a specific consumer segment may adversely affect existing mass-marketed services, such as the catch-all television shopping channels.
- The use of increasingly sophisticated audience databases will allow new services to do a better job of targeting individuals and households, reducing the importance of mass marketing.
- In the near future, switched television technology (similar to that of the telephone network) may allow the delivery of customized messages to individual homes, opening the door for new services that will compete with existing television retailers.

• Other electronic retailing services, including on-line shopping over the Internet and commercial on-line services, will proliferate as the penetration of the Internet increases, again offering additional competition.

Other Factors to Consider

When evaluating the future of television retailing, consideration of the social role played by television shopping and other forms of television retailing will be necessary. The most important social dimension may be the personalities who host the programming offered by each form of television retailing and the parasocial relationship that viewers have developed with these hosts. Just as celebrities have always been important in commercial advertising, they will continue to play an important role in hosting and, in some cases, in creating their own "signature" lines of merchandise to take advantage of these parasocial relationships.

As new television retailers enter the marketplace, existing television retailers must devote considerable attention to differentiating their services from those of these new competitors. Differentiation could include providing a variety of presentational features, as well as increasing brand identity in the minds of consumers.

A final concern is the development of international markets. Although the primary focus of this chapter is television retailing in the United States, many television retailers, especially QVC, have made significant inroads into markets in other countries. Increasing globalization of the media should lead to greater globalization of the television retailing industry.

CONCLUSION

In reviewing the brief history presented in this chapter, the relative age of the industry should be used to provide some perspective on television retailing. The industries discussed in this chapter are virtually in their infancy, still struggling to define their role with respect to traditional retail outlets and traditional media.

The primary factor influencing the growth of each form of television retailing will be the acceptance by the audience of the retail medium. Many people will point to technological factors as the primary impetus for growth, but the lessons from the brief history of television retailing indicate that technology has always been subordinate to social factors.

In this respect, television retailing offers a number of important lessons for other forms of electronic retailing. The most significant of these is that television retailing is not comparable to catalog shopping. As Internet and on-line retailing become more established in the marketplace, it will be important to determine whether they more closely resemble catalogs or television retailing, a unique combination of the two, or something else altogether.

In any case, television shopping, infomercials, and direct response television advertisements have established themselves as important retailing phenomena. As such, these retailing forms should be expected to play an increasingly larger role in all areas of television as they continue to mature.

NOTES

1. In fact, Turner's reliance on DRTV advertising resulted in the formation of a new subsidiary that handled DRTV advertising for all Turner networks. At one point, this company was spun off from WTBS, but was later reacquired. Virtually all advertiser-supported Turner networks continue to air DRTV announcements.

2. Two of the most consistent phenomena regarding television ratings are the lead-in effect and the lead-out effect, which describe the manner in which television ratings affect and are affected by the ratings of the programs scheduled on the same channel immediately before and after any program.

3. This program evolved from Rivers' talk show, *The Joan Rivers Show*. The program lasted only one season and again demonstrated the problems with inserting television shopping programming into competitive time periods on broadcast television stations.

4

Electronic Sales Force Management at Mary Kay

Walter A. Bradley and S. Kregg Jodie

Mary Kay, Inc., originally a small, regional cosmetics firm, is now a fully integrated manufacturer and distributor of personal care products in 25 countries worldwide. Sales totaled more than $2 billion at the retail level in 1996, the company's ninth consecutive record year. Mary Kay, Inc., is a direct selling company that does business through independent contractors called beauty consultants. There are more than 100 national sales directors, more than 9,000 directors, and more than 400,000 independent beauty consultants worldwide selling to nearly 25 million customers. The largest direct seller of skin care products in the United States, Mary Kay is the number-one brand of facial skin care and color cosmetics in the U.S. (based on the most recently published industry sales data). Mary Kay manufactures and distributes more than 200 premium products in nine categories: facial skin care, color cosmetics, hair care, body care, nail care, sun protection, fragrances, men's skin care, and nutritional supplements. Mary Kay's direct selling approach creates a unique environment and opportunity in which to apply electronic marketing concepts and techniques.

The story of Mary Kay's humble beginnings is now legendary. In 1963, after the man she had trained and mentored as a subordinate was promoted to become her superior, Mary Kay Ash went out on her own and started Mary Kay, Inc. Knowing she would not change the business world by accepting it as it was, she began her own business for the purpose of providing a healthier environment and better economic opportunity for women—therein "changing" the business world. Even today the first item on the company's purpose statement is to provide "unparalleled opportunity for women"—our primary focus and customer is the independent sales force. Since inception, the vision has not changed. A majority of the sales force consists of women. However, the pursuit of that vision has changed immensely. Today, an "unparalleled opportunity" requires embracing technology and electronic marketing concepts to add value to a Mary Kay career.

Before going further, it is important to describe key principles in Mary Kay's business plan and provide a brief description of the direct selling industry. All independent beauty consultants buy products from Mary Kay at the same volume-discounted wholesale price and sell those products to consumers at retail. Consultants also recruit others to sell products to the consumer. As a consultant adds recruits and sells more products, she moves up to become a director. If she develops a substantial organization around her, she may ultimately attain the prestigious position of national sales director.

As a director, she manages many consultants and continues to sell products to the consumer. The director is compensated on her own sales as well as sales attributed to her recruits—who become known as her unit. Managing her unit includes teaching, coaching, motivating, and recognizing her consultants. This is a career opportunity for women that not only includes compensation but also recognizes a job well done. Such congratulations come in the form of prizes (pink Cadillacs are but one) and in the form of public recognition, either at unit meetings or at companywide events. Compensation is important, but we cannot overemphasize the importance of recognition—ask any consultant about the thrill of walking across the stage at the company's annual sales seminar and you can only then begin to appreciate the power of this visible type of recognition for the sales force. This is important to remember as we move into our attempts to bring technology to the sales force.

A discussion of the direct selling industry is really a topic worthy of an entire book, much less a paragraph in a chapter of a book. However, it is important to understand the basic principles and how they relate to Mary Kay, Inc. The direct selling form of retailing focuses on the idea of providing personalized service to the end consumer—individual-to-individual, point-of-sale—as contrasted with typical over-the-counter retail sales at fixed business locations. At Mary Kay, our personalized service comes in the form of beauty classes and personal contact with potential and existing customers. For potential customers, independent beauty consultants hold skin care classes to demonstrate our product and how to use the product. For existing customers, the consultant continues to provide personal care and product information as products change. For Mary Kay and other direct selling organizations, personal sales is an integral part of the power of direct selling, with the mission of providing total customer satisfaction. Personal sales and independent contractors present some interesting challenges and opportunities, especially regarding electronic marketing and sales automation. With independent contractors and customers in distant locations and decision making distributed across a vast number of people, the success of any direct selling organization, including Mary Kay, is how quickly, reliably, and effectively it interacts or communicates with these people. Electronic marketing and sales automation can greatly enhance our ability to manage and support independent contractors economically and will play a key role in successful direct selling organizations in the future. The benefits of any direct selling organization's electronic marketing and sales automation efforts should include:

- Speed of communications
- Cost-effective and improved communications and service
- More valuable and timely information
- Improved sales force service
- Automation of nonvalue-added tasks

Time is very critical to independent contractors, who typically work on a part-time basis. Any reduction in nonvalue-added tasks or increased support in marketing the product will result in a more productive sales force.

FIRST ATTEMPTS AT AUTOMATING THE SALES FORCE

Known for its legacy of creating profitable, fulfilling relationships dependent on interpersonal contact between its sales force and consumers, the simple mantra of Mary Kay, Inc. is "Nothing happens until someone sells something." Our direct selling environment and personalized service would seem in contrast to the current rate of technological evolution and certain societal trends toward electronic commerce, convenience buying, "chat-room dating," and other manifestations of the cyber-world. The sales force should spend its time meeting with customers and recruits, not playing on a computer. This concept was actually validated in our first attempt to bring technology to our sales force.

In 1982 we introduced a sales force automation tool-set written for a DOS environment and using a Tandy computer. The objectives were simple and straight forward—provide the sales force with tools that would help its operations be more efficient. The software provided contact management and inventory and financial analysis capabilities. Contact management allowed the consultant to track personal and product information on each customer. Inventory and financial analysis tracked inventory reorder points and expenses and income information necessary for tax reporting. However, it required the consultant or director to rekey information from paper reports sent to her monthly through the mail.

Unfortunately, our sales force was not composed of off-duty programmers or early adopters of new technologies. But even if it had been, it didn't matter. Our product, created by a technology staff working autonomously, was cumbersome and a poor replacement for a manual process, which though repetitive and slow, got the job done. It did little but create impressions that technology was, in fact, counterintuitive to the business of direct selling and that we had done little more than transform outstanding customer-oriented sales people into data entry clerks.

The system never gained wide acceptance. At its termination some seven years later, less than three hundred directors were using the system. The limited functionality, high price (Mary Kay originally priced the software at $699 but reduced it to under $500 a couple of years later), its manual, redundant nature, and expensive hardware were attractive to only a few. In addition, the software offered nothing *unique* from Mary Kay, Inc. There was no network connection to

Mary Kay to exchange critical information. Mary Kay has extremely valuable information for the sales force, such as sales production, contests, promotions, and product information. For example, only Mary Kay can provide access to company-developed information and plan changes. Only it can provide e-mail addresses for *all* of its consultants. Only Mary Kay would know about new promotions and special product offerings that might be included on an order form. Only Mary Kay knows about inventory back orders and out-of-stock products. We did not include these capabilities. By the end of its era, many third-party vendors offered similar capabilities for a fraction of the cost.

It failed. Resoundingly. This failure appeared to validate the thought that *our* business was not an appropriate one to advance new technology—"high touch" (our people-to-people principles) *meant* "low tech." We lived with that impression for six years, during which we saw other companies and other direct sellers make equally uninspired attempts with similar results. In reality, however, it was not the technology that failed, but how we approached and implemented the technology.

A DIFFERENT APPROACH

After this less-than-illustrious start, we approached the automating of our sales force from a wholly fresh perspective. Although lessons had been learned from the first attempt, the information systems leadership team had completely changed hands. Unencumbered by history, our second attempt was from the customer's perspective. The end result was a very successful product we call Mary Kay *InTouch*™. The product is sales and marketing driven for our sales force; it is based on four principles.

Focus First on Sales Productivity, Not Operational Productivity

The sales force at Mary Kay is motivated by recognition *and* compensation. If we could deliver a product and processes that would increase its potential for more revenue and recognition, we would be successful. Operational components would be delivered and, in some cases, have a major bottom line effect; however, our focus was and remains on consultant sales productivity. The sales force, we believed, would embrace a technology that increased its own *earnings* and *recognition* potential. Mary Kay would benefit, of course, but *only* if the sales force did.

Become Your Customer

We often remind our staff that we must do more than *think* like customers, we must almost *become* them. That frame of reference—the customer's—is critical. Our information systems' legacy has scattered among its wounded and dead the remnants of systems built by programmers. These same systems, which may contain more technological brilliance than the world will ever know, often fail to fully solve the underlying problem.

Our staff is now conditioned to listen. To do that, several of our programmers and analysts practically lived with their customers. From an "over the shoulder" vantage point with our top sales directors, they observed the business as it actually occurred, not as they wanted it to occur or as they had *heard* it occurred. The team made priceless observations one cannot make without being there. For example, often our directors work at peculiar hours—either very late or very early—around other work schedules or the pressures of running families and households. Since our "available" hours were inconsistent with theirs, they would have to queue certain activities to work around us. Since *becoming* customers, we have a greater sensitivity to how our business affects theirs. And, more importantly, how ours must change for them.

The result has been a vastly superior system, one that has gained widespread acceptance with minimal marketing. The difference has been profound; *InTouch*™ works in ways our independent contractors can relate to and addresses *their* needs.

Make It Simple, Simple, Simple

If we accomplished nothing else in our efforts to develop a good product, it had to be easy to use. Our product had to be kiosk-like. We knew we could not personally train all our directors or consultants, a largely PC-illiterate group. The software had to interact on an intuitive level and be very consultant friendly. At times we had to give up flexibility and functionality to avoid complicating the product.

And as much as it had to be simple, it also had to be fun to use. Yes, fun. People will inadvertently teach themselves new tricks and develop new skills if the training environment doesn't look like work. *InTouch*™ presents such a visually appealing contrast to their manual systems that consultants enjoy working with it. The feedback we get from the directors is filled with the delight they feel when they discover a feature or new way to use the system. People are pleased when their own curiosity yields results. We know the novelty will wear thin eventually, but "fun" will be as much a part of the future success as it is with the current success.

It would have been easy to succumb to the notion of accommodating all of the great ideas we found in the field. Because our sales force consists of different types of business people having different ideas on how to run a business, we aimed for a middle ground where the most effective directors got something of value and the least effective got tools that let them emulate the best. There were many brilliant opportunities left on the cutting room floor, perhaps to be included in later releases. To keep it simple, we accommodated those practices we believed best exemplified the standards of a well-run firm, irrespective of business acumen and experience.

Don't Go for the Home Run

We certainly have a vision of how technology can revolutionize how our company and sales force do business; however, we also know that we have to evolve toward that vision. Rather than develop our tools around how the sales force *should do* business, we knew we had to build tools around how they already *did* business. The change in the way the sales force did business needed to be gradual. Too much change too quickly would have resulted in failure. The new tools would be adapted to their current frame of reference before process improvements would be made.

An ideal example is in the *InTouch*™ Communications Manager. Among other features, this software sends company information such as newsletters and announcements to the sales force electronically. In its first iteration, our weekly *Director's Memo* looks much like its paper ancestor—only in electronic form. Directors already know how to read the *Memo*, what it typically contains, and where to find what they need. They did not need us to reinvent things they already knew how to use, even if it meant our developers had to wait to make the productivity gains they knew were possible. Whatever *our* thinking, the sales force has to be ready.

Likewise, from a system development standpoint, our focus was to phase in applications over time. We would build on success after success to gain momentum; this also allowed us to learn in an iterative fashion. We needed to be somewhat cautious because everything we were doing was a new way of doing business at Mary Kay.

AN ATTITUDE SHIFT

As mentioned, Mary Kay, Inc. historically viewed the "high touch" aspects of its business as contradictory to "high tech." If consultants were working on computers, customers and unit members were presumably not getting the critical personal contact they needed to reach their respective potentials. Given our results from automation efforts in the 1980s, management had a right to be skeptical.

Recent experience with technology has proven otherwise. Today our business focus is still on the high touch aspects of Mary Kay, but with a fundamental shift in attitude toward technology. Mary Kay, Inc. now recognizes that high tech is a tool to support and enhance the way it does business. The two are not contradictory. Nor are they merely complementary. Rather, technology has the potential to enable one to reach unprecedented proficiency—a synergy can be created, making the new whole more than its parts. In our business, that means technology will enable a consultant to spend more valued-added time with unit members and customers than she would otherwise have had available, and on matters of the highest impact.

We had unknowingly placed an incredible administrative burden on our consultants—the result of an increasingly complex business and our desires to gather new information. For example, placing product orders is a massive endeavor for our sales force. Maybe it shouldn't be a complicated, time-consuming activity, but it is. A large, complex, manually prepared order for a new consultant, for example, can take 2 to 3 hours or more. With the *InTouch*™ Order Manager, that same order takes a fraction of the time.

We are no longer accused of making computer operators of our consultants. And, incidentally, the automated order is much more accurate than the manual one. In the past, 80 percent of the orders had some flaw that required attention. The Order Manager significantly reduces errors at the source.

SOLUTIONS WE ARE DELIVERING—MARY KAY *INTOUCH*™

Electronic marketing means different things to different companies. Given the relationship with our independent sales force, it means providing the directors with information about the people they are mentoring and managing. This information includes production and sales information, general communications, product promotions and/or marketing plan rules or changes. This information is critical in improving sales force productivity.

As mentioned previously, the result of our different approach was Mary Kay *InTouch*™. Figure 4.1 illustrates the buttons and a brief description of all the functions and capabilities of *InTouch*™. The following four sections outline the major functions and benefits of Mary Kay *InTouch*™.

Sales Production Tracking and Reporting

Again, a critical success factor of Mary Kay's marketing plan is recognition and motivation. With timely information on how someone is performing and where she stands in terms of contests, sales rankings, and so forth, a director can work with the right person at the right time with the right message. The result will be a more productive unit. Previously this information was either severely dated, not available, or required a great deal of work to retrieve and put into the appropriate format. The information is now delivered to directors on a daily basis.

Figure 4.1. Mary Kay *InTouch*™ Functions

Mary Kay *InTouch*™ Services Screen Buttons	
Button	**Description**
Datebook	The sales force can track appointments and significant events, manage address information, maintain a To Do list, and keep a personal journal.
Reports Manager	Vital sales information can be viewed, graphed, copied and pasted, printed, or exported to other software packages with only a few clicks of the mouse button.
Communications Manager	Communication is facilitated by the ability to send and receive electronic mail as well as electronic documents.
Order Manager	The sales force can realize significant time savings and virtually eliminate calculation errors by using blank or company-supplied sample electronic order forms to create product orders on their PC.
Setup	The sales force can elect to receive electronic documents in Spanish as well as English.
Connect	A single button click initiates the CompuServe connection that downloads electronic mail, electronic documents, and sales information.
Download T.O.C.	A list of the information received on the most recent successful download can be viewed easily.
What's New	Important Mary Kay *InTouch* program notes display automatically following a successful information download.
News Flash	Time-sensitive or critical Mary Kay business information can be communicated via News Flash messages.
WinCim	CompuServe's online services are accessible from within Mary Kay *InTouch*.
Exit	A single button click closes all Mary Kay *InTouch* modules and returns to Windows.
Help	Each Mary Kay *InTouch* module provides detailed online help.
Hints	The Hints button activates *balloon help*, which provides brief explanations of the areas touched with the mouse pointer.
Support	Questions, comments, or program enhancement suggestions can be sent directly to the Mary Kay *InTouch* Support Center via a pre-addressed electronic mail message.

Electronic Documents

We now electronically deliver documents directly to the desktop of a director that once came through the U.S. mail. The information is delivered more quickly and in a format that can be shared easily within the sales unit. The electronic documents can easily be stored and retrieved for use at a later time. In addition, a director will be able to search for a particular subject within the electronic documents. See Figure 4.2 for an example of a document that was originally sent only through U.S. mail but is now sent electronically once a week. The electronic document is identical to the paper document and requires no additional formatting by Mary Kay before being sent to directors.

Figure 4.2. Director's Memo

E-mail

We provide easy-to-use e-mail as part of the infrastructure of our system that facilitates quick and efficient vertical communications. Electronic mail does not replace the telephone, but rather provides a way to share information with an entire group and extends the type of information that can be shared to a visual still form (that is, news fliers, spreadsheets, word processing documents, and so forth). Our support team also uses electronic mail to communicate software changes to the sales force, which in turn offers suggestions and criticisms.

Electronic Order Entry

Electronic order entry will not only give us significant operational benefits, it will also help the sales force market the right products. This application allows the sales force to create an order on the computer, saving endless hours of calculating, erasing, and transferring order information onto the paper order forms. With the Order Manager, the sales force can quickly perform what-if analyses and leverage sample orders provided by the system or their own predefined order templates targeted to their own customers' preferences to make quick, accurate business decisions regarding their orders.

The system promotes additional sales by providing information on various discount programs and any special promotions at the time an order is prepared. The system also promotes up-selling by suggesting how much more investment is needed to reach the next discount level. This helps to alleviate concerns that it takes a caring, thinking human to *improve* the transaction. In fact, since a disproportionate share of our business comes in the final week of a calendar month, the telephone order staff is under tremendous pressure to simply process the calls. *InTouch*™ does not respond to pressure and simply suggests the best deal possible for the consultant. The average order amount is expected to increase with electronic ordering because of the benefits it provides.

PC HOME MARKET SHARE AND WOMEN USING PCS

Our approach assumes that our sales force has access to personal computers and that the sales force will be able and willing to use them. This issue will be irrelevant in 10 years, when all women will be just as likely as men to have PCs and will be educated in using them. However, the real question for us is whether a 39-year-old woman (the average age of a director) will have access to a PC and be willing to use the PC or learn how to use it today or next year. Is this reasonable? We obviously think so.

In 1995, there were more PCs sold than TVs, more e-mail messages sent than postal messages (95 billion versus 85 billion), and more data traffic than voice traffic for the first time in history. Bandwidth concerns not withstanding, PCs will continue to encroach into our daily routines until the television, telephone, mail systems and shared data networks will become one. In addition, user demographics for on-line systems, especially the Internet, are drastically changing. No longer are men the only surfers on the Internet; women are being attracted more and more to it. The number of women going on-line is projected to more than triple from 5 million to more than 18 million in the next five years. Why is this? Some reasons are that technology is easier to use, on-line services are common in the workplace, and on-line services are being targeted to women (Delhagen and Eichler 1996).

Depending on whom you believe, 30 to 40 percent of all American households currently have a PC. This percentage increases dramatically when household income is more than $50,000 a year and the family is well educated. In 1995 our consultants earned an average annual household income of $47,000, compared to a national average of $31,000. Eighty percent of our consultants have at least some college education, compared to 36 percent of all U.S. women. Consultants are better educated and earn more income than the average woman. In addition, the number of households owning a PC continues to rise, and the cost of PCs will continue to go down. Industry is doing everything possible to exploit the home market, and this includes ideas such as inexpensive dumb terminals that will give the consumer access to the Internet. We believe that our consultants either already have access to a computer or will in the near future.

Will Mary Kay consultants use the PC for business purposes? Baskin (1995, p. 72) noted that in 1994

the number of women who influenced home PC purchases grew 25 percent and represent 42 percent of all home PC buyers. Women don't get carried away by the gadget nature of PCs like men—they like high performance PCs if and when it helps them excel at their jobs and manage their personal lives. Women will use the PC if it helps them make money and they do not have to be a computer programmer to use the PC.

We agree with Baskin.

AFFORDABLE NETWORKS AND TECHNOLOGY

How do we affordably network consultants all over the United States and provide them with software tools? The advent of on-line services and the Internet has made this possible. It costs a consultant $15 a month for the network connection. The network allows Mary Kay to send information and program updates to the consultants at the touch of a button.

When we entered the market in 1982, we offered a $4,000 8 MHz Tandy computer with 640k memory and 20Mb storage running Tandy's proprietary operating system and a $699 software and database package. In 1996, *InTouch*™ requires, at a minimum, an Intel® 486-based PC with 8 Mb of RAM and 20Mb of available hard disk space. The software requires much more power, but the PC can be purchased at half the price of the Tandy that Mary Kay originally required. (In fact, it is hard to compare the two systems because it was not possible to construct this much computing power in an off-the-shelf system in 1982.) And in terms of the software tools costs, we can distribute our database and tools necessary to run the programs at no cost to the end user.

There is obviously a cost associated with programming and supporting *InTouch*™. However, rather than charge the consultants for the software, we provide it free by recognizing the incredible dividends its use will pay back to Mary Kay. Only the third-party network costs are recurring, and we will absorb them if we must for increased sales force penetration. Consequently, the technology is affordable to an increasingly larger segment of the sales force.

HAVE WE BEEN SUCCESSFUL?

Our experiences from the 1980s left some with impressions that our business could not lead the market in technological innovation or that the information systems team was incapable of delivering on its promises. We will not be measuring our success against that failure—the threshold for success would be too low.

Currently we offer *InTouch*™ only to directors. The 9,000 directors represent the most productive of our consultants. It is critical that they buy into the new paradigm that one can do business with Mary Kay without having to speak with a human for every transaction. Our vision includes making more productive people of our directors. To that end, we have already had an impact.

That we have achieved a 25 percent penetration rate with our directors with little marketing in approximately one year is remarkable. For a company renowned for its marketing prowess, this seems to point to an incredible, latent demand for richer, more timely information. This argues the case for reaching the remainder of the sales force—the consultants—as soon as possible.

But we know that the next 25 percent penetration will be harder to reach than the first 25 percent. We now begin to reach into less progressive and less profitable directors and units. We know that the most progressive among our directors are also the most likely to have the willingness and resources to adopt new technologies and business practices. That our 25 percent penetration represents almost 50 percent of net sales is evidence of this correlation. Now our challenge is to provide such unquestionable value to those lesser units that they are compelled to seek the product for its productivity gains.

Other measures of our success include whether *InTouch*™ is being used and if its use is reflected in the performance of the units. Because our directors are independent business people, we rely a great deal on anecdotal evidence. The stories they offer are compelling; see Figure 4.3 for illustrative testimonials.

Empirical evidence does exist, however, and it corroborates these less scientific anecdotes. We know, for example, that when using *InTouch*™ the call frequency and durations into our voice response system (which "reads" daily results to callers) are dramatically lower for those who are experienced with the system. The savings are realized at corporate and, when *InTouch*™ is fully deployed, will eliminate a significant telecommunications cost. We also know what the costs are for printing, handling, and mailing voluminous month-end reports. These savings, too, are sizable. In recent years we've reduced the production quality—not the content—of our field communications, such as eliminating four-color images and buying cheaper paper. Certainly, the costs of sending color on premium stock are greater than when the medium is electronic. Finally, we spend upwards of $1 million per year printing and distributing order forms. Most of these forms we will never see again, nor are they used to prepare telephone orders. After *InTouch*™ is fully deployed, these paper orders—and their associated costs and environmental impact—should disappear.

Figure 4.3. Mary Kay _InTouch_™ Testimonials

Just a note to let you know how much _InTouch_™ means to our unit. In the past six months our unit has nearly doubled in size, and we have just won our first Cadillac. The fast information access provided by _InTouch_™ was a big factor in our success _Cathy Burrell, Director_	_InTouch_™ made it possible, both visually and especially timewise, for me to track my unit in June for End of Year Production. We had our best month ($40,000!!!) in 10 years! The tracking that _InTouch_™ made possible helped me to believe we could do it _Marjorie Haun, Sr. Director_
I am really delighted with the _InTouch_™ program. This time last year I didn't know how to use a computer. Now I can send e-mail! I have set up a fabulous recognition system that my secretary oversees. I have made up form letters, greeting cards, on-target cards, etc. I am able to track directors and the size of their personal teams with a regular letter, depending on whether team size is growing or not. I am seeing some definite results. _Anita Garrett-Roe, Sr. National Sales Director_	Wilma had a new recruit who placed her $600 order, only it turned out to be $596.00 and would have not qualified for the free product. _InTouch_™ saved the day, allowing Wilma to follow-up and get it corrected, averting a crisis for a newcomer. More positive impact is the ability to get info daily without the large amount of time spent on the phone and the stress of trying to write it all down. _Costa, Wilma Dunias' husband, Director_
I'm a great _InTouch_™ success story of hope. I still am afraid of our TV remote control and can barely turn on the VCR to play a movie. I gave up on computers a long time ago, before _InTouch_™. I have been labeled one of the "electronically challenged." I can't say I breeze through all this now, but I can get what I need and get it fast. Thank you for bringing me into the 21st century! _Jill Beckstedt, Exec. Sr. Director_	Yesterday somebody placed a $3,600 wholesale. She was from out of town and she needed the order ASAP. Normally it will take me half a day to do a big order like that and a headache to figure the tax, etc. Did you know it only took me 20 minutes to do her order? _Evelyn Ruffer, Sr. Director_

No test is adequate to judge the success of our effort save the test of time. But, then, time passes quickly in this age of the electron.

LOOKING TOWARD THE FUTURE

We see opportunities in the future to extend our system's utility well beyond operational support systems. Operational support systems are those that help conduct business, such as inventory control, sales contact management, order entry and submission, and package tracking. We will always have initiatives to improve the efficiencies and economies of our business by redefining and refining the processes supported by these systems. But at best they make us more efficient—they do little to genuinely and radically improve our market position.

Likewise, in the future we will go beyond our current analytical systems. Analytical systems that support a better understanding of the business, such as financial reporting, sales reporting, and marketing analysis, will be packaged as decision support systems (DSS) or executive information systems (EIS). Well-developed analytical tools provide information that can be viewed in various contexts so that intelligent, trained analysts can with time detect trends and anticipate outcomes against different scenarios. But many decisions can be made from simple tests applied against easily interpreted information. Computers can be taught to perform these simple tests and communicate the actions suggested.

As technology becomes a common denominator, its existence in a firm ceases to be a distinguishing factor. The market will reward those who assimilate, synthesize, and act on the information provided by technology. We have already seen empirical evidence that information that is actionable is worth money to us and to our customers.

Our focus has shifted to what we call "thinking systems." The passive-sounding name should not be mistaken—these are the most actionable of systems. These systems either learn (such as with artificial intelligence) or are taught (as with rules) to suggest actionable tasks—in essence, thinking *for* their users. Rather than have to draw a conclusion, the system clearly says "Call Jane Doe at 555-5917 and encourage her to place a $100 order before month-end to qualify for her Grand Am." Or, perhaps the system sends Jane an urgent electronic mail message with a return receipt. If no receipt is processed in the next day, the "call Jane" message would appear on the director's daily task list. The possibilities are seemingly unlimited.

To some, this background on technology might seem askew with the marketing theme. After all, isn't marketing creating impressions in minds and influencing future decisions? In fact, we are very much marketing Mary Kay in a unique way by helping the consultant reach her potential. The fact that we readily share information that was once regarded as proprietary exemplifies this new view of her and demonstrates—or markets—our goals for her success. It helps identify and hold her. It helps solidify the corporate image. It helps her develop the best possible outcome for her efforts by incorporating over thirty years of "smarts" being built into the system. It is, in every sense, a marketing tool. But it is and will be much more.

The vision for *InTouch*™ is to extend the little gray box (or TV) on a director's or consultant's desk into a business assistant ready to greet her each morning with information such as who needs a call that day and why—a business partner empowering the director/consultant to provide personalized encouragement and recognition to each consultant in her unit and personalized service to each customer. Multimedia training and recognition will be standard tools for a successful director or consultant.

The five-year vision for the creation of this cyber assistant involves components of communications, order entry, back office support, and unit development. Figure 4.4 illustrates this five-year vision.

Figure 4.4. Mary Kay *InTouch*™ Five-year Vision

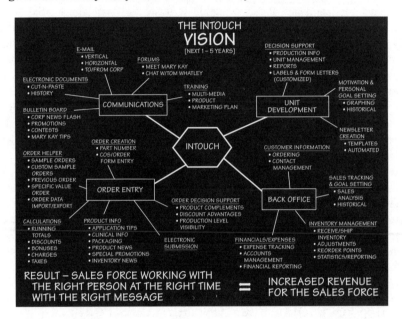

As shown in Figure 4.4, the five-year vision incorporates several major themes. One theme is *productivity*. Collaboration rather than duplication. Just-in-time motivation rather than after-the-fact condolences or congratulations. No other technology supports productivity as well as a wide-area enterprise network such as *InTouch*™. In an information age, and within a direct selling environment dependent on motivation and response, *InTouch*™ should profoundly affect sales force efficiency well into the 21st century.

Another key theme is *personalization*. We have recognized that from a profiling perspective our consultant is no longer a "she;" instead, she is a "them." This is a profound admission on our part. For example, past marketing efforts were targeted to a profile or to a narrow range of profiles. In the 21st century, our consultants and their customers will demand personalized services. In essence we will have closer to 400,000 profiles, all requiring some measure of support tailored to them as individuals, and we will have to recognize their unique needs and adapt to them. This represents a huge challenge, a challenge that only well-conceived technology can possibly support.

A final theme is *convenience*. Certainly we must provide tools that make our consultants more productive and that can be personalized to the way they do business. But it must also be convenient to access and must be available when needed. Currently, we can only be reached through a specific machine that has all the software installed properly. This makes a mobile operation difficult and will therefore change.

Of particular interest to those of us in the information technology field is the behavioral trend toward providing information to users when they are ready for it and not just when the information is ready for them. This trend helps justify efforts into user-based tools, data warehouses and datamarts, networks, real-time all-time information, and graphical interfaces. We are embracing the trend by providing consultants with information they can use and suggesting when we think it will be most useful to them. This rarely matches when we most conveniently (read: economically) can make it available.

Today, Mary Kay consultants receive the poorest customer service at the time they need it most. During those last few days of the month, the avalanche of inquiries and orders from directors and consultants strains our capacities. Unintentionally, we have made it inconvenient for consultants to conduct the most crucial of all transactions—the ones where money changes hands. This changes in the *InTouch™* vision. In the vision, a consultant conducts business with us at *her* convenience. There are no waiting lines. There are no on-hold queues. There are no harried or overbearing order takers. There are no set hours of operation. And thus the vision of *InTouch™* eloquently supports Mary Kay's own of providing a healthy, profitable relationship for women around the world, women who have complete control over their daily lives and schedules.

IF OUR FOCUS HAS BEEN ON THE SALES FORCE, HAVE WE FORGOTTEN THE END CONSUMER?

Undoubtedly, we have a unique business challenge: everything we know about our consultants is based on what they tell us and what they *buy*. Nowhere in the current business model is information about what they *sell* made available to us. Their selling activity may well provide more useful information to us than their buying activity. Sales are often a poor barometer of demand because promotions, contests, and other incentives mask consumer behavior. We are somewhat insulated from consumers.

Today we gather information about our consumers anecdotally, from industry statistics, and from focus groups in which we try to anticipate behavior from responses. All of these forms are woefully inadequate against empirical data, if they existed, that would *prove* behavior. We would be wary of scenarios where we extract sales and inventory information from our consultants' systems—even if such systems existed. Because no systems currently provide this information, we are investigating an extension to *InTouch™* that would allow us to extract generic sales and inventory information with the consultant's approval. Perhaps we will provide incentives to encourage participation and temper our results against any deviations resulting from our unrepresentative population. In any regard, it is a place to start.

Obviously, this information is worth much to us. Not appreciating the inventory in the field, for example, has caused us to misjudge the impact of a promotion or to over- or under-manufacture products. Because all of our revenues come from the field, avoiding these costly mistakes can only reduce our costs of business and improve the quality of our product and promotion launches. Mary Kay and the sales force will both benefit.

Our sales force is granted broad geographic territory. Under current rules and with few exceptions, consultants are bound only to their contracted country and have no other geographic constraints. For the U.S.-based consultant, this means that her business could and occasionally does extend from coast to coast. Even so, because of the personal nature of the product and a very mobile society, many consultants have not adequately served customers too far removed for personal contact.

This challenge of finding and serving her customers without regard to geography is not unique to our business and may be quite harmonious with the linking capabilities promised by an information superhighway available to us all. After all, in the future not even the geography of a country will be confining. Borders will become "soft." Mary Kay is already in 25 countries and will add new countries to the portfolio every year. It is but a matter of time before the geographical borders that separate them give way. Rather than physical and jurisdictional, these soft borders might include language, interests, experiences, lifestyles, belief and value systems, and occupations.

Retention is another major aspect of great interest in direct selling that technology has the potential to impact. Consultants or their customers relocate for various reasons, but the result is often a severed relationship between the company and the customer, sometimes between the company and the consultant. If we can help overcome this geographic distance between them, we have an opportunity to retain them both.

A test in progress involves the World Wide Web. At present, the Mary Kay Web site functions solely as an advertising medium. However, the lure of convenience and the sophisticated thinking of customers about products and services may change the Web into a more powerful sales support device in the future.

There are other possibilities of Web support for the Mary Kay sales force. Taking a what-if scenario—what if a customer, after being taught by a consultant how to use the product and get the most from it, is able to replenish the product on-line? The reorder goes directly to the picking line, the product directly to the customer, the commission check directly to the consultant. Or what if Mary Kay's *Preferred Customer* program, a follow-up mail campaign direct to consumers with revenue linked to consultants, were subscribed on-line?

Again, the ordering, delivery, and commission process is automatic, and the consultant builds revenue without investing time. This would seem to offer a formula certain to encourage tenure for both the consultant and her customers.

Surely the consumer has much to gain from these new tools and prospects. And, no, Mary Kay has not forgotten her.

CONCLUSION

Those who find ways to create and maintain electronic relationships with their customers will dominate the future. We aren't just debating whether we protect our market from entreaties by others—that's defensive. Rather, we are debating the creation of new markets and how our markets change because of the technologies we deploy. We know that our use of technology says a great deal about us to our customers. Just ask any of them if they'd be affected if a report were not on time, their 1099 statement was wrong, or they were unable to get through to someone on our telephone system. We are convinced that properly executed technology presents a tremendously positive image of our company that may beckon prospective consultants.

We can't know with certainty how the role of marketing will change with these new tools, but we are assured that it will change. We also know new definitions of marketing will emerge. In the past, we were judged by our price, our product, our performance, and our claims. Now customers will also be comparing the value they get from our technology—which may be very separate from our prices, products, performance, and claims.

Finally, there are trends influencing our decision making at Mary Kay regarding technology and how it relates to electronic marketing, sales force management, and information services in general. These trends represent both challenges and opportunities, and if we do not correctly anticipate their impact, we will be at a definite disadvantage as we turn toward the next century. The trends influencing us at Mary Kay include the following:

- Geographic borders are yielding to social borders.
- Network technology is connecting us in new ways and creating richer relationships among us that counter concerns that it will depersonalize us. High touch, in fact, *requires* high tech.
- The urgency of business information precludes its being reduced to paper. News that did not happen today or yesterday will be too old to report.
- Multimedia technology liberates our creative initiative; most of its uses have not yet been demonstrated.
- Consultants and consumers are demanding personalized services only achievable through wise technological implementation. Markets of one are becoming reality.
- Our consultants *will* have access to information technology. Based on education and income levels, our consultant base is among the fastest growing users of PC technology—even after considering gender-based influences.

- Intranet and Internet technology is enabling new forms of mass applications, much as the printer has had an impact on correspondence. This, though, is not *all* positive.
- The mainframe computer is reemerging in the role of warehouse for massive quantities of data that belie truths about our customers and how they behave—truths we must understand and appreciate.

5

Real Shopping in a Virtual Store

Raymond R. Burke

"Retailing will never be the same." So proclaimed the cover of the July 26, 1993, issue of *Business Week*. The magazine described how home shopping through interactive television would revolutionize retailing. Fiber optic cable, digital image compression, video servers, and powerful TV set-top boxes would bring 500 or more channels into consumers' homes, providing new applications for home shopping, banking, and video on demand. The world was captivated by this new technology. Major agreements were announced between cable, telephone, computer, and entertainment companies to develop and deploy interactive television. Everyone expected that these would be major successes. Jupiter Communications forecast that interactive TV sales would approach $10 billion by 2002, with 17.6 percent of U.S. households shopping by television. R. Fulton Macdonald, president of International Business Development Corp., was even more optimistic, predicting that home shopping would grow to $250 billion in ten years. Unfortunately, the industry agreements collapsed and the new services never materialized.

Today, people are making similar claims about the Internet. Business publications, consultants, academics, and high-tech companies trumpet the news of how the Internet will revolutionize the way we work, play, shop, bank, communicate, and learn. But business history suggests that we should be pessimistic. Are these claims true? Will retailing never be the same? And if it will be different, how will it be different and how will this affect consumers and their relationships with manufacturers and retailers?

WILL CONSUMERS SHOP IN A VIRTUAL STORE?

Electronic shopping has been available for several years through various computer on-line services, including America Online, Compuserve, and Prodigy, as well as the Internet and television shopping channels (e.g., QVC and HSN). The sales results have been unimpressive. Of the $2.2 trillion in U.S. retail sales, only about $60 billion are through non-store retail formats, including catalogs, television, and direct mail. TV and other electronic sales account for just $3 billion, or one-seventh of one percent of the total. And 40 percent is jewelry! If we look just at sales through the Internet and on-line services, the total for 1995 was only about $350 million, or less than 0.02 percent of the total.

Despite its poor performance to date, electronic retailing may still become a significant force in the future. First, consumers' acceptance of nonstore retailing is higher than what sales figures suggest. About 45 percent of American households purchase products from catalogs each year, and about 7 percent buy via television. Sales are limited, in part, because few products are available through these channels. Once consumers are able to purchase high-volume items like groceries and drug products through the Internet, we may see a dramatic increase in electronic sales.

Second, electronic retailing may become a significant force because of the rapid growth in home computing and the Internet infrastructure. Home computers are now estimated to be in 30 to 40 million homes. Most of the new computers sold have advanced communications and multimedia capabilities. There has also been a steady growth in computer connections to on-line services. The Internet has an estimated 23 million users in the United States, with 16 million people using the World Wide Web. America Online and Compuserve together serve about 9 million subscribers and are adding about 10 thousand subscribers per day.

A third reason to wax optimistic about electronic retailing is that new developments in three-dimensional (3-D) computer graphics promise to make personal computers dramatically easier to use. In the past, users had to learn a complex set of commands to shop electronically. While this was a surmountable barrier for the experienced computer user, it was usually an impossible obstacle for the computer novice. Keep in mind that 72 percent of the U.S. population does not have a college education and that most adults do not know how to program their VCRs. People are also reluctant to buy products "sight unseen" from a text-based shopping interface. For electronic commerce to become a mass-market phenomenon, consumers must be able to move transparently between the physical and virtual worlds of retailing, seeing and interacting with products in the same way in both environments. With 3-D graphics, consumers can use their extensive knowledge of the physical marketplace to shop for brands in the virtual store.

WHY SHOP IN A VIRTUAL STORE?

Consumers will only shop electronically if it provides significant advantages over conventional shopping. While this may seem obvious, few of the firms developing interactive shopping applications have conducted research on consumers' needs and desires for such services, instead focusing on what is technically possible.

In the past, two major consumer benefits have driven the emergence of new retail formats: convenience and economy. The first gave us convenience stores, offering consumers a limited selection of products at convenient locations with extended hours of operation and little or no waiting. At the other extreme, it drove the development of huge (200,000+ square feet) supercenters, which sell groceries, prepared foods, general merchandise, soft goods, and a variety of other items, all under one roof. Consumers have responded positively to the convenience of one-stop shopping. For example, people now buy more nonprescription drug products and flowers from supermarkets than from drug stores or florists, respectively.

The second major benefit, economy, drove the development of warehouse clubs (e.g., Sam's, Costco, BJ's) and mass merchandise outlets (e.g., Wal-Mart). These channels are designed to maximize operational efficiency. Through bulk purchasing, centralized inventory, inexpensive store locations and fixtures, and continuous replenishment, warehouse clubs and mass merchandise stores are able to cut costs and pass the savings on to consumers.

The virtual store has the potential to deliver both convenience and economy. In conventional retailing, the physical store handles all of the distribution functions, including providing product information, taking orders, delivering the merchandise, and handling post-sales customer service. There is a natural tension between offering high levels of convenience, customer service, and product variety and minimizing costs. This conflict does not exist in the virtual store. It splits apart the distribution functions, providing product information and taking orders electronically, and then delivering merchandise to a consumer's home from a centralized fulfillment center. By eliminating the expense of a conventional retail store and handling deliveries from a dedicated warehouse, virtual shopping can cut distribution costs by 25 to 30 percent while offering a larger product assortment and reducing out-of-stock conditions.

For several reasons, the following discussion will focus on the electronic sale of grocery products. First, groceries are an important part of the U.S. and global economies. In 1995, U.S. grocery sales were about $400 billion, or one-fifth of total retail sales. Half of the world's population is involved in the production, distribution, or sale of food products. Second, everyone has to eat, and shopping for food in a conventional store takes a considerable amount of time. Each week, consumers spend an average of about 1.5 hours grocery shopping and make 2.5 trips to the store. Third, grocery shopping is incredibly inefficient. A shopper who purchases the same products week after week is still forced to walk up and down the aisles of the store. An analysis of the average customer's shopping basket reveals that about 85 percent of the items are simply replenishment purchases (e.g., milk, bread, paper towels, and soft drinks). Fourth, most people don't like grocery shopping. A 1990 University of Michigan study asked people to rank 22 daily activities by how much they enjoyed doing them. Grocery shopping ranked next to last, just above housekeeping.

To measure consumers' reactions to the concept of virtual shopping for frequently purchased, nondurable products, six focus group interviews were conducted in the eastern, midwestern, and western regions of the United States. Each group consisted of eight to ten people, screened to include individuals who were the principal grocery shoppers in their household. Participants had the opportunity to shop for groceries and over-the-counter drug products using a 3-D shopping simulation developed by the author.[1] Within the virtual store, shoppers could "pick up" a product off the shelf, rotate and examine its packaging, and then purchase the item by dropping it into a shopping cart. People were then asked to discuss their likes and dislikes concerning the system.

People were generally favorable toward virtual shopping, but their reactions varied by consumer segment. The consumers who were most positive had significant time or mobility constraints, including dual-income households, single-parent families, and the disabled. They perceived grocery shopping as an unpleasant but necessary task and complained of long lines at the supermarket and poor service. In contrast, the people who enjoyed grocery shopping had ample time available. Shopping provided a chance to get out of the house and socialize with others. Stay-at-home mothers used grocery shopping as an excuse to get away from the children and have some time to themselves. Retirees also enjoyed grocery shopping for entertainment and social contact.

Both the perceived costs and benefits of the system related to convenience, information, and economics. On the dimension of convenience, shoppers appreciated the ability to visit the virtual store at any hour and to conduct other activities (like exercise, cooking, and child care) while shopping. They could shop when transportation was unavailable and avoid crowded parking lots and bad weather. The simulation eliminated drive time and checkout time, and allowed access to stores at great distances. The weight and bulk of packages were no longer constraints. Participants had concerns related to the timing and handling of deliveries. They worried that delivery times might be inconvenient (especially for products needed immediately, such as milk and bread), and that perishable items might spoil or melt in transit.

Participants commented on the differences in the quantity and quality of information provided in the real and virtual shopping environments. On the one hand, the simulation did not allow physical product contact with the merchandise, so participants could not touch, smell, or taste the products. Selections were made at the level of the individual product type or shopkeeping unit (sku), so it was not possible to pick the ripest fruit from a display or the dairy products with the best expiration dates. On the other hand, shoppers expected that they could often make better and faster decisions in the virtual store. They could construct their shopping lists at home as product needs would arise, and with the input of family members. Once the shopper entered the virtual store, the computer would display only the relevant and desired product categories and brands (deleting, for example, the pet food aisle for non-pet-owners, and high salt and cholesterol products for consumers with dietary restrictions). The computer could also enrich the information environment by facilitating comparison shopping, by providing additional product information, recipes and meal planning, and by highlighting new products and store specials. Consumers would have more time to shop because the entire task would not need to be compressed into a single weekly trip. Shoppers also expected that a greater selection of products would be available in the virtual store because the displays were not constrained by physical floor space.

Participants noted several economic costs and benefits of virtual shopping. In contrast to their willingness to pay shipping and handling fees for catalog purchases of durable and soft goods, some participants objected to charges for grocery delivery. They compared groceries to fast food, which was delivered for free. Many shoppers said they would be willing to pay a fixed charge for grocery delivery but would amortize the cost by making less frequent, larger orders. Consumers expected that delivery charges would eventually be eliminated as competition between retailers increased; as retailers became more efficient at picking, packing, and transporting groceries; and as the overhead of physical stores was eliminated. Many participants also expected to shop more efficiently in a virtual store, having the ability to electronically access, clip, and redeem coupons and to continuously monitor the total cost of products purchased.

Study participants also mentioned other advantages of virtual shopping, including the safety and entertainment of shopping from home and the ecological benefits of eliminating short driving trips. People were split on the implications of this technology for social welfare. Some felt that electronic shopping would isolate consumers from the real world, removing the sensory stimulation of the physical store, the contact with other shoppers, and the exercise of walking the aisles. Others argued that virtual shopping would free up time for more fulfilling discretionary activities. The latter believed that the time taken by the mundane task of grocery shopping could be better spent with family and friends.

HOW WILL CONSUMERS SHOP IN A VIRTUAL STORE?

As people begin to shop in virtual stores, manufacturers and retailers must consider how the simulated environment will affect consumers' purchasing behavior. Given the variety of ways in which physical and virtual stores might differ, one would expect that we will see substantial changes in purchasing. The design of the shopping interface may encourage or discourage planned purchasing, make product information more or less accessible, facilitate or inhibit the purchase of certain brands, and so on.

To explore these issues, a panel of consumers was recruited from a suburban community in the northeastern United States and asked to keep a written record and receipts for all grocery purchases made during a seven-month period (Burke et al. 1992). At the end of this period, panelists were brought into the laboratory and asked to use two types of home shopping systems. The first, a text-based system, displayed alphabetical lists of brands and the associated sizes, prices, and promotional information for each product category. Shoppers highlighted their preferred items and typed in purchase quantities. They were free to delete undesired items entirely from the list. The second, a graphical system, displayed realistic images of product packages, shelf displays, and shelf tags, arranged as in a conventional store. Respondents selected items from the shelf using a trackball.

For both home shopping systems, product category sales were 50 to 100 percent higher than the sales levels observed in the physical store. These results are consistent with the experiences of commercial home shopping companies. This may be a consequence of consumers' freedom from the constraints of available cash and carrying capacity when placing orders electronically. (A similar increase in order size was observed in 1936 when Sylvan Goldman introduced the shopping cart to replace the hand-held basket.) Another explanation is that shoppers might place larger but less frequent orders to amortize the fixed fees for delivery. Although total orders were larger, the distribution of preferences across brands was similar in real and computer-simulated environments. Correlations between estimated brand shares ranged from 0.70 to 0.96 across product categories. The electronic shopping systems did not bias preferences in favor of national or private-label brands.

Across shopping trips, there was significantly less brand switching in the two simulated stores than in the physical store. The simulations minimized extraneous events that might disrupt habitual purchasing, such as out-of-stock conditions, manufacturers' coupons, and the activities of other shoppers. This inertia in brand preference is likely to be even greater in commercial trials if consumers are given the option to recall their last shopping trip and place the same order again.

On a number of dimensions, the text-based and graphical shopping systems produced different patterns of consumer behavior. Shoppers took significantly longer to make purchases in the text-based system than in the graphical system, particularly during the first few shopping trips (where brand selections would often take several minutes per category). The text-based shopping system did not provide shoppers with the familiar, visual cues of package location, shape, and color, so they were forced to recall and search for the names of preferred brands from the alphabetical lists. Shoppers were also significantly more price sensitive in the text-based simulation than in the graphical simulation or the actual store. Although the graphical system displayed price tags in correct proportion to the shelves and packages, the text system gave the prices, sizes, and brand names equal prominence. Another consequence of the visual-versus-textual display of information was that consumers tended to buy the same sized packages in the graphical system that they did in the real store, but did not buy the same-sized packages in the text-based system. This suggests that shoppers typically use a package's appearance rather than its measured size as a purchase cue, and become confused if they must rely exclusively on the latter.

Of course, these two systems provided only the most basic levels of shopping functionality. One can speculate about how further enhancements of the shopping interface might produce more dramatic changes in consumer behavior. If the interface is designed to allow shoppers to enter and recall shopping lists, to access product categories directly (rather than in a fixed sequence), and to electronically access and apply coupons, then consumers are likely to make more planned and fewer impulse purchases. If the computer allows shoppers to sort brands on price per ounce, nutrition, and performance dimensions, this may commoditize categories, shifting preference to high-value products and reducing interest in premium-priced, branded merchandise. Gross margins may drop as the market becomes more efficient.

As consumers seek to enhance their shopping efficiency, they may reallocate their time across categories, reducing the time spent shopping for household and other functional products (perhaps by automating these purchases) while increasing the time spent shopping for food, health and beauty aids, and entertainment products, where variety is highly valued. As a consequence, high-value brands in functional categories will achieve high loyalty (inertia), whereas specialized, niche products may see increased opportunity in food, personal care, and other sensory categories. With direct category and brand access, home shopping systems will also make it easier for consumers to find desired products. John Kaula, president of the Point of Purchase Advertising Institute (POPAI), quotes statistics indicating that this benefit alone may increase retail sales by an average of 6.7 percent.

WHAT'S NEXT?

As we have moved from the country store to modern retail formats and as branded merchandise has proliferated, consumers have become comfortable with the concept of buying products without physical product contact. This change in behavior, along with the development of interactive media, creates the opportunity for the emergence of virtual stores. Yet, consumers continue to have reservations about buying some products (like perishables and soft goods) without handling them. In the short term, interactive retailers can address these concerns by building consumer trust through familiar store names, branded merchandise, conventional prices, delivery checking, and product guarantees.

Another barrier to adoption is that many people are reluctant to try new technologies. Interactive shopping systems must be made psychologically as well as physically accessible to customers. This will require firms to go beyond the existing text-based interfaces to more intuitive and familiar graphical representations of stores and their products. The benefits of convenience, faster and better decisions, and economy must also be delivered to shoppers for this technology to gain broad acceptance.

In the longer term, virtual stores can be seen as a natural extension of the food industry's Efficient Consumer Response initiative to streamline the logistics of getting products from manufacturers to consumers. One research participant noted:

> You know what I expect? You'll have warehouses and then you'll have 7-11s and that would be it. . . . All the major stuff would come out of these central locations. . . . You're interested in the cheapest cost for the product that you want. Then you go to the convenience stores for the last-minute things that you need.

Although traditional supermarkets will probably not disappear, even a small shift in purchases from traditional to virtual stores will have dramatic implications for manufacturers and retailers. The current retail vacancy rate of 13 percent is estimated to rise as high as 33 percent. Channel power may shift from conventional retailers and distributors to manufacturers. New forms of competition will emerge as companies gain access to new markets. For example, grocery stores may compete with fast food restaurants to deliver prepared foods and beverages.

Unlike conventional stores, the virtual store can carry an unlimited variety of products, styles, flavors, and sizes. New products can be "stocked" that do not yet physically exist but that are produced in response to customer orders. The store can be tailored to the preferences and purchasing habits of individual shoppers. Products can be shown in a variety of entertaining and informative contexts, including, perhaps, a model of the consumer's home. The virtual store thus becomes a channel for direct, personal, and intelligent communication with the customer.

NOTE

1. For additional information on the virtual store, see Burke (1996).

6

Electronic Marketing:
The Dell Computer Experience

Kenneth Hill

Dell Computer Corporation is a $7 billion corporation. Ninety-two percent of its revenues are derived from corporate accounts. This percentage tends to surprise many people since Dell is often (wrongly) considered to be a consumer-oriented company. Although it is "consumer" or, more properly "end-user" oriented, its business model is focused on business-to-business marketing. In particular, Dell uses a business model that it calls "direct." Dell employees speak with literally thousands of customers every day over the telephone and an additional few thousand through its Web site at Dell.com. We call the telephone model "ear to ear," and we are now trying to replicate that model on the Internet.

If a company does not know anything about telemarketing, it must learn about it before developing an Internet strategy. Forty years ago, when companies first started using telephones, senior executives were reluctant to give each employee a telephone unless the employee could mandate it for his or her responsibilities. Think about that! Today, everybody has a telephone, and not only does it impact the business coming in, it also has the same kind of impact for marketing, service support, sales, and all these kinds of things. The parallels between telephone communications and Internet communications are phenomenal. There are many important lessons to be learned from the experiences of companies regarding the deployment of telephones that can be applied to marketing over the Internet.

Go back 12 years in time to a little company by the name of PC's Limited. Close examination would reveal several insights about how to be successful with the Internet. For anyone who has not made the connection, PC's Limited was the name of the company now called Dell Computer Corporation. PC's Limited sold $6,000 Intel 8080 computers over the telephone. There wasn't a research person, a business analyst, or a magazine or newspaper writer who said this fledging company was going to be able to sell a $6,000 computer over the telephone.

They also said there was no way people were going to provide their credit card number over the telephone. Well, everyone knows what happened. The direct-to-customer computer revolution was born, and Dell Computer soon became the world leader in selling computers direct. What Dell learned back then, and what is still true today, is that it can deliver high levels of customer satisfaction, customer services, and products by using the telephone, facsimile machines, the mail, and private delivery services. Every computer company had telephones, facsimile machines, the use of the U.S. Postal Service, and private delivery services back in 1985, but Dell used them better than any of these companies. It later augmented them with field-based account executives to gain access to senior executives in large companies. Now we have telephones, facsimile machines, the U.S. Postal Service, the private delivery services, one of the best field-based sales forces in the industry, and the Internet. The Internet is a recent weapon in our competitive arsenal and can deliver much value to our customer base.

DELL'S INTERNET PRESENCE

Dell has an Intranet site today that is currently accessed by about 60 percent of our computer-user workforce. We are presently rolling out connections in Europe, Asia, and Australia, and we just finished rolling out Canada. What makes our Intranet interesting is that it is connected to practically everything that we consider a legacy system. Dell categorizes legacy systems as anything that has important data, data that if taken away would have huge ramifications to the business. If one views a legacy system in these terms, it is obvious that systems like the Lotus Notes databases in research and development become legacy. These databases can be just as important as the databases that are used in financial services. Dell's Intranet, Inside.Dell.com, is connected to the public Internet, Lotus Notes systems, our Tandem computers, and it is currently in the process of moving over to SAP as part of the global roll out. Essentially, the Intranet connects our data infrastructure to our employees. As we connect our data to our employees, we look at the types of data that can add value to our customers and then connect them to the infrastructure as well. Our goal is to make Dell's data infrastructure become our customers' biggest asset. Think of it as Direct, Phase Two!

Why will this approach work? An example from eight years ago exemplifies why the approach will work. Field sales force automation was a hot topic eight years ago and still is today. Data show that nine-out-of-ten field force automation projects usually fail. They fail for many of the same reasons that Internet projects and sites are failing today. The most common reason for failure is a focus on making the home or back office more efficient, not the sales force. The value should accrue to the sales force in automation projects and to the customer on the Internet. Dell has 300 people out in the field; these are senior executives who sell to CEOs and CIOs. They are responsible for the relationship part of the business. We started a sales force automation project two-and-a-half years ago to automate these people. I happened to be one of the persons in the field at the time and was asked to come back and run that project. As I began looking closely at all the software programs that were available and then looked at what we were really trying to do at Dell, I said, "Wait a second, we're direct." Let's just automate our customers and drag the field sales force along with them. Back then that was fairly revolutionary, but the company embraced the idea and soon started trying to find a way to do it. Shortly thereafter we started building Dell.com. (See Figure 6.1 for an overview of the structure, functions, and benefits of Dell.com.)

Figure 6.1. WWW. Dell.com

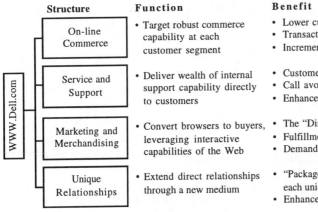

Structure	Function	Benefit
On-line Commerce	• Target robust commerce capability at each customer segment	• Lower customer costs • Transaction cost reduction • Incremental revenue
Service and Support	• Deliver wealth of internal support capability directly to customers	• Customer satisfaction • Call avoidance • Enhanced service
Marketing and Merchandising	• Convert browsers to buyers, leveraging interactive capabilities of the Web	• The "Direct" experience on-line • Fulfillment cost reduction • Demand generation
Unique Relationships	• Extend direct relationships through a new medium	• "Packaged" services for each unique customer • Enhanced relationships

Dell launched its initial Internet site back in 1994, before the World Wide Web really began to get hot. We focused on delivering technical support. Today, Dell.com has over 240,000 unique visitors a day. We sell more than $3,000,000 a week in computers through our Internet store, and growth is phenomenal. These numbers have been achieved with no advertising, direct mail, or public relations. That will change shortly!

Recall what the industry analysts were saying back in 1985 about selling computers by telephone. These same people are out there today saying the same thing about the Internet. Don't believe it! If you offer value, customers will embrace your business. Eighty-five percent of the customers who buy from the Internet store are brand new to Dell. They have never bought from the company before. The average system selling price is higher than what we sell over the telephone. A lot of companies would like to have a $150 million revenue stream in less than 90 days, especially when there are only 27 persons running the business. When talking about infrastructure and scale, this revenue generator is potentially very significant.

A big opportunity for Dell is system service and support. Dell is in a unique position because it sells something that is necessary for connecting to the Internet, a computer. We can load all types of items on the computer that take advantage of the direct business model that we use. Today, we have a fabulous service area on our Web site. Thirty-five thousand pages are currently part of this area on our site. This makes our service and support site alone larger than 75 percent of the Web sites on the Internet today. The lesson to be learned from this is simple: to add customer value, a firm cannot just sell a product; it must also service what it sells.

As a company starts looking at its business and tries to figure out how to take advantage of Internet technology, it must ask itself a simple question. What else does the firm do besides sell products that can add value to its customer relationships? Is there customer feedback detailing likes and dislikes, and can the company take advantage of the Internet in dealing with it? What "nonselling" information can a company provide its customers that will add value to the customer relationship? Here is an example of value-added information in the area of research and development. Assume that a customer wants to find out where technology is going, what Intel is doing, what the status of the $500 NC is, or what is happening with an IEEE specification that is coming out that could change the way computers work. Answering these questions adds value for the customer, and our customers can literally find these answers on Dell.com. Thus, the Internet can be used to educate customers, not just sell to them.

Further, for example, why would a company put its annual report on the Internet site since customers don't generally care about annual reports? At Dell we know that our stockholders and investors need our annual reports, so we put them on the Internet. People love information if it helps them become empowered. In a world of technology, savvy customers will usually choose Dell.

Real-time stock and financial information on Dell is a very important part of our Internet site. In fact, the financial side of Dell.com is actually quite large. It connects a visitor directly to the SEC so that 10Ks and 10Qs can be instantly accessed. Virtually any public financial information is available on Dell.com. Everything is instantaneous. Whatever we do, whether it is a filing or a press release, it is put on Dell.com. The site is connected to multiple stock price retrieval systems. In certain instances the site is actually connected to research information. If investors or customers want financial information about Dell, they can visit the Internet site and click to places like Edgar and conduct research on the company.

As an aside, there seems to be a relationship between financial information and activity on the Internet site. Every time the executive staff communicates information about quarterly financial performance, makes a significant announcement through an analysts' conference, or even sends out a press release, we see an increase in traffic on Dell.com. We view the Dell.com site as another opportunity to deliver consistency in the corporate message.

Reflect a little more on the Dell Internet strategy. We are going to sell our products, service our products, and provide information to our customers and prospects so that they can make educated decisions. We will use our employees to deliver the personal touch that many customers desire. All of these things in the value chain work together to deliver the best possible experience for our customers. We believe Internet technology is an integral part of our communication system. This is because the Internet is not about technology. It is simply a new way of delivering better services.

The Internet applies to all of our customers, but in different ways. The household customer uses the Internet very differently than does the small business, the medium-sized business, the large business, the federal government, state governments, and educational institutions. Consider this example. If a person works for a government agency, that person knows the state government probably has a contract with every major supplier in the city where the agency is located. As such, the agency may have the right to purchase at a discount. So, when the person visits an Internet store site, the first question is, "Can I buy at a discount from this vendor?" But if the person works for a large business, the route taken in the purchasing process is very different. Business customers look to see what the Internet store offers and then ask questions about price. Another difference is the consumer versus the chief executive officer (CEO) of a major corporation. The CEO has access to a T-3 Internet connection. The person at home doesn't. These are differences that most business people are not used to dealing with. More generally, 60 percent of the users on the Internet at some point during the day have access to ISDN, T-1, or T-3 connections. It is because they are part of a big workplace network. Hence, if you are marketing on the Internet, do not assume that it is a 14.4 or 28.8 world. Most people have jobs and through them access to big networks.

Remember, though, personal interaction is still going to be a big part of any business. CEOs of *Fortune 500* firms do not want to have a relationship with a computer. They want to have a relationship with someone who can come in, help solve some real business problems, and tell them where computing will be in six months, 12 months, or 24 months. Can we package information for these CEOs, manage their transactions (e-mail and those kind of things), and add that to the relationship? You bet. Can we set up preferred areas where CEOs can come in and get information and chat with Michael Dell, and do things like that? You bet. You must figure out where your customers are, and who the people are that you are trying to develop a relationship with, and you must start delivering services to them. This is what we are doing with our Internet site today. Figure 6.2 outlines the Internet information management approach that Dell Computer is currently using.

Figure 6.2. Dell's Internet Information Management Approach

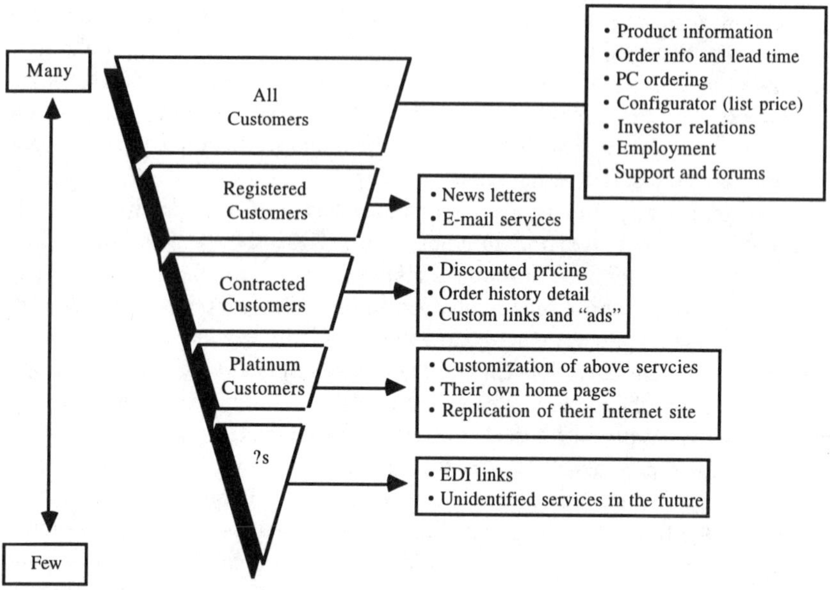

Many

All Customers

- Product information
- Order info and lead time
- PC ordering
- Configurator (list price)
- Investor relations
- Employment
- Support and forums

Registered Customers

- News letters
- E-mail services

Contracted Customers

- Discounted pricing
- Order history detail
- Custom links and "ads"

Platinum Customers

- Customization of above servcies
- Their own home pages
- Replication of their Internet site

?s

- EDI links
- Unidentified services in the future

Few

Personalized Services

One decision that must be made when constructing a Web site is the extent to which personal services are going to be built for specific customers. Such services would allow customers to build their own Web sites, register for products, promotions, or information, and build a personal data base. Dell is learning that less than one percent of the people coming to most Web sites actually take advantage of such site features. We think it is because they are scared to death to give the vendor their personal information.

If one begins to treat certain types of data as personal, then an entirely new type of conversation will take place with customers. As an example, Dell offers list prices and discounted prices. We view the discounted price as a customer-specific piece of data. Therefore, it is personal. Everyone gets a price on the product, but if a customer has an existing contract with us, it receives a discount. Dell must deliver what we call a "one-off" to that customer. Other types of one off or unique data include order history, service tag information, BIOS updates, video drivers, and all kinds of hardware and software that go along with an individual computer. These data constitute personal information.

Imagine being the purchasing director of a *Fortune 500* business and obtaining services over the Internet from Dell that are unique to your firm. You could come to Dell.com, enter a personal ID number, and view a list of computers, purchased this year by your firm, with warranties about to expire.

Dell would then automatically offer your firm the opportunity to extend the expiring warranties.

Another type of personal service is a vehicle that we call "registered." This level of service is individualized. You can come to Dell.com and look at the hierarchy of information on the Internet site, thousands of pieces of information, and indicate that you are a desktop, multimedia user at home and that you want particular types of information. This information may be about new products, prices, R&D letters, a new service, or perhaps even a newsletter. You select the information that you desire and tell the Internet server to notify you by e-mail or have the information ready when you come back to the site. If any information changes, your selected method of notification begins.

An important reason for a personal service in the business world is to assist in delivering the proper "value information." Assume that there are three individuals in a firm who want personalized service from your company—the vice president of the help desk operations (the person who is in charge of supporting all the employees in the company), the CIO (or chief information officer), and the vice president of purchasing.

Even though they work for the same firm and all have a relationship with your company, each individual requires a different type and level of information if he or she is to be kept as a customer. This requires being able to deliver unique services to each of these three users. The CIO, the VP of purchasing, and the VP of the help desk operations would each visit the site and register for information that interests them. The help desk vice president would want lots of technical material, the purchasing vice president would want new product and pricing information and materials on "deals" and things like that, and the CIO would want strategic-level data that may be confidential. At Dell, we would pro-actively send each of them information every time something in his or her interest area changes. The personalized services for customers that are "contracted" are considered very "personal."

How would you like to own a computer and know that anytime something was found to be wrong with the computer, or a new application like Windows 95 or OS2 or NT came out, we would automatically send you an e-mail telling you "the three things you need to do to the computer to make that new operating system work?" These types of informational activities tend to build loyal, repeat customers. The other thing to keep in mind is that you are probably not the first person to experience the problem you may be having with your computer. Chances are somebody else has had the same experience. Since Dell is centralized, if a telephone call or e-mail arrives describing a problem, the company can resolve the problem and embed the solution in the technical support function of its Internet site. If anyone else experiences that problem, the troubleshooting process can be short-circuited. Solve a problem for one, post the solution to many!

Another service that we provide our largest ("platinum") customers is a personal Web site. We build these sites because these customers buy in volume and have unique needs. Big companies often have their own Web sites that include information on products they buy, the service information that they need for those products, the special prices they pay, their Dell account teams, regional information, and how to contact us all over the world. In some cases, we have actually tied the coding mechanism in the site to the customer's own purchasing system. This allows the customer's end-users to get on-line and not call purchasing any more. They simply "click" and say, "I want one of those." The site launches an e-mail back to the central purchasing office at that account. This e-mail is received by the purchasing agent telling him or her that Fred in accounting wants a particular PC. This starts the purchasing approval process at the company. In brief, Dell.com connects Dell to its customers' systems and Web sites, as well as simply serving as an information service or purchase contact. This can be especially important in developing and maintaining business-to-business relationships.

THE ISSUE OF CHANNEL CONFLICT

Any time a company enters a new sales channel, such as the Internet, there is the possibility of channel conflict. In the case of Dell Computer, the fixed sales force and telemarketers are busy building customer relationships and then, all of a sudden, customers can order from the Internet site. Channel conflict is an interesting issue at Dell because the company does not have a channel in the traditional sense. Our "channel" is our salesforce. There are no intermediaries. Even so, we have not completely resolved some of the conflicts that the Internet could create for employees tasked with selling. We know our customers value the Internet connection, so there is some level of risk involved. We are, however, thinking about ways to deal with some of the issues the Internet is raising.

Dell could, for instance, pay field-based account executives a bonus to get their customers off of the telephone and onto the Web. This could be a relatively inexpensive solution. Since Dell revenues are growing at 56 percent a year, many members of the sales force view the Internet store as a way to eliminate the time-consuming transactions that a customer may have and use that time to focus on account relationships. Since there is an identification number assigned to each sales representative, there is no reason a customer cannot enter that number when placing an order. Dell's largest accounts are already assigned to individual sales representatives, and the representatives are paid more when they sell more profitable computer systems. There is no reason the representatives cannot be paid to move their customers to a more efficient transaction system.

Sales representatives who have strong relationships with their customers do not view Dell.com as a threat. Sales representatives who do not focus on relationship building and who do not add much value beyond picking up the telephone and saying "hello" view the Internet as a threat. The latter representatives think that they now have competition. To counter this perception, sales representatives have been told that if they talk to a customer on the telephone and they are really worried that Dell.com might take the order away from them, they should give the customer their sales rep number so that the customer can enter it on the order. Dell will then pay the sales representative for moving the customer to the Web. Under these circumstances the representatives view the Internet store as their friend. Are we 100 percent confident that our sales force is engaged? No. Do we have questions that need to be addressed? Absolutely. It will take some time before Dell.com is completely integrated into the corporate culture.

THE NEXT NINE MONTHS

What is Dell going to do to its Internet site in the next nine months? The short answer is that Dell will continue to add more services to its Internet store and the service and support area. An expansion of personal services, products in the store, service and support and a continuation of legacy system connections are all in the company's short-range plan. Service and support will continue to be a focus for us. We want to add all types of interactive services to our site. Imagine coming to Dell.com with a computer problem, clicking on "query my computer," and then entering an interactive session with our Internet server as it diagnoses your computer's problem. These are the kinds of things that the Internet permits.

Because Internet technology changes all the time, we plan to change our site every time technology can add value for our customer. An example is our real-time order status systems. Customers can come to our site and type in their customer number, and our Internet server will report the complete order history of everything that was ever purchased from us. Since we build to order, a real-time data connection to the factory can deliver a level of service that our competitors cannot even comprehend. Figure 6.3 overviews some of Dell Computer's Internet activities and functions that will be addressed in the near future.

If you look up one of our ads, you will see the Internet address there. Three or four months ago, Dell started integrating Dell.com into its advertising through some tests. We are now getting ready to release full-blown service ads on the Internet site. We don't see Dell.com as a competing channel. We see it as a complementary channel. A lot of people visit Dell.com and then call us on the telephone and buy. Is that a bad thing? No, because we just made five telephone calls go away. It takes six to eight telephone calls to sell a computer, and we just made five of them go away, with a commensurate reduction in operating expenses. So, Dell.com is not replacing an existing channel, or even competing with it; it is simply making the existing channel more efficient.

Figure 6.3. WWW.Dell.com Plans

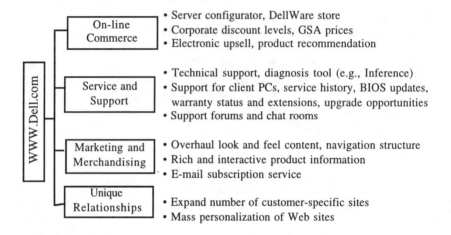

There are a lot of myths associated with the Internet. One of the myths is "don't send me e-mail unless I ask for it." It is a cardinal sin, and if done on a wholesale basis, has even been given a derogatory name—"spamming." Despite the nature of using e-mail in marketing, Dell started testing some interesting things. One question was particularly intriguing: what if someone was already a customer; would he or she mind getting an e-mail from us? About six months ago we sent out 35,000 e-mails that said "Dell is thinking about adding some services and here are some of the services that it is thinking about. If you would like to 'unsubscribe' to this, please reply." Less than one percent unsubscribed, and the myth about e-mail was dead, at least from Dell's perspective. We also had a very low rate of incorrect e-mail addresses, especially compared to direct mail, where a sizable percentage is returned because of incorrect addresses. Not only were we able to confirm that the message was received, customers told us that our hypothesis was correct. The moral is not to be afraid to test things and always keep the customer in mind.

The Internet store that Dell has up today is not as pretty as it could be and quite frankly could be more intuitive. Even so, it is difficult to argue with the benefits that it offers both the customer and the company. The store contains a wide array of Dell products and services. When a visitor makes a request by, for example, clicking on the XPS button, the button sends a message to a database that pulls information from Dell's Tandem database. The request may be to provide an sku for every product description and every price that is available on the Dimension XPS PC right now. If the price changed during the day, it is reflected on the monitor. The request produces what we call a bundle or product configuration. One of Dell's competitive advantages is that it does not carry much inventory, so as prices fall, the savings are passed along to customers. The Internet allows us to deliver that savings instantaneously.

With a few mouse clicks, a shopper can systematically configure a personalized computer. When finished, the shopper is told he or she is entering a secure transaction system. How the order is ultimately transacted is not of much concern. Many customers print the price quotes found in the Internet store and fax them along with a purchase order or credit card number. As long as we offer a service that facilitates purchasing, we have added value to the process for the customer. In fact, Dell has a large telephone service if Internet shopping or buying is not a customer's "cup of tea." How many companies take 2.5 million telephone calls a year? Not very many.

The Dell.com site has been re-launched every ninety days or so since December, 1995. It keeps getting better and better and better. Every day we get more unique visitors to our Internet site than we get telephone calls into the company. We view the Internet as just another type of dial tone. If you treat it that way, with all of its dynamics, you can be successful with it. If you treat it as a "marketing thing" or an "advertising thing," you will not be successful.

7

Electronically Connecting Retailers and Customers:
Interim Summary of an Expert Roundtable

Fred Phillips, Andrew Donoho, William W. Keep,
Walter Mayberry, John M. McCann, Karen Shapiro,
and David Smith

This chapter reports on a collaborative study, still underway, of a particular aspect of electronic commerce—the use of electronic communication technologies to link retailers and their customers. The form of the study is an "electronic roundtable" of experts, a modified Delphi process consisting of two rounds of formal submissions supplemented by informal e-mail, telephone and personal exchanges, and much Web surfing.[1]

The study aims to achieve a balanced presentation of the subject by correcting two erroneous directions in the current literature on electronic commerce. The first is the overemphasis on payment transactions as the holy grail of electronic commerce. Much has been written in recent years about relationship marketing. Like strategic alliances, relationship marketing is made necessary and desirable by the greater ability of the parties to exchange information, usually through communications technologies, and both are in contrast to the older, arms-length-transaction model of business. It seems senseless and retrograde for electronic commerce, effected by and through communications technology, to focus exclusively on the transaction. Equally important is the fact that the right kinds of information sharing reduces costs for both buyer and seller. Of course, transactions are what makes money for the seller; but there is a wide—and more immediate—scope for *saving* money through electronic retailing.

The second erroneous direction is overemphasis on the World Wide Web (WWW or Web). Table 7.1 lists many communications technologies other than the Web, as well as their uses in electronic commerce. Each communication technology has its own advantageous uses and its own interesting synergies with the others. Some of them are well-suited to helping fixed-location retailers retain competitive advantages against newer, locationless retailers. As the latter point

Table 7.1. Electronic Connections between Retailers and Customers: Examples by Medium and Type of Customer Connection

Electronic Medium	Product and Store Information	Answer Customer Queries	Refer to Other Media	Persuasive or Image Advertising	Purchase Transactions	Feedback and Market Research
• World Wide Web (WWW)	Amazon Books, AA, Delta Airlines	Powell's Bookstore	PBS posts transcripts of TV specials; MS/NBC	Samsung on Yahoo	Best Western Hotels	*Communications Week:* on-line subscription qualif.
• On-line services	Public libraries	Compaq: user support over Compuserve		BofA cosponsors startup disk with AOL	Many vendors on AOL, Compuserve	
• Electronic kiosks; Arcade games	Ikea, Nordstrom, Barnes & Noble		Mall games refer to game reviews on WWW			
• Phone/voice-based info services	Radio stations: free cellular calls	800 numbers	AT&T links WWW and telephone	Telemarketing		Phone surveys, viewer polls
• Pagers/Beepers						
• CD-ROM			Bill Gates' *The Road Ahead* refers to MS s/w products	Pepsi		
• Television/Radio	Local video networks beamed to food court		Toyota: URL on TV ads; NPR Music Resource	Almost all retailers		
• ATM Machines		Banks			Visa, MC, Amex	
• Video Phones/ Conferencing, Whiteboards	Netframe					
• Agents	Bargainfinder	B&Bs			Idealist	
• E-mail, Usenet, Listservs						E-mail surveys
• Virtual Reality	Virtual "walk-thru" real estate properties					
• Smart Cards, Digital Signatures, Electronic Wallets				Phone cards	Phone cards, debit cards	

Continued

Types of Customer Connections

Electronic Medium	Increased Selection	Frequent/Preferred Buyer Clubs	Connect Customers with Each Other	Contests/ Tie-ins	Personal Shopping Services	Ameliorate Waiting Time
• World Wide Web (WWW)	Music Boulevard		GM Saturn Division	KVO's "Where's Pierre"		
• On-line services		Lexus			Nordstrom	AA, Delta
• Electronic kiosks; Arcade games		Easy-SABRE Valley View Center Smart Shoppers Club (Dallas)				
• Phone/voice-based info services				900 numbers		
• Pagers/Beepers				Pepsi, Videoland beeper giveaways		Restaurants beep when table is ready
• CD-ROM						
• Television/Radio						Warner, Disney stores
• ATM Machines						All banks
• Video Phones/ Conferencing, Whiteboards			NetFrame			
• Agents						
• E-mail, Usenet, Listservs			Newsgroups for users of product X			
• Virtual Reality						
• Smart Cards, Digital Signatures, Electronic Wallets						Phone cards: "No fumbling for change"

implies, we also hoped that the study would shed light on the tension between all-electronic retailers (nonusers of retail real estate space) and traditional mall and center retailers (users of retail square footage), and on implications for providers of commercial real estate.

This chapter begins with an examination of how electronic marketing reinforces relationships and reduces costs. We next look at the range of electronic media that can be brought to bear on these tasks and at some creative examples drawn from industry. Although we list several reasons why the World Wide Web is "not ready for prime time" in regard to electronic commerce, we conclude that the momentum to make the Web into a significant commercial channel now exists. We provide some guidelines and cost data for retailers who wish to get started on the Web, as well as three short cases of diverse companies' early experiences on the Web. The chapter concludes with implications for traditional retailers and some forecasts about retailing's future electronic environment.

ELECTRONIC MARKETING REINFORCES RELATIONSHIPS AND REDUCES COSTS

Knowledgeable people with whom we have spoken generally agree that

- True electronic commerce is not yet here and will not be for some years.
- Businesses are not yet making money using Internet marketing; they are *saving* money by using Internet marketing. Like US West (Moylan 1996), companies begin Internet marketing "with the hope of eventually making money" but with the knowledge that, with exceptions, returns on their Internet investment will be indirect at first.

These points indicate that retailers interested in cost savings should focus on the cost-reducing benefits of electronically communicating with customers instead of on the actual execution of payment transactions with customers. These benefits can include providing reliable store and product information directly to customers, thus reducing costs and uncertainties of sales force training; capturing customer queries about location and availability of merchandise; and increasing customer satisfaction by reducing customer waiting times.

Management Horizons (*Supermarket News* 1996) reported that information system advances have been applied primarily to the supply/distribution end of retail businesses (e.g., Wal-Mart, The Gap), not the customer end. But Greco (1995) claimed that the key to taking advantage of information technology is to cost-effectively create a "one-to-one" relationship with individual customers. Technologies for electronic commerce have been advancing rapidly, and Baig (1996) noted that customers have now become accustomed to "friendly amenities such as . . . touch screen computers" at Nordstrom, Ikea, and Barnes & Noble.

Cost-reducing benefits of communications technologies are tied to the consumers' pursuit of (or indifference to) shopping benefits. In other words, discussing cost-reducing benefits for the retailer is not meaningful without discussing consumer buying behaviors that make such reductions possible. The cost reductions are of two kinds: reductions in costs because of incorrect demand forecasts, and reductions in the direct costs of marketing.

Reduce Demand Uncertainty and Cost of Goods Sold

The retail income statement inset below suggests the first kind of cost-reduction results, when electronic commerce helps reduce demand uncertainty for the retailer. If the retailer can more quickly and more accurately identify those products that sell well and those that do not, and respond appropriately, the retailer's cost of goods sold as a percentage of sales will decline. For each dollar of sales, the retailer will retain more as gross margin. Although certain operating expenses associated with the buying process may also be reduced, the most significant impact will come from reducing the cost of goods sold. In the case of Internet shopping, when the customer base on the Internet represents a significant proportion of the retailer's market, the speed with which the customer responds to the available products will allow the retailer to adjust stocks accordingly. Fewer unplanned mark-downs, improved buying, and faster inventory turnover will result.

Retail Income Statement

Sales
– Cost of Goods Sold
_____

GROSS MARGIN
– Operating Expenses
_____

PRETAX PROFIT

Reducing Marketing Expenses—Active/Passive and Interactive/Noninteractive Forms

The second kind of cost reduction is reflected in the operating expenses associated with marketing. Electronic marketing is essentially a form of communication. Because marketing expenses are overwhelmingly communication expenses, the potential for cost reduction is significant in this area. Consider the separation of electronic communication according to two characteristics: active/passive and interactive/noninteractive. Active electronic communication occurs when the seller reaches out to the buyer, such as through e-mail, facsimiles, pagers, electronic signs, and so forth. Passive electronic communication requires the buyer to actively seek information, such as in searching the Internet or loading a CD-ROM (although in the latter case the retailer may have been active by virtue of sending the CD-ROM through the mail).

When making the active versus passive decision, the retailer must calculate the frequency with which the consumer will be exposed to the message. Whereas frequency is well understood and easily measured for some media (e.g., newspapers and radio), consumer usage of newer media, including specific media areas (e.g., the apparel shopping section of the Internet), is less well known. Thus, if a passive electronic form, such as information available on the Internet, is substituted for more active nonelectronic forms, such as placing an advertisement in the local newspaper, different exposure frequencies could result in higher costs even if the electronic form has a lower out-of-pocket expense. Alternatively, if the retailer substitutes a less expensive active electronic form like e-mail for a more expensive nonelectronic active form like direct mail, and the frequency exposure is similar, there may be a significant cost reduction. The retailer will have to answer three important questions: Can the electronic form be targeted as accurately as the nonelectronic form? What is the frequency of message exposure for the various media involved? Will the response rate of the electronic form differ from the response rate of the nonelectronic form?

The active versus passive distinction is not a strict dichotomy, because exposure to a message typically involves some active participation on the part of the consumer (e.g., reading the newspaper, traveling a road that features billboard advertisements, or surfing the Internet), as well as some passive exposure. Underlying this issue is the more fundamental one regarding consumers' frequency of exposure to marketing communications, and the cost-effectiveness of these exposures.

Finally, interactive electronic forms seem to offer the greatest potential for cost reduction because the variable costs associated with responding to the individual customer are lower than other currently available interactive means, such as person-to-person selling (store and nonstore) and telemarketing. It is not yet known how best to present information in an interactive format. Some retailers use pictures (gifs, jpegs, and so forth) of groups of products similar to those that are found in a catalog-type format (e.g., www.spiegel.com/spiegel/vol2.04/cover/index.html), whereas others use pictures that attempt to more closely highlight the qualities of a single product (e.g., www.londonmall.co.uk/tmlands/default.htm). How useful are generic interactive approaches such as "frequently asked questions" (FAQs) on the Internet? Nonetheless, interactive electronic commerce promises to reduce those selling expenses directly associated with responding to the customer. There will also be cost reductions in other support areas. For example, not only will interactive electronic commerce reduce labor costs associated with selling, they will also make other tasks, such as changing prices, faster and less expensive. Dabholkar (1996) showed that (for service businesses) expected savings in waiting times and expected reliability of the electronic device or technology are very important determinants of the consumer's willingness to substitute an electronic self-service capability for contact with a human assistant.

Cost Savings and Customer Satisfaction

What is the magnitude of the cost savings from electronic marketing? The Aspen Institute (Bollier 1995) estimated that 10 times the units can be sold with 1/10th the advertising budget and with 25 percent less cost than direct marketing. As an example, Internet Shopping Network (http://www.internet.net) is a virtual computer store having no physical inventory or telephone operators. All transactions are handled on-line. Transaction costs are 20¢ to 50¢ per transaction, compared with $5 for 800-number telephone sales and $15 for retail store sales. Most of the savings comes from distribution expense, which is widely thought to constitute 50 to 80 percent of the cost of consumer products. An exception is banking, where there is little transportation or storage of material goods: "Cyberbanking costs about 20 percent of net operating income versus 60 percent for branch transactions" (Borsuk 1996).

So much for the cost savings. Of possibly greater magnitude is the benefit of increased customer satisfaction and loyalty stemming from quick, reliable information delivered by electronic means. There is not enough space here to look in detail at the many benefits to the retailer of reducing headcount, reducing employee training expense, hiring lower priced employees for less demanding jobs, and ensuring that uniform, correct, and timely information is, nonetheless, delivered to each customer. As one sage notes, "Try going into a shoe store in a mall and saying to a clerk: 'I have a pronation problem. What shoe do you recommend?'" Interactive information services can solve this problem with accurate, on-demand answers even to obscure questions.

THE MEDIA-SERVICE MATRIX

The columns of Table 7.1 show twelve positive roles for communication technology in retailer-customer relationships, in addition to simple purchase transactions. The rows show the variety of such communications technologies and devices, and the cell entries provide examples of the use of each technology to enhance each customer relation and marketing function. The table illustrates the following:

- The media represented in the rows are in a process of convergence; some rows that are displayed separately in the table will soon be actualized by a single device and no longer thought of as separate technologies.

- The multimedia and interactive nature of the WWW make many applications possible, resulting in examples in almost every cell of the WWW row.
- Retailers use each medium to refer the customer to their presence on other media, thus reinforcing the relationship with the customer. (See the third column.)
- Many of the businesses noted in the cells—for example, the automobile makers and Microsoft—do not now deal directly with customers. But disintermediation may well occur. For example, airlines now sell tickets directly to customers, and electronic services threaten to eliminate the traditional retail travel agent. By offering electronic marketing support to their independent dealers and retailers, producers of goods and services will eventually take advantage of the interactive contact with customers to sell directly to them.

Creative Applications

Some of the more creative retailers represented by cell entries in Table 7.1 are included in the following descriptions.

- The Idealist, a source for bargains on Macintosh products, solicits subscribers through electronic-mail discussion groups. Interested consumers subscribe by returning e-mail to Idealist. The company represents any manufacturer offering a close-out or extraordinary bargain on Apple-related products, and e-mails periodic notices to subscribers.
- A company called Dial-A-Book lets users look at the first chapters and other excerpts of books before purchasing.
- AT&T utilizes an Internet phone (real-time two-way audio to and from the customer's desktop computer) to allow customers to talk to sales representatives. Customers activate the I-phone connection using a hot button on the company's World Wide Web site. Being able to speak to a representative will make transactions safer than sending credit card numbers over the Internet, AT&T says.
- NetFrame allows HP9000 UNIX customers to track their own case histories, audit their environment, and access pertinent product information.
- Anderson Consulting's Bargainfinder agent tracks down the WWW retailer charging the lowest price for a specified compact disc.
- Amazon.com Books (http://www.amazon.com) offers a personal notification service for new releases. Dell Computer's Web site (http://www.us.dell.com) allows buyers to custom configure, price, order, and check the shipment status of their computers. Security First Network Bank, FSB (http://www.sfnb.com), a bank based in Pineville, Kentucky, now serves customers worldwide for U.S.-based transactions. At Charles Schwab & Co. (http://www.schwab.com), customers can trade stocks and mutual funds, check account information, and access investment research over the Internet. The University of Minnesota on-line course registration system

(http://www.umn.edu/registrar) includes a current camera shot of the length of the check-out lines in the campus bookstore.

- eShop Plaza (http://www.eShop.com) is an excellent example of a virtual mall. It includes retailers like Tower Records, Spiegel, Avon, 1-800-Flowers, and "The Good Guys," and allows consumers to download free shopping software to emulate a real shopping environment. The company was acquired by Microsoft in June 1996. Its technology is being integrated into the Microsoft Merchant System and the mall into Microsoft Network (MSN).
- Clodfelter and Overstreet (1996) reported on a grid of receivers in store ceilings picking up infrared transmissions from shoppers' carts, resulting in a map of "hot" and "cold" spots in the aisles. They also noted that not only restaurants but also pharmacies, automotive service centers, gift wrap counters, and one-hour eyeglass centers use pager systems to inform customers when their orders are ready.

Fit the Marketing to the Market

The columns of Table 7.1 can be divided into six categories: corporate identity/public relations, sales/marketing, order taking/distribution, payment/collection, service/support, and new product research/market feedback. Clodfelter and Overstreet's (1996) comparable categories are customer tracking and database marketing, entertainment and visual merchandising, information and shopping assistance for customers, and on-line shopping services. All contribute to successful retailing. Compare these functions with current WWW business usage patterns: 30 percent of businesses now using the Web do so to publish product information; 75 percent to gather product information; 30 percent to purchase products; and 38 percent to provide customer service; but only 15 percent do so to sell products (CommerceNet 1996).

CURRENT LIMITATIONS OF THE WORLD WIDE WEB FOR ELECTRONIC COMMERCE

Electronic commerce on the World Wide Web requires a lot of work to reach a still-small audience. It is hard for the information provider to make the most of WWW contact once it is made, and hard for the customer to find and assimilate the right information. This is not a promising situation for marketing. In particular, there are several disadvantages associated with the Web:

- A chaotic, unorganized abundance of sites and information makes it difficult to find value, even after overcoming technical roadblocks. High tolerance for uncertainty and lots of spare time are prerequisites for surfers and seekers.
- It's slow. Unless you have a high-speed line, the payoff may not be worth the wait.
- There are 500,000 channels with no quality control. (Unlike TV, where there is nothing on 50 channels, on the WWW almost

everything is there on an infinite number of channels.) Anyone can create a Web site. No authorities separate the "prime time" players from those "not ready for prime time."

• Both providers and users get lost in hyperspace. Organizing Web information for "intuitive" customer access is an even harder problem than graphic design of the Web page, which is difficult in itself.

• A real danger is that you put things up (on a Web site) and then forget that you have to maintain the site.

Although the Web is a giant step forward, it still is not a user-friendly environment. It is chaotic, variable in quality, and unindexed. Users must hassle with their Internet service providers (ISPs), and each browser and home page points people in idiosyncratic directions. It is time consuming, one can't look at everything, and when a user stops browsing, he or she does not know what has been missed. Moreover, 14.4 modems are slow, browsers are buggy and will crash a system, Web pages give huge gratuitous graphics, servers are busy or missing, and navigation is poorly planned. The provider doesn't know whether the user will download material (should the producer minimize Mbytes to be downloaded?) or read on-line (will the user be nervous about paying the ISP for connection time?).

A provider may use certain extensions to HTML to build an exciting page, but it cannot be viewed effectively without a browser that supports these extensions. This is like a TV broadcaster not knowing whether the audience is using PAL, NTSC, or some other kind of receiver.

Only 12 percent of the U.S. population currently has access to something other than e-mail on the Internet, and not all of these individuals use their access. Of those that do, only 14 percent have purchased a product or service through the Internet, and the number of non-U.S. total users is still quite small.

WWW-based electronic commerce can be fairly passive, requiring the potential customer to take the initiative to search out the product while providing retailers with limited ability to target potential customers. Other electronic formats, such as CD-ROM catalogs, faxes, and infomercials, can be more aggressively directed at pre-targeted consumers.

There are schemes afloat to resolve the bandwidth shortage by charging for Internet access that has been free heretofore. Demand elasticity surely exists, and use pricing will drive down demand in the short run. *Business Week* (August 26, 1996, p. 66) reported that most Internet users already believe access cost is a problem. Most users also told the magazine that slow access, hard-to-locate information, and difficult connections were at least minor problems. Only 16 percent of the users called their Internet experience "excellent."

There are also more current negatives. Incompatible products are typical, and competing standards are proposed. Investment is quickly made obsolete by new developments. Inadequate security and lack of privacy place users and their assets at risk. Fear of obscenity scares off decent folks. Conduct is often not guided by existing laws, and existing laws are often not enforceable. Current retailers and distributors of products often have geographically based exclusive sales rights. Because the Web is blind to geography, it is difficult to enforce exclusivity in some territories and not in others. Web commerce, having no location, in the worst scenario may be taxed in all locations in the future.

These negatives, however, do not minimize the potential impact of the Web. It will get a lot better. Expect more distributed access, more bandwidth, interactivity, and media richness. The Web is "cool," currently newsworthy, and user demographics are highly desirable. Historically, the greatest transformations in commerce have occurred when new vehicles for product distribution and retailing were invented. Each has been driven by the goal of selling higher volumes of products more cheaply by reaching a wider universe of consumers through more efficient distribution systems. Earlier examples have been catalog sales pioneered by Sears Roebuck and super stores pioneered by Wal-Mart. Given observed rates of change in Web growth and innovation, the "long run"—in which most of these problems are resolved—could be a mere five years. For these reasons, we devote the next section to the costs of setting up various innovative retail functions on the World Wide Web.

WEB SITE STRATEGIES AND COSTS

A recent International Data Corp. (IDC) survey found that *Fortune 500* companies spent from $804,000 to $1.5 million just to get their Web sites up and running. This estimate is probably inflated by a number of collateral costs. A more plausible analysis from the Gartner Group reports that start-up costs for a Web presence range from $104,000 to $285,000, with additional annual costs ranging from $49,000 to $110,000. In most cases, big companies try to do too much on the Web before they have learned enough about the medium. Retailers should focus on the most important purpose of the site, the measurement criteria and goals, then tailor the effort and cost to that purpose.

We estimate Wal-Mart's investment (www.wal-mart.com) to be among the largest to date. At Wal-Mart's site, the company polishes its image through information about its community involvement programs, corporate information, and even a visitor's center where one can see Sam Walton's pickup truck and his wife's wedding dress. Bloomingdales, another positive example (www. bloomingdales.com), looks ultra-hip, as any big New York concern should. At the opposite extreme, consider K-Mart's site (www.kmart.com), which one can safely assume required an out-of-pocket investment of no more than $20,000. The site reflects little long-term strategic planning, direction from marketing, or involvement by professional Web designers. The result is a Web site that reminds consumers of the wrong side of K-Mart's image, instead of reinforcing a better image of value and selection.

Both Wal-Mart and K-Mart maintain a copy of their monthly circulars on-line. These modest efforts may cost them roughly $10,000 per month, especially if the circulars are designed up front for conversion to electronic media. In a much more exciting example, Bloomingdales opened its site in September 1996 by offering special on-line deals and four $1,000 shopping sprees given away in the month following the opening of the store. The estimated additional cost for the promotion program is roughly $50,000, which includes developing and maintaining content and programming to support the promotion, the prizes, managing the entries and the selection process, and awarding the prizes. (This merchandising is entirely consistent with Bloomy's image, and the price tag is lower than what the company might pay in other media for the same level of design and production.)

The Internet serves as a great channel for quick answers to common questions, so consumers feel a retailer is convenient and responsive. One simple point: Wal-Mart's store locator lets a potential customer find stores by city, state, zip code, or area code. We estimate the cost of this capability at about $20,000, plus perhaps $5,000 every quarter to keep the database on-line and up to date.

Commercial software is available to implement real-time communication ("chat") or message-board communication (threaded discussion) for customers. KVO has implemented such capabilities for prices starting at $10,000, although a large retailer may need to invest $20,000 or $25,000 for a nationwide audience. This is just the setup cost; the larger cost is in the time it takes to monitor these communications capabilities to direct conversations and prevent abuse. Each customer communications service can require at least a half-time position for monitoring alone.

A $100,000 Web project may be seen by tens of thousands of upscale consumers ($50,000+ household income) over a three-month period; a similar investment in TV advertising would have negligible impact. Although a Web site does not have to do everything, it must do one or two things extremely well. With the proper focus (e.g., the use of a microsite), a retailer can accomplish one or two specific goals (e.g., market research and coupon distribution) at costs starting below $100,000.

Some Examples

The NECX Direct Experience.   One revealing case study is the NECX Direct (www.necx.com) computer-products catalog company, which opened an on-line semiconductor and components store. The Web site cost roughly $1 million to develop and requires a staff of forty to operate, including webmasters, developers, networking staff, graphic designers, telephone sales and support personnel, merchandisers, buyers, and management. A substantial investment, to be sure, and NECX Direct already had much of the back-end EDI in place. Still, in its first nine months (April to December, 1995), the Web site generated $5 million in revenue, and the company expects that to balloon to $50 million this year. It's interesting that 30 percent of the income comes from advertising (banner ads placed on its site) and merchandising fees.

Ordering, payment, invoicing, and inventory management are handled electronically. "We've learned that it's expensive to operate a Web site," says Randall Ashley, NECX's director of MIS, "but on an ongoing basis, this is a cheaper sales channel than other media because we have fewer people involved per transaction. The biggest expense is just to maintain the site, to keep it fresh and keep it changing . . . launching the site really being the easy part."

When NECX began its development, there was very little commercial software to facilitate an electronic store. Today, many new products speed the effort and reduce the cost. For example, iCat Corporation of Seattle recently announced its Electronic Commerce Suite, which "allows companies to create interactive catalogs, deliver them on the Internet, and accept electronic transactions from shoppers. Key features of Version 2.1, priced from $1,495, include support for the First Virtual Internet Payment System, e-mail order verification for merchants, over 250 predefined catalog templates and user interfaces, improved catalog searching capabilities, and compatibility with Sun-O/S and Digital Alpha NT Internet Server platforms." Such products are relatively new, so retailers should expect a considerable engineering effort to configure, test and debug electronic stores based on them. Still, the overall investment is now plummeting to half or less of the original overall cost of the NECX Direct project.

The Bank of America Experience. Bank of America (BofA) has $237 billion in assets, eight million checking-account customers, 95,000 employees, 6,700 ATMs, and more than 2,000 global retail locations in 37 countries. The Internet is important to BofA not only for getting the word out, but also for bringing banking into the home.

Bank of America was the first major bank on the Web, going "on-line" in September 1994. The "Build Your Own Bank" theme premiered in October 1995, and the home banking launch in June 1996. The bank's early Web presence featured limited applicability, was not sufficiently interactive, and did not allow enough control over placement of graphics.

The current, in places whimsical, Web site reflects a lesson the bank has learned: the more mysterious the message, the more people will come (see The Nike Experience, below). BofA has also learned that on-line ads are not driving sales. Companies selling on the Internet have to advertise off-line anyway, and technological complexity forces them into strategic alliances that generally slow their progress even while making continued progress possible.

Banking regulations prevent some of the services listed on BofA's Web site from being available to customers outside California. Until this situation is resolved, it will continue to cause frustration for non-California visitors to the site.

The Nike Experience. Nike's Digital Media Group began with a problem of "legacy communications"—its new electronic ads had to match the feel and quality of the company's traditional communications. In Nike's case, this meant action sports video and exciting sound. These capabilities were not available on the WWW, at least prior to the 1996 Olympics, making the Web unsuitable for Nike's consumer advertising.

Although not an Olympic sponsor, Nike obviously had an interest in the games being a showcase for its products and for its endorser athletes. Because of the human drama of the games, these athletes would be highly visible to Nike customers; and in any situation, the athletes are inherently more interesting than are the shoes. The trademark and copyright situation surrounding the Olympic games did not mean athletes could not wear shoes and apparel with the Nike swoosh, but did mean that Nike ads could not mention the Olympics or Atlanta by name. These considerations led to Nike's Olympic WWW strategy: Develop Nike's first Web site. Direct its content at journalists covering the Olympic games, but avoid mentioning the legally unmentionable (the site was called "@lanta"). Do not reserve copyrights on any of the site's text or photos. Coyly pretend that the site is not meant for consumers. (The home page stated, in artistically fuzzy-edged Courier type of varying sizes, "The purpose of this site is not to sell shoes. Or glorify apparel. Or market a brand. For the time being, Nike.com exists only to provide useful information about Nike athletes to the press. If you're not a member of the press, you can still sneak in and see the stuff they get to see. Just don't expect anyone to try to sell you anything.")

The site provided sportswriters, and of course ordinary folks, with up-to-the-minute coverage of Nike athletes' Olympic performances and scores, as well as downloadable digital photos of athletes, transcripts of all their press conferences, and personal profiles. A rolodex-style database interface led visitors to material on any desired athlete. The site was one of the most heavily accessed during the games. (Nike will not disclose the number of hits.) Nike received exceptional exposure by leveraging the best of the then-current Web technology, namely news text, downloadable audio clips, digital photography, and a database search. It provided grist for daily press stories about Nike athletes, increasing the value of the endorsements. It was able to thumb its nose at the Olympic committee by demonstrating that Nike did not need to pay the exorbitant Olympic sponsorship fee in order to get first class exposure from the games.

The mission was to provide a "living media guide" for the 1996 summer "events." At the Barcelona games, the slickly printed Nike media guide had been outdated in days. This year brought the interactive, continuously updated "@lanta press box '96." It had a Netscape graphics version, a text-only version, and a special version for the America Online browser—the latter because surveys show 40 percent of the journalists who use the Web go in through AOL.

No single Web development company was up to this task. Consequently, Nike hired a team of companies to provide the graphics, database, servers, a publishing system for continuous updating, translation (into 26 languages), Web access stations for the press in Atlanta, and telecommunications.

After the games, analysis revealed 78 percent of the hits were from the United States. Canada and Japan were clearly the largest source of non-U.S. hits. Seventy-seven percent of the site's hits were from Netscape users. Although this would seem to confirm that a significant number of nonjournalists were browsing the site, apparently it is possible to access Internet via AOL, then invoke the Netscape browser to view Web sites, and Nike suspects this is what happened. A large number of Windows 95-sourced hits—and 60 percent of all those traced to ".com" domains—indicated that business (presumably press) users outnumbered home computer users.

Now that the games are over, Nike's Web site needs a new mission. The home page now reads, "The number you have reached is no longer in service. Nike.com will be dark for several months while we rebuild the site and prepare for the future. So thanks for thinking of us and be sure to come back when we go on-line again. Don't worry, you'll hear about it."

IMPLICATIONS FOR TRADITIONAL RETAILERS

Don't Rush to Electronic Payment

The only evidently secure Internet payment system, "e-cash," is disliked by retailers (because it is anonymous, no customer information is captured) and by governments (currency is effectively issued independent of central banks) alike. Rumors circulate on Internet listservs that the long-awaited Visa/Mastercard secure transaction protocol has been compromised. Recent articles detail hackers' ability to sweep consumers' personal information from on-line service files and Usenet archives. *Business Week* has categorically advised consumers not to reveal credit card numbers on the Internet (Baig 1996). As noted above, a focused microsite can be a more effective Web presence than an attempt at a complete virtual store.

The consulting firm Arthur D. Little has just conducted an on-line survey to gauge the effects of electronic commerce on business. It reported that while more than 30 percent of the businesses surveyed ranked other customer-related electronic communications as a current priority, "performing consumer transactions in real time . . . were ranked top activities by less than 10 percent of the respondents," which is consistent with the CommerceNet survey cited earlier. But rather than explore why this is so, an Arthur D. Little vice president (http://www.adlittle.com; see also http://www.gigaweb.com) urges all businesses to regard electronic transactions as an untapped opportunity that must be pursued immediately.

We disagree. While the worst consequences of a credit card receipt discarded in a restaurant may be a few unauthorized charges and a $50 liability for the cardholder, a misrouted credit card number on the Internet can result in many large, simultaneous charges and dissemination of the number to numerous databases. The conflict between the shopper's desire for privacy and the electronically facilitated tendency of industry and government to collect and disseminate personal data is likely to persist. With likely resistance to electronic transactions from consumers, credit card companies, government, and even retailers, retailers are wiser to pursue the more clearly beneficial aspects of electronic commerce—cost reduction and relationship building.

A Niche Channel with High Uncertainty

Anyone surfing the WWW can conclude that Web-based selling is still most suited to

- reaching geographically dispersed customer populations with specialized interests. Hobbyists, collectors, and scientists are examples of such populations. Because there is no efficient physical location for stores to serve these groups, the WWW takes on a role similar to that of sales catalogs.
- information-based products. Software, computer games, weather reports, and research reports can be distributed directly over the Internet. Moreover, these products appeal to the consumer segments that are heavy Internet users. As our colleagues at MIT would say, "bits, not atoms" are the natural products for the early stages of electronic commerce.
- small sellers with nothing to lose by trying the WWW. As an inexpensive advertising medium, the WWW is an ideal alternative to leased space for a small start-up business bootstrapping its way into the marketplace.
- low-cost, low-risk goods. These are the goods most likely to be bought sight-unseen from a nonlocal retailer with whom the consumer may not be familiar.
- upscale, high-risk goods only when presented by sellers with ultra-high reputations. Lands' End, REI, and Eddie Bauer are brand names known for quality. They and other such producer-merchants are able to sell expensive goods electronically because their names are trusted.

Retailers do not yet know (no one does) how new technologies will change the Internet. Agents, expert system Web crawlers, and virtual reality, to name a few, will continue to present a high level of technological uncertainty to Internet-based merchants.

Also, as with many retail decisions, the decision to adopt an electronic format may require significant up-front costs with little certainty of return. Naturally, the accuracy with which the retailer will be able to forecast demand will be in large part based on whether electronic customers are representative of nonelectronic customers. Ideally, as in the case of Peapod, all customers are electronic customers. In these instances customer databases containing demographic and shopping behavior information will become important for forecasting sales. As retailers become increasingly familiar with their customer bases, purchases from retailers will better match demand and become less costly. At some point retailers such as Wal-Mart will have some customers shopping electronically, others shopping only in stores, and still others shopping both ways. Similarities and differences between the groups will greatly affect the retailer's ability to forecast overall demand for specific products in specific geographic areas. The retailer's ability to develop a rich and accurate database is very important.

The same can be true for other electronic commerce forms such as electronic kiosks, CD-ROMs mailed to targeted customers, and ATM machines. Because these forms of electronic commerce are location based, the retailer will be able to use the demographics of the customer base to project demand for products and services in the area. The result will be accurate placement of product inventory and service potential.

There are certain issues to which a retailer will need to be sensitive in this period of transition. First, interactive electronic commerce may be a poor substitute in the eyes of some consumers for interactive, person-to-person contact. Second, interactive electronic commerce may be a poor substitute for noninteractive store retailing. Many store customers rely on self-service and have only minimal contact with retail personnel. That they could have more interactive contact through on-line shopping is really of little consequence, especially since they will have to wait to acquire their purchases. Third, some electronic forms offering limited interactive capabilities, such as CD-ROMs, or no interactive capabilities, such as videos, may be considered poor substitutes for some noninteractive, nonelectronic forms, such as mail order catalogs. Sitting at a computer monitor or television is not quite the same as curling up in bed with a good catalog. Finally, some noninteractive electronic forms may or may not substitute for some interactive nonelectronic forms. For example, in what instances can a video or CD-ROM successfully replace a person-to-person sales presentation?

Avoid What is too Unfamiliar to the Customer

Not surprisingly, the products consumers are most willing to purchase via electronic means are those they are the most familiar with. Products such as music CDs, videos of favorite movies, previously purchased apparel items, and basic computer equipment lend themselves to purchases through electronic means. Shopping situations where the consumer feels the need to acquire product information through a tactile experience, where the consumer is uncertain as to the specific product being sought, or where the consumer pursues nonproduct-related shopping benefits (e.g., social benefits) are slower to successfully adapt to an electronic format.

As a result, successful electronic retail formats tend to be those that offer either products well known to the customer base or products not well known to the customer base but have high nonprice costs. Peapod Interactive (currently available on a limited number of on-line systems with information posted at www.peapod.com) provides a good example of an electronic retailer offering products well known to experienced supermarket shoppers. A large percentage of household supermarket purchases are repeat purchases; therefore, in many product categories uncertainty is fairly low for the electronic shopper. Furthermore, familiarity with product categories means textual and pictorial information can provide meaningful information to the consumer, even for products new to the product category. Web pages offering computer hardware and software to the experienced computer user are another example. There are, however, important differences in presentation quality, product information, and service among the various Web sites. Thus, although some initial supermarket shopping sites by Big Bear and Winn-Dixie (available on some Compuserve and America Online systems [for information on Big Bear see http: www. bearhug.com/index.html]) offered products well known to the consumer, they did not offer the price information, presentation quality, or service necessary for a critical level of shopping benefits. These systems will, of course, develop over time.

Some on-line and Web sites, CD-ROM catalogs, and infomercials may offer products not readily available in the local marketplace, such as jewelry designed and sold only in Las Vegas (see http://www.manifest.com/jewelers/index.html). Since the nonprice costs of acquiring these products is high (i.e., travel to another geographic area), the retailer can put together a viable geographically dispersed market even though some potential shopping benefits are reduced. In these situations the consumer has lower nonprice costs but an acceptable package of potential shopping benefits. In the jewelry example, the consumer cannot touch the product but does receive important information regarding product quality and endorsements from previous customers, some of whom are internationally famous. It should be noted that mail-order catalogs have historically offered customers products that were and were not readily available in local markets. In the latter case, mail order catalogs did secure local market share but frequently found it difficult to increase that share over time.

Location-based versus Virtual Retailing

Table 7.2 shows, in its columns, a view of what characteristics of the shopping experience retailers can offer consumers. The upper portion of the table gives the expert panel participants' view of the importance of these characteristics to three important customer segments: teens, baby boomers, and seniors. Of course, each of these age groups could well be subdivided further, and the table entries are called "presumptive" because the panel did not perform primary research to confirm them (although the entries conform well to Kang,

Table 7.2. Presumptive Utility of Various Dimensions of the Shopping Experience for Three Customer Segments, and Ability of Retailers to Provide the Utility

	Sensory Experience	Social Experience	Local Community Experience	Global Community Experience	Convenience	Selection	Safety	Price
Customers' Utility								
Teens	high	high	mid	low-mid	low	?	high	mid
Boomers	low	mid/low	high	low-mid	high	?	high	mid
Seniors	low	high	high	low-mid	high	?	high	mid-high
Retailers' Ability to Provide								
Traditional centers/ retailers	high	high	high	low	mid-high	mid-high	?	mid
All-electronic	low	low	low	high	high	varies by category	high	high

Kim, and Tuan's (1996) study of very comparable characteristics). The figure's bottom portion assesses, separately for users and nonusers of retail real estate, retailers' ability to provide customers with positive characteristics of the shopping experience. The table implies that traditional mall and shopping center retailers would do well to emphasize the social and local community aspects of shopping, as well as the sensory advantage that accrues from the high bandwidth of actual physical presence. The participatory layout of The Sharper Image, Disney Stores and Tandy Incredible Universe—and the free foot massages at the Texas and Colorado outlets of Larry's Shoes—make the most of this sensory advantage (Rosenburg 1996; Clodfelter and Overstreet 1996).

Note that Table 7.2's ratings of retailers' abilities to provide "Social Experience" and "Local Community Experience" are more ideal than real. Shopping in a traditional retail center in a city, and in most large towns, is a solitary activity because the individual has little or no contact with other shoppers. And most retail centers do little, if anything, to tie their centers into the surrounding community. Thus the traditional retail centers should be given high marks for neither the social experience nor the local community experience. All-electronic retailers may prove to dominate on these dimensions if efforts by firms such as Microsoft (with its planned thrust into local electronic newspapers with heavy community content) are successful.

CONCLUSION AND FORECASTS

The Internet is "here for the interim." What we will see in two to five years will be completely different from what we see today.

Sites will coalesce around a "conceptual proximity" that we do not yet understand. Because there is no clear definition of "distance" in Internet hyperspace, we are a long way from the theory of geographic trading areas that has been long established for physical space. We will learn what consumers look for in a Web site and why they click on links. In response, Internet business functions will converge as, for example, more access ramps offer content.

Research, references, decision support, self-servicing, and e-mail will improve with agents, personalization, advanced retrieval, and storage capabilities. In plainer language, better software will enable WWW users to benefit even more from the Web.

Broadband delivery will merge the Internet, full-motion video, picture phones, on-line shopping, games, and so forth. Exchanging more bits per second will allow greater multimedia, multisensory interactive experiences on the WWW—some of which are available now only at a lower level of interactivity through the telephone or television, and some of which are not yet imagined.

In every business sector, the best, the brightest, and the bravest (not to mention the youngest) are creating Internet businesses around the things consumers already do in their lives. "Killer applications" that will keep users coming back again and again are on their way.

The interactive nature of WWW means, for example, that gardening ads can be targeted to a customer who is reading about gardening *now*. Customers will be more receptive to pitches when they're already thinking about a topic. This means general WWW malls (analogs of physical shopping malls, intended for undirected browsing) will not flourish in the long run.

The retailer's ability to capitalize on the cost-reducing benefits of electronic commerce will stem from two areas. First, the cost of goods sold as a percentage of sales will decline if electronic commerce allows the retailer to better understand market demand. Second, electronic commerce holds the promise of lowering the marketing expenses associated with communicating with customers. In each instance, however, the retailer is pursuing cost reductions while altering potential consumer shopping benefits. In some cases this trade-off will succeed nicely, whereas in others it will not.

There is a movement underway, led by IBM, Microsoft, and others, to centralize control of computing resources by marketing near-passive network computers (NCs, as opposed to powerful PCs with floppy drives and locally resident software). This movement seeks to make the Internet an advertising medium, more like television. It may work in some sectors. But unlike the early days of television, today significant segments of users are in a position to fight back and make the Internet a truer community than television—with its crude community-access products—has been.

New telephone modem technologies will provide leaps from today's 28,800 bits per second to 10,000,000 bits per second. This is the speed that is coming soon from cable companies via cable modems, telephone companies via entirely new technologies, and perhaps from start-up companies such as Teledesic via satellite connections. This new change is so dramatic that retailers will have to learn how to think about it without being able to use their existing experiences as models or guides. They need to learn how to plan new in-store environments and new in-home environments based on powerful, cheap computers connected at high speed and low cost to multimedia servers. The in-store environment will come first because it is much easier and cheaper for the 1.4 million U.S. stores to install this equipment than it is for more than 150 million U.S. households to do so. Thus, the store is likely to serve as the gateway to the world for the next five to ten years; homes will then become that gateway. Stores will lead the way in applications like computer visualization of cosmetic makeovers or fitting of men's suits, applications that must prove themselves on specialized or fast equipment that is not yet ready for the desktop or the Internet.

This is especially true because the ultra-high bandwidth applications must be wired, often at specialized institutions such as large stores. Individual consumers will be slow to accept mobile (wireless) applications that are appreciably slower than those at the desktops in their homes and workplaces. To avoid ionizing the atmosphere (and perhaps vaporizing small animals), the bit speed of wireless units will top out at much slower levels than those connected to cable or fiber.

NOTE

1. This chapter is a summary of the participants' first-round submissions. It benefited from a presentation by Steven Gehlen, Director of Nike's Digital Media Group, to the Oregon Multimedia Alliance. The participants' complete submissions will appear in a paper for the research sponsor and on the Oregon Graduate Institute of Science and Technology's WWW page.

8

Consumer and Corporate Adoption of the World Wide Web as a Commercial Medium

Sunil Gupta and Rabikar Chatterjee

Among the different forms of electronic media that have the potential to develop into significant vehicles for conducting marketing transactions, probably none has generated as much excitement and received as much media attention in the last two years as the World Wide Web (WWW, or Web) on the Internet.[1] This chapter examines the evolution of the World Wide Web as a marketing medium, drawing on empirical data gathered since the early stages of the Web's development.

A basic characteristic of the evolution of a new marketing medium such as the Web is that it must be adopted simultaneously by the companies wishing to transact commerce and by Web users who are potential customers of these companies. In this "double diffusion" process, the rate of adoption of either group is circular in the sense that it is potentially dependent on the other group. Thus, companies should be more likely to open a Web site if there is a large pool of potential customers on the Web, whereas users are more likely to adopt the Web as a commercial medium if there is a large pool of companies on the Web (e.g., Chatterjee and Gupta 1995). Completely understanding the commercial implications of the Web, then, requires carefully examing the rate and nature of adoption by both groups.

We first profile the on-line buying behavior of Web users, examining differences across product and service categories. Next, we study the evolution of vendors (companies having a commercial presence on the Web) and investigate the extent to which this evolution relates to users' buying behavior across the product and service categories. Data on Web users' information seeking and buying behavior are based on the biannual HERMES/GVU survey of Web users conducted in collaboration with James Pitkow of Georgia Tech and the Georgia Tech Research Corporation. For more details and complete results, visit http://www.umich.edu~sgupta/hermes/.

To track the evolution of corporate use of the Web, we developed counts of "births" and "deaths" of commercial Web sites from on-line directory services. Specifically, we collected data weekly on the new commercial Web sites from two major commercial directories, Yahoo (www.yahoo.com) and Open Market (www.directory.net). These sites have become virtual registries for new on-line businesses. These data allowed us to create the birth database. Data regarding deaths were created by sending out on-line "bots" that canvass the sites in the birth database for continued activity. If a site cannot be contacted on three consecutive occasions, we deem it "temporarily dead." If the site is still unavailable a month later, we declare it dead. Both databases are classified by industry and checked for duplicate entities.

INFORMATION SEEKING AND BUYING
BEHAVIOR OF WEB USERS

To understand why shoppers adopt the Web, we found it useful to break down the shopper's decision process into an information-seeking (search and evaluation) stage and a buying stage (ordering, paying for, and acquiring the product or service). In this section, we discuss how the Web impacts both aspects of shoppers' decision processes for all product categories. We then examine differences across product categories.

Information Seeking for Products and Services

The extent of information seeking for commercial products and services on the Web depends on the costs and benefits of searching for and evaluating commercial offerings through the Web relative to other sources. Search costs (or the costs of locating a vendor) consist of (1) the setup costs of getting connected to the Web, (2) the actual time and effort needed for the user to locate an on-line vendor's address (using on-line search engines, links from related pages, getting suggestions from newspapers/magazines/friends), and (3) the time it takes to obtain (download) information from the on-line vendor (which depends on the speed of the connection, usage charges, traffic on the network, traffic at the site, and the kinds of information being obtained). Clearly the costs will be lowest for those shoppers who already have computers, have high-speed connections to the Web, and have the computing skills to use the available resources efficiently. In turn, the kinds of products and services that are of greatest interest to these shoppers are likely to be among the more successful during the initial stages of Web development.

Evaluation costs have to do with judging the credibility of the information provided by a vendor, comparing the offerings of competing vendors, and arriving at some evaluative summary. Because it is easy to travel from one vendor's site to another on the Web, it is often easy to compare their offerings. Some Web sites further simplify this process by providing side-by-side comparisons of competing products on the same page (e.g., the Bargainfinder and QuickQuote sites). In addition, the availability of increased computing power can better support the evaluation process by aiding human memory and analytical skills. Formal decision aids, such as loan calculators (e.g., the Bank of America site), preference predictors (e.g., the BizRate site), and sophisticated sorting and ranking of databases (e.g., the NetWorth site) are increasingly available. Thus, the actual cost of thinking and making the necessary comparisons can be greatly reduced.

In addition to reducing search and evaluation costs, the Web has the potential to provide new benefits by enabling the discovery of a better fit between the buyer's and seller's needs (creating new exchanges that might have been too expensive in the off-line marketplace). For example, consider a vendor who knows how to make a single product that can be shipped without undue expense (or even transmitted electronically). Assume that customers are very sparsely located in any single geographical market area, but the total number of customers is sufficiently large to support this vendor. Because of the distribution and advertising expenses involved, demand in any given region may be insufficient to justify marketing the product. The target customers would then have to buy some commonly available, but idiosyncratically less preferred, alternative. On the Web, however, demand can be aggregated across all of the markets, making it possible for at least some vendors to provide the more preferred alternative.

The global reach of the Web, combined with the small, minimal cost of establishing an on-line presence (for as little as $15 per month) can make barriers to entry in the Web-based marketplace considerably smaller than those of more traditional off-line markets. This further increases the customer's probability of finding a more preferred alternative on-line. Some examples of successful on-line companies that have been able to take advantage of such agglomeration of demand, and which might not exist otherwise, are Hot! Hot! Hot! (a site that specializes in hot sauces from around the world), Arctic Adventours (a Norwegian company specializing in rugged adventures), and All India Internet Radio (an Internet-based radio station providing news and music from India in Hindi and English).

In general, then, marginal costs for search and evaluation are expected to be lower, and the possibility of finding a better fit between vendor offerings and personal preferences is, a priori, higher on the Web. For these reasons, we expect the Web to become an important source for seeking and evaluating commercial offerings. In fact, our surveys of Web users show that despite complaints about transmission speed (resulting in higher search costs) and concerns about vendor credibility and reliability (resulting in higher evaluation costs), seeking information about commercial products and services is the third most popular use of WWW resources (see Figure 8.1).

Figure 8.1. Usage Intensity of WWW Resources[a]

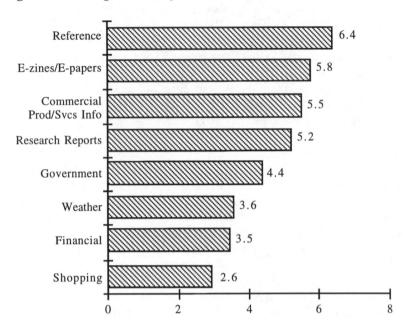

[a]Respondents were asked to indicate how often (7 = all the time, 1 = not at all) they have used the Web for each of the eight categories.

Source: Fifth HERMES/GVU WWW User Survey, April 1996.

Further, Web users express a clear preference for gathering purchase-related information through Web sites rather than through traditional methods. On a five-point scale measuring agreement with the statement, "On the whole, I would prefer to gather purchase-related information through WWW vendors," the average was 4.1. They use commercial Web resources more frequently than even direct mail advertising and brochures as sources for shopping-related information (see Figure 8.2), although still not as frequently as print media.

Buying and Acquiring Products and Services

From the consumer's perspective, the costs and benefits of buying and acquiring products on-line, rather than off-line, will depend on the price/quality trade-off (the ability to buy at cheaper prices and the possibility of finding higher quality products and services on-line), the relative speed and costs of shipping and delivery (for some products, such as books and software, electronic delivery would increase the speed of delivery and reduce associated costs substantially), and other transaction-related risks (e.g., the ability to cancel orders, return products, and get after-sales service, and the possible misuse of personal and credit card-related information by the vendor or miscreant third parties).

Figure 8.2. Sources of Shopping-related Information[a]

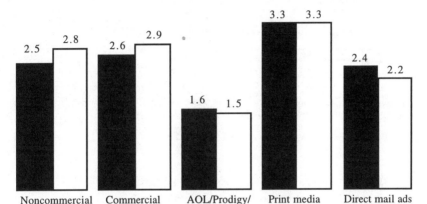

^aRespondents were asked to indicate how often (5 = very frequently, 1 = not at all) they have used (expect to use) each of five information sources in the past (next) six months in their purchasing decisions.

Source: Fifth HERMES/GVU WWW User Survey, April 1996.

Overall, Web users are not yet as inclined to make purchases on-line as they are to seek information. On a five-point scale measuring agreement with the statement, "On the whole, I would prefer to buy through WWW vendors," the average response was only a 2.9. In fact, on-line purchases are less likely than those made through alternative in-store and nonstore channels (see Figure 8.3).

Why does this purchasing reluctance exist? Among the reasons cited by our respondents (see Figure 8.4) are security and privacy concerns. Sixty percent of all respondents and 71 percent of female respondents agreed somewhat or strongly that security concerns are a primary reason for not buying on-line. Those issues relate to the credibility and reliability of Web vendors—users believe that Web vendors are inferior to traditional vendors when it comes to providing after-sales service or processing order cancellations and refunds—and less than compelling merchandising; Web vendors are seen as providing a more limited variety of offerings than off-line vendors.

Figure 8.3. Preferences for Buying: WWW Versus Traditional Sources[a]

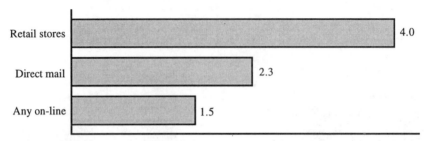

[a]Respondents were asked to indicate how often (5 = very frequently, 1 = not at all) they have made any purchases from each of three sources in the past six months.

Source: Fifth HERMES/GVU WWW User Survey, April 1996.

Figure 8.4. Relative Importance and Perceptions of WWW Vendor Characteristics[a]

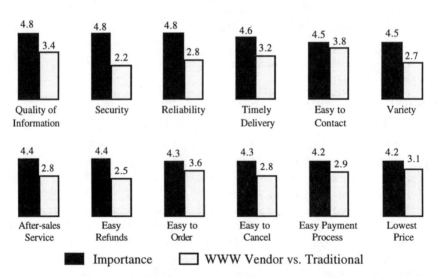

[a]Average scores on five-point scales for all respondents. Higher numbers signify greater importance in choosing a WWW vendor; scores above 3 indicate WWW vendors preferred over traditional vendors.

Source: Fifth HERMES/GVU WWW User Survey, April 1996.

In general, then, the data indicate that the Web has already established itself as a source of information and of vendor evaluations. For various reasons, however, it has not been readily accepted as a venue for actually concluding transactions. We next examine how these general findings are accentuated or mitigated for specific product and service categories.

Differences in Information Seeking and Buying Behavior Across Product and Service Categories

We propose six factors that can help explain why one product or service category can be more successfully marketed on the Web than another product or service category. Success is more likely under the following six conditions.

- The product category has a good fit with the profile of the typical Web user. Table 8.1 reports selected characteristics of Web users over the past couple of years. While the demographic profile of users has been trending toward that of the adult population in the United States, differences between the overall population and the population of Web users can have important implications for marketers. For example, because Web users are more likely to be male, we would expect products such as jewelry to not do as well as through other venues. However, as the proportion of women increases, the proportion of Web users buying jewelry on-line should also increase.
- The product category requires that the shopper process a lot of information (e.g., buying stocks or bonds) because of the complexity of the product (e.g., homes) or because the rapid pace of change associated with the product category (e.g., technology-based products, some home electronics appliances). Where such information can be readily presented in a digital manner, chances of success are likely to be even greater. Although the consumer may need a lot of information for certain kinds of jewelry or art work, providing such information in a digital format may not be very difficult.
- Products in the category have moderate-to-high prices, resulting in significant savings if the cheapest vendor could be quickly located. When price comparisons are hard to conduct in a consumer's off-line environment (e.g., if the consumer lives in an area where store-level competition is limited, or if the price comparison process is likely to be long and tedious), the Web may provide a means of reducing search and purchase costs. Computer hardware and software, cars, and insurance policies would be some of the categories in which the Web can play an important brokerage function.
- Information and transactions are time sensitive. Financial information, news and weather, and certain kinds of software fall into this category.
- Products or services can be tried or delivered digitally. In this case the user would gain substantial benefits through faster and cheaper evaluation and acquisition of the product or service. Software, music, news and information, and books illustrate some of the categories representing this condition.
- Buyer and/or seller markets are thin, or customers are not concentrated in a single geographical area. In such situations (e.g., certain collectibles, used oil well drilling equipment, gourmet foods), the Web can play an important agglomerative function and help create markets that might not otherwise exist.

Table 8.1. Some Characteristics of Web Users

	Survey Wave				
	First (Apr 94)	Second (Oct 94)	Third (Apr 95)	Fourth (Oct 95)	Fifth (Apr 96)
Age (average)	28	31	35	33	33
Income (average)	N.A.	$59,600	$69,000	$63,000	$59,000
Male (%)	95	90	85	72	68
Single (%)	N.A.	47	43	39	41
Education Undergraduate degree (%)	N.A.	34	35	32	33
Grad/professional degree (%)	N.A.	39	32	25	24
Occupation Educational (%)	43	31	24	31	30
Access to Internet through educational institution (%)	N.A.	51	27	32	27
Hardware and software used for Internet access Mac/PC (%)	8.5	48	78	82	88
Unix/other (%)	91.5	52	22	18	12

N.A. designates data not available.

Source: HERMES/GVU WWW User Surveys, April 1994–April 1996.

Figure 8.5 presents the percentage of Web users who have sought information about certain product or service categories or have actually purchased a product or service from a category on-line. As noted earlier, across product and service categories, looking for information is more common than making purchases. However, there are important differences across the categories: computer hardware and software constitute the most popular categories with respect both to information seeking and buying, and, contrary to expectations, home electronics is not a very popular category for on-line purchases. This is despite the known affinity among Web users for such products, the ability to describe (and perhaps even simulate use of) these products digitally, and the potential benefit of comparing prices across competing vendors. Perhaps the frequently stated concerns of Web shoppers about insufficient variety, repairs, returns, and after-sales service can explain this lack of popularity. Moreover, the relatively small number of merchants in this category may also limit its popularity.

Figure 8.5. Percentage of All Respondents Who Sought Information or Bought Products/Services On-line Over the Past Six Months[a]

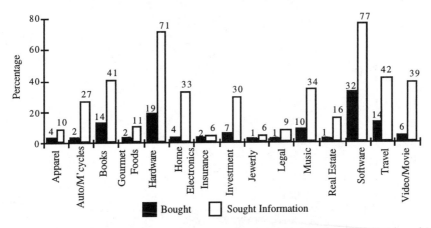

[a]Respondents were asked to indicate whether they have sought information about (or bought from) each of 15 product or service categories on-line in the past six months.

Source: Fifth HERMES/GVU WWW User Survey, April 1996.

Of particular note is the popularity of travel, books, and music. These categories, although not technology related, fit the on-line user's profile, can be transmitted or tried digitally, and provide the opportunity to easily compare offerings across vendors. It is interesting to note that travel is one of the fastest growing categories for on-line purchasing. With each subsequent survey, the proportion of users making on-line purchases has grown by about five percentage points (5 to 10 to 14).

In contrast to the travel, books, and music categories, the apparel category attracts relatively small percentages. The typical reason provided for such small numbers is the inability of the digital medium to allow the consumer to properly evaluate the offering (no touch, no feel). However, this category has some of the highest direct marketing/catalog sales, media that also preclude touching and feeling. Future research needs to examine the extent to which on-line merchandising and the variety of offerings compare favorably with those off-line.

CORPORATE USE OF THE WEB

Although the Internet grew out of academic and noncommercial origins, the advent of the Web resulted in its rapid use for commercial purposes. Figure 8.6 shows the rate at which commercial sites (those that intend to communicate or transact business with customers) has been growing on the Web. The overall growth rate is regular and rapid.

Figure 8.6. New Commercial Web Sites: Cumulative

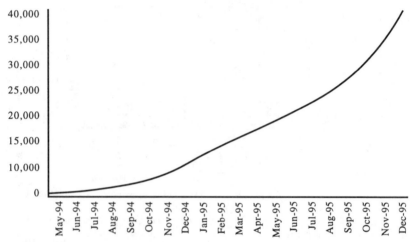

Table 8.2 shows the rate at which new commercial Web sites have been growing in 42 industries since May 1994. While the growth rates vary from month to month and across industries, note that new firms have been joining the on-line world at a rapid pace. In fact, the total number of commercial sites on the Web has doubled every four to five months. This is considerably higher than the estimated 12 to 15 months it takes to double the number of Web users (Cyber Atlas, http://www.cyberatlas.com/market.html). Table 8.2 also shows the industries in order of the number of sites at the end of 1995. As expected, software, hardware, and Internet-related companies are the most likely to use the Web. Companies whose products allow digital comparisons, trials, and purchases are also well represented (e.g., automotive, music, books, investments, and real estate). Highly specialized companies providing offerings in product categories in which the supplier and buyer sides are likely to be thin (e.g., arts and crafts, gourmet food, collectibles, and games) are also common.

Among the less-well-represented industries (in absolute numbers) are several business-to-business industries (e.g., manufacturing, industrial supplies, office supplies, aerospace, aviation, energy, and chemicals). Given the rapidly growing Internet connectivity among businesses, the larger volume of business that needs to be transacted, and the greater importance of acting in a timely manner, we should expect many more corporate buyers and sellers to use the Web. Among the possible reasons for the smaller numbers could be the presence of well-established existing relations and the use of other, private networks. As the Internet becomes more secure and reliable, the growth rates in these industries may increase.

RELATIONSHIP BETWEEN WEB ADOPTION
BY USERS AND COMPANIES

Thus far, we have separately examined the adoption of the Web for commercial purposes by both users and companies across various industries. We now examine the extent to which adoptions by the two groups are related. Table 8.3 shows the number of sites, the proportion of Web users who have bought a product on-line, and the proportion of consumers who have sought information on-line at the end of the first quarter of 1995. The correlation between the number of new commercial sites at the end of the first quarter of 1995 (Q1 95) and the percentage of users who had purchased on-line (Bot3) is 0.92; that between Q1 95 and the percentage of users who had sought information on-line (Sot3) is 0.76. Thus, the two diffusion patterns appear to be closely related to each other. Further, at the end of 1995, the pattern of correlations remains essentially unchanged (0.86 between Q4 95 and Bot4, 0.77 between Q4 95 and Sot4), suggesting some stability in this relationship. It is also instructive to examine whether the percentage growth rates in the numbers of new commercial sites across industries are related to the levels of user activity in information seeking and buying. The correlations between the percentage growth rates in numbers of new commercial sites and the percentage of users buying or seeking information on-line are not significant. Thus, for example, in industries such as software and hardware, which have high levels of information seeking and products/services purchased, as well as large numbers of sites, the percentage growth rates in the number of sites are no larger (if anything, smaller) than other industries with more limited Web-based commercial activity.

Finally, we examine the rate at which companies are abandoning their Web efforts and the factors that influence abandonment. Table 8.3 shows the percentage of commercial Web sites started during 1994 that are no longer accessible (Dead 94), for each of the industries studied. Overall, almost two out of every five sites are no longer accessible. A separate analysis showed that of the firms establishing Web sites during 1995, about 29 percent are no longer accessible. Although the more recent adopters are less likely to have abandoned their efforts (this may be a function of the time period analyzed), the death rates for both groups are significant. An examination of the industries with above- and

Table 8.2. Growth of New Commercial Web Sites

	May-94	Jun-94	Jul-94	Aug-94	Sep-94	Oct-94	Nov-94	Dec-94	Jan-95	Feb-95
1.Software	59	0.63	0.43	0.42	0.27	0.23	0.20	0.19	0.23	0.19
2.Presence Prov	27	0.37	0.35	0.40	0.44	0.32	0.17	0.16	0.25	0.21
3. Hardware	60	0.38	0.25	0.35	0.26	0.19	0.18	0.18	0.18	0.18
4. Music	5	0.20	1.33	0.86	0.73	0.49	0.46	0.40	0.27	0.26
5. Investment	12	0.42	0.53	0.88	0.27	0.32	0.24	0.25	0.28	0.19
6. ISPs	21	0.48	0.52	0.21	0.30	0.28	0.21	0.10	0.19	0.37
7. Real Estate	3	1.67	0.75	0.36	0.47	0.21	0.29	0.23	0.26	0.34
8. Sports		1.00	4.00	1.20	0.09	0.92	0.48	0.44	0.35	0.50
9. Travel	5	0.20	0.17	1.14	0.40	0.67	0.51	0.36	0.21	0.21
10. Books	6	1.00	2.22	0.59	0.24	0.32	0.21	0.21	0.26	0.23
11. Arts & Crafts	6	0.50	0.44	0.46	0.11	0.43	0.43	0.35	0.34	0.33
12. Entertainmen	6	0.17	0.00	0.29	0.56	0.36	0.37	0.69	0.23	0.31
13. Television	2	0.50	0.00	0.00	1.00	1.50	0.27	0.21	0.13	0.46
14. Inet Conslt	7	0.14	1.00	0.25	0.45	0.31	0.24	0.30	0.34	0.24
15. Food	2	0.00	2.50	0.57	0.64	0.83	0.58	0.38	0.44	0.29
16. Automotive		3.00	0.33	2.25	0.31	0.24	0.38	0.72	0.40	0.31
17. Apparel	6	0.00	0.33	0.50	0.33	0.31	0.81	0.42	0.31	0.21
18. Law	3	1.33	1.00	0.63	0.38	0.22	0.23	0.11	0.53	0.24
19. Collectibles				3.00	1.00	0.17	0.43	0.40	0.57	0.55
20. Gifts				5.00	1.40	0.42	0.82	0.52	0.13	0.21
21. Health & Fit	3	1.00	0.50	0.67	0.60	0.38	0.18	0.28	0.18	0.14
22. Games	2	0.00	0.50	1.67	0.13	0.33	0.08	0.31	0.35	0.39
23. Radio					6.00	0.83	0.27	0.07	0.07	0.00
24. Newspapers	5	0.60	0.50	0.83	0.23	0.26	0.21	0.12	0.09	0.18
25. Corp Svcs	2	1.50	0.40	0.29	0.22	0.64	0.06	0.16	0.23	0.37
26. Electronics	3	0.00	0.33	0.75	0.14	0.25	0.10	0.27	0.50	0.24
27. Insurance	1	1.00	1.50	0.60	0.13	0.33	0.08	0.23	0.19	0.26
28. Mnfg				3.00	0.00	0.00	0.33	0.00	0.50	1.00
29. Jewelry	1	2.00	0.00	1.00	0.67	0.10	0.45	0.38	0.23	0.15
30. Indl Supp	2	0.50	0.33	1.50	0.20	0.33	0.06	0.12	0.11	0.24
31. Hotels		4.00	0.25	0.60	0.38	0.18	0.15	0.27	0.26	0.25
32. Audio	1	0.00	0.00	0.00	1.00	0.00	0.00	0.50	0.67	0.00
33. Aerospace	5	1.00	0.20	0.08	0.00	0.08	0.14	0.06	0.06	0.06
34. Research	3	1.00	0.50	0.11	0.00	0.70	0.12	0.00	0.74	0.12
35. Aviation				2.00	0.00	0.50	0.67	0.00	0.00	1.00
36. Energy								1.00	3.00	0.50
37. Chemicals	1	0.00	0.00	0.00	0.00	1.00	0.50	0.00	0.00	0.33
38. Off Supp	2	1.00	0.25	0.20	0.17	0.86	0.23	0.25	0.10	0.09
39. Maps	1	0.00	0.00	1.00	0.50	0.00	0.33	0.25	0.40	0.14
40. Restaurants	2	1.00	0.75	0.57	0.36	0.00	0.13	0.06	0.00	0.17
41. Cosmetics						1.00	1.00	1.00	0.25	0.00
42. Firearms					1.00	0.00	0.00	0.00	0.00	0.00

Each shaded cell indicates the first period in which the existence of a commercial site in a category was recorded in our database. Thus, categories with a shaded cell in May 1994 probably got started in an earlier period. The unshaded cells show month-to-month growth rates (e.g., the number of commercial sites related to computer software grew 63 percent in June 1994 compared to May 1994).

Continued

	Mar-95	Apr-95	May-95	Jun-95	Jul-95	Aug-95	Sep-95	Oct-95	Nov-95	Dec-95	95 Sites
1	0.16	0.18	0.16	0.16	0.19	0.20	0.24	0.20	0.17	0.14	3316
2	0.20	0.21	0.22	0.21	0.22	0.20	0.25	0.28	0.27	0.23	2148
3	0.16	0.16	0.15	0.15	0.15	0.14	0.12	0.13	0.15	0.14	1562
4	0.22	0.19	0.18	0.18	0.16	0.18	0.18	0.24	0.29	0.25	1434
5	0.24	0.24	0.23	0.19	0.22	0.24	0.24	0.22	0.20	0.19	1433
6	0.30	0.26	0.27	0.19	0.18	0.20	0.19	0.17	0.18	0.17	1390
7	0.29	0.30	0.28	0.30	0.35	0.34	0.30	0.34	0.33	0.28	1357
8	0.37	0.29	0.32	0.30	0.28	0.32	0.25	0.28	0.26	0.28	1307
9	0.25	0.23	0.22	0.25	0.37	0.30	0.28	0.29	0.26	0.28	1171
10	0.18	0.16	0.15	0.14	0.15	0.19	0.18	0.22	0.20	0.22	889
11	0.32	0.27	0.24	0.20	0.21	0.20	0.25	0.23	0.20	0.18	817
12	0.35	0.10	0.31	0.31	0.31	0.29	0.27	0.23	0.26	0.28	774
13	0.42	0.35	0.37	0.32	0.41	0.39	0.34	0.35	0.31	0.22	747
14	0.16	0.21	0.20	0.23	0.20	0.22	0.22	0.23	0.25	0.26	730
15	0.18	0.18	0.18	0.18	0.17	0.16	0.14	0.15	0.15	0.16	617
16	0.26	0.23	0.21	0.18	0.21	0.22	0.30	0.14	0.14	0.12	579
17	0.21	0.19	0.19	0.19	0.19	0.31	0.23	0.23	0.19	0.17	576
18	0.47	0.37	0.21	0.27	0.26	0.26	0.21	0.19	0.20	0.18	567
19	0.44	0.22	0.23	0.26	0.34	0.42	0.29	0.27	0.25	0.22	443
20	0.09	0.00	0.01	0.28	0.24	0.20	0.20	0.24	0.38	0.31	366
21	0.24	0.08	0.07	0.27	0.26	0.32	0.21	0.15	0.14	0.10	356
22	0.38	0.09	0.27	0.21	0.30	0.28	0.24	0.27	0.30	0.29	323
23	0.00	0.00	0.06	0.24	0.00	1.67	0.75	0.57	0.44	0.40	310
24	0.19	0.21	0.14	0.14	0.16	0.16	0.13	0.20	0.20	0.23	299
25	0.27	0.26	0.24	0.25	0.24	0.20	0.21	0.20	0.24	0.21	296
26	0.04	0.07	0.07	0.39	0.51	0.35	0.31	0.27	0.29	0.34	254
27	0.29	0.29	0.30	0.29	0.30	0.26	0.26	0.24	0.16	0.19	237
28	1.67	0.00	0.00	0.34	0.49	0.44	0.29	0.22	0.22	0.17	207
29	0.13	0.17	0.20	0.22	0.20	0.21	0.23	0.25	0.24	0.23	204
30	0.27	0.03	0.06	0.19	0.02	0.45	0.28	0.40	0.22	0.32	185
31	0.23	0.00	0.05	0.23	0.02	0.35	0.33	0.40	0.22	0.22	183
32	0.80	0.11	0.00	0.90	0.00	0.84	0.86	0.54	0.37	0.30	178
33	0.47	0.18	0.12	0.11	0.10	0.13	0.18	0.20	0.10	0.15	91
34	0.08	0.00	0.03	0.10	0.07	0.17	0.25	0.10	0.12	0.06	91
35	0.20	0.00	0.25	0.40	0.00	0.43	0.23	0.43	0.17	0.24	77
36	0.33	0.00	0.00	0.38	0.09	0.25	0.40	0.67	0.37	0.50	72
37	0.75	0.00	0.14	0.50	0.00	0.33	0.56	0.40	0.29	0.24	56
38	0.08	0.15	0.03	0.10	0.03	0.11	0.10	0.02	0.02	0.11	50
39	0.75	0.00	0.00	0.43	0.00	0.00	0.35	0.22	0.06	0.23	43
40	0.05	0.00	0.05	0.17	0.00	0.04	0.04	0.10	0.09	0.11	39
41	0.40	0.00	0.00	0.00	0.00	0.29	0.33	0.50	0.06	0.32	25
42	0.00	0.00	0.00	0.00	0.00	2.00	0.67	0.40	0.57	0.36	15

below-average death rates revealed no clear pattern in terms of their characteristics. However, when related to user behavior, a significant and negative correlation (-0.45) was found between Dead 94 and the percentage of Web users seeking information in that industry (Sot4). A somewhat smaller negative correlation (-0.17) was found for the percentage of users buying on-line (Bot4) in that category. Thus, unlike the percentage growth rates, death rates appear to be driven by actual results, particularly the extent of information seeking. If users are not visiting sites in a certain category, the results are quickly felt by site sponsors, leading to a decision to abandon the firm's Web effort.

CONCLUSION

Drawing on empirical data collected during the early stages of the Web's development, this chapter examined the manner in which the World Wide Web evolved as a marketing medium. Our results show that across industries, the Web has already become an important source of product-related information for its users. However, for various reasons (including security and privacy concerns, credibility and reliability of Web vendors, and poor merchandising), on-line transactions have significantly lagged information seeking. Multiple surveys of Web users also revealed considerable variation in the Web's impact on the buying process across product categories. These differences appear to be related to six characteristics of product and service categories: customer fit, information need, moderate to high prices, time sensitivity, digital trial or delivery, and thin buyer and/or supplier markets.

Turning to corporate adoption of the Web, we found regular and rapid growth in the number of new commercial sites. Commercial sites have doubled every four to five months. This is considerably faster than the 12 to 15 months it takes to double the number of Web users. Further, the general pattern of rapid growth holds across a wide range of product and service categories. The category-level differences in the total number of Web sites established by the end of 1995 appear to be related to the same six factors identified in the analysis of Web users. In fact, the total number of Web sites in a product or service category was found to be closely related to the percentage of users buying and seeking information on-line. In addition to the rate of Web-site adoption by companies, we also examined the rate of abandonment. Overall, we found a significant rate of abandonment of Web efforts, although the rate declines the shorter the time a site has been in existence, as might be expected. Finally, our results showed that, unlike the percentage growth rates, death rates appear to be driven by actual results, particularly the extent of information seeking by Web users.

Table 8.3. Web Adoption by Users and Corporations

Industry	Number of new sites by end of		Growth	Dead 94 (%)	3rd Survey		4th Survey	
	Q1 95	Q4 95			Bot3 (%)	Sot3 (%)	Bot4 (%)	Sot4 (%)
Apparel	104	576	4.5	37	6	11	4	10
Auto/M'cycles	116	579	4.0	38	N.A.	N.A.	2	27
Books	201	889	3.4	39	14	39	14	41
Gourmet Foods	158	617	2.9	38	2	10	2	11
Hardware	468	1,562	2.3	21	18	69	19	71
Home Electronics	27	254	8.4	18	5	35	4	33
Insurance	33	237	6.2	45	N.A.	N.A.	2	6
Investment	31	1,433	45.2	41	7	27	7	30
Jewelry	35	204	4.8	60	1	4	1	6
Legal	84	567	5.8	30	1	8	1	9
Music	268	1,434	4.4	30	11	38	10	34
Real Estate	117	1,357	10.6	22	N.A.	N.A.	1	16
Software	732	3,316	3.5	28	30	70	32	77
Travel	131	1,171	7.9	45	10	44	14	42
Video/Movie/Play	72	774	9.8	26	6	41	6	39
Average			8.0	39	7	26	8	30

N.A. designates data not available.

Legend:

Q1 95, Q4 95—Number of new commercial Web sites established in each industry by the end of the first and fourth quarters (1995), respectively.

Growth: (Q4 95–Q1 95)/(Q1 95)

Dead 94:   Percentage of commercial sites established during 1994 that are no longer accessible.

Bot3, Sot3:   Percentage of users who have bought or sought information on-line in each industry based on third-wave results.

Bot4, Sot4:   Percentage of users who have bought or sought information on-line in each industry based on fourth-wave results.

The patterns of behavior among both Web users and vendors cover only the early stages of World Wide Web development. It will be interesting to see how these patterns change as the Web evolves further as a commercial medium.

NOTE

1. For a description of the World Wide Web and what it has to offer the marketer, see Ainscough and Luckett (1996).

9

Is There a Future for
Retailing on the Internet?

Sirkka L. Jarvenpaa and Peter A. Todd

In this chapter, we explore the Internet's World Wide Web (Web) from the consumer's perspective.[1] The Web is a multimedia hypertext technology embodied in browsers such as Netscape, which use hypertext links to form conceptual relationships between otherwise unrelated sites. This allows consumers to navigate among sites and search for information about products and services or place orders (Hoffman and Novak 1996).

Much of the research on the Internet as a retail channel focuses on estimating the customer base, developing customer profiles, or determining what people are buying and how much they are spending. Reasons why consumers might shop and what they expect from shopping on the Web have been largely overlooked (Berthon et al. 1996). Instead, customer attitudes about Internet shopping appear to be embodied in a set of largely untested myths. Thus the "need to understand Internet consumers is vital for both existing businesses and those who are considering a shop in cyberspace" (Fram and Grady 1995, p. 63).

To address this need, our research tries to identify factors that are salient to consumers when forming attitudes and intentions to shop through the Web. We use data collected from consumers while shopping on the Web to explore prevailing, but as yet untested, myths about retailing on the Internet.

BACKGROUND

Discussions of the Web as a retail channel generally focus extensively on technological issues. This technology-centered view assumes that the impediments to consumer acceptance of Web shopping are rooted in technology-based factors such as slow transmission lines, insecure electronic payments, and the lack of affordable full-motion demonstrations of the merchandise. Other retail innovations such as videotext, home banking, and home TV shopping have also been driven by this view, which has been linked to their failure to be widely accepted by consumers (Herbig and Day 1992). Although overcoming technical limitations is important, it is not sufficient to ensure growth. It is also necessary to consider functional advantages that the new channel offers to consumers. In the case of the Web, the often-touted impacts are enormous.

Many suggest that the Web will experience exponential growth as a consumer retail channel. Although last year Web shopping revenues were estimated at only $200 million, a negligible portion of the overall retail economy, by the year 2000 electronic commerce on the Internet is estimated to include almost $3 billion for consumer content (Hoffman and Novak 1996).

By the end of 1995, 7,000 retailers (*Boston Business Journal* 1995), including half of the supermarkets in the United States (Raphel 1996), had developed an Internet presence, including such direct marketing stalwarts as L. L. Bean, Lands' End, Eddie Bauer, and The Sharper Image. Wal-Mart opened a commercial site in March 1996. Developing sites gets easier all the time. Merchants can now download software such as Intershop Online (http: //www.intershop.net) that allows novice business users to create "branded secure feature-rich on-line storefronts including inventory tracking capabilities with a minimum of time and effort" (*Business Wire,* July 30, 1996).

Many expect revolutionary impacts on the consumer as well as on retailing, where electronic communities will become "vast, new global marketplaces in which billions of dollars in products and services will be sold" (Champy et al. 1996) that have the potential to "radically change the way firms do business with their customers" (Hoffman and Novak 1996, p. 50). At the same time, although electronic commerce was predicted to "spread like wildfire across the Internet" (*Economist,* July 9, 1994, p. 85), some say it has not happened and that on-line shopping has failed to live up to its overhyped promise (*Information Week,* August 5, 1996).

Many blame the commercial infrastructure and fears about security for the slower than expected start (*San Diego Daily,* May 28, 1996). Others see the small number of Internet users and the uncertainty over the actual number of users as the largest barriers (*New Media Age,* March 28, 1996). Yet, many with experience in shopping on the Web point to the mechanical and static nature of the storefronts (Burstein and Kline 1995) and the lack of compelling incentives for people to switch from traditional channels (Wingfield 1995). Some also suggest that current Web surfers are not among the target markets of many retail merchants (Fram and Grady 1995). In particular, women who are still the primary shoppers in most households are not on-line in large numbers.

Others acknowledge that business has been slow but that the Web is now ready to "rock and roll" (*San Diego Daily,* May 28, 1996). The security features built into Netscape Navigator 2.0 and 3.0 are expected to alleviate many of the concerns over credit card use. Still others claim that low estimates of shopping activity are incorrect in the first place: "approximately one out of three net surfers engages in shopping while on-line" (International Data Corporation, May

6, 1996, http://www.idcresearch.com), or "commerce is higher than expected" (*Business Wire*, May 6, 1996). "Other estimates place the cyberspace consumer population as high as 100 million internationally" (Fram and Grady 1995, p. 63). Gattuso (1996, p. 7) reminds us that although "only four percent of the population had been on-line in January 1995, by November 1995, 19 percent of the population had been on-line—a 400 percent increase. Some 31 percent of the people have access to the Net, whereas 66 percent have access to a PC on a daily basis. Eighty-four percent of Net users say that they are likely to buy."

As the above review suggests, many conflicting trends are depicted in the literature. In Table 9.1 we identify a number of common statements, or myths, about shopping on the Internet and assess them using data we have collected. We call these initial statements myths because they are often presented in the popular press as if they were facts, although to our knowledge they have not been validated or even studied systematically. The myths address the reasons why consumers shop or do not shop on the Web and what they expect from their shopping experiences, from Web merchants, and from the electronic channel itself.

Table 9.1. Myths

Myth 1:	The biggest obstacle to Internet shopping is the lack of security.
Myth 2:	Internet shopping appeals only to young male computer nerds and yuppies.
Myth 3:	The biggest potential advantage of Internet shopping is time saved and convenience.
Myth 4:	The Internet consumer has access to a broad selection of lower-priced goods and services.
Myth 5:	Web storefronts offer high-quality, personalized encounters.
Myth 6:	The Web is a retail channel very different from other direct marketing channels.
Myth 7:	Nobody knows you are a dog on the Internet.

RESEARCH APPROACH

The original data that we report were derived from an experiential Internet shopping study with a sample of 220 consumers in Austin, Texas. A mail solicitation asking the primary shopper to participate in a study was sent to a random sample of 1,500 local area households that met the demographic characteristics of the Web population along dimensions such as household income and age and education level of household head. Because we solicited the primary shopper, the sample consisted predominantly of the adult female in these households. Females are still the primary shoppers in most households in the United States (Dholakia et al. 1995), even though they so far have not played a major role on the Web.

Of the 220 participants, 184 were female. The average age was 44, the average employment experience was 15 years, and the average household income was in the $50,000 to $75,000 range. The most common educational experience was a college degree. Seventy percent of the participants had Internet access; 47 percent of those had access from home. Fifty-four percent of the sample had previously used Web-browsing software, with six months being the average length of time that the Web-browsing software had been used. Eight percent of the study participants reported previously shopping on the Web.

Because even among Web users electronic shopping is relatively low, we wanted to use a research methodology that ensured at least a minimal exposure to shopping on the Internet. An experiential survey methodology provided participants with an informed basis for answering research questions about Internet shopping. Web pages were created that outlined the shopping tasks and provided links to various shopping sites and facilitated searching for specific products and services (http://www.bus.utexas.edu/~jarvenpaa/shop). Participants in the study performed three Internet shopping activities: a 10-minute familiarization task in which they browsed among different shopping sites, a 20-minute gift-shopping exercise to try to find a gift for a friend or relative, and a 20-minute personal shopping exercise in which they tried to find something to buy for themselves. The tasks were meant to be typical of those that a consumer might routinely perform. Each participant was paid $20.

The shopping sessions were held in a computer lab at The University of Texas at Austin. The lab was equipped with Pentium workstations, 17-inch monitors, and high-speed Ethernet access to the University's backbone network. Lab assistants were present to answer questions, help the participants find specific sites, and assist in navigation over the World Wide Web. The data were collected from groups of 10 to 25 participants over five days in January 1996.

Data were collected from participants both while they were browsing and shopping and after they browsed and shopped on the Web. An open-ended questionnaire, a structured questionnaire, and focus group sessions were used to explore the salience of different shopping factors related to product value, shopping experience, customer service, and consumer risk that we thought, on the basis of prior research, might influence consumer attitudes and intentions toward shopping on the Web. Half of the 220 shoppers also attended a 30-minute focus group session that was used to explore themes surrounding the shopping factors (for additional details of the study, see Jarvenpaa and Todd 1996).

The open-ended questionnaire asked participants to discuss a Web site they respectively had and had not liked and why, as well as why they would or would not shop on the Internet. Responses to the open-ended questionnaire were categorized into factors relating to product value, service quality, shopping experience, and risk.

The structured questionnaire contained multiple items to assess consumer responses to these same factors—product value, service quality, shopping experience, and risk. Questions incorporated a seven-point scale ranging from strongly disagree (1) to strongly agree (7). For simplicity we classified the two extreme points on each end of the scale as representing either a generally negative or generally positive view, and the three middle points as representing a neutral view.

RESULTS

Table 9.2 indicates the percentage of study participants who responded positively, negatively, or neither positively or negatively to the survey questions. Table 9.3 reports the regression results from analyzing the relationship between the four shopping factors and, respectively, attitude toward Internet shopping and intention to shop on the Internet within the next six months.

Attitude toward shopping on the Internet was significantly influenced by perceptions of product value, shopping experience, and risk. Perceptions of service quality did not influence attitude. Collectively the four factors accounted for 48 percent of the variance in attitude. Intention toward shopping on the Web was significantly influenced by perceptions of product value, shopping experience, and service quality. Perceptions of risk did not influence intention. The four factors collectively accounted for 34 percent of the variance in intention.

We supplemented these results with excerpts from "think-aloud" protocols that we had collected from 40 pilot study participants to the study described above. All of the pilot study participants were University of Texas staff members or graduate students.

DISCUSSION

Myth 1: The Biggest Obstacle to Internet Shopping is the Lack of Security

Perhaps the most widespread belief about Internet shopping is that consumer product sales are hindered by Internet security issues. There is still a popular perception that credit card numbers are not safe from hackers on the Web (e.g., *Information Week*, August 5, 1996).

Table 9.2. Descriptive Results from the Structured Questionnaire

Shopping Factor	Each factor defines the degree to which consumers perceive that . . .	Percentage Response		
		Negative	Neutral	Positive
Product value		7.3	53.9	37.4
• price	the Web provides competitively priced merchandise and attractive promotions and deals.	10.0	63.0	25.6
• variety	the Web provides a wide range of goods and services, including those that consumers are not able to get elsewhere.	9.1	42.0	48.9
• product quality	the Web is a source of high-quality goods and services, which meet customer expectations.	4.6	52.5	41.1
Shopping Experience		5.5	30.6	63.9
• effort	the Web saves time and makes shopping easy.	26.5	36.5	36.5
• compatibility	the Web fits consumer lifestyles and the way they like to shop.	22.4	54.8	22.8
• playfulness	shopping on the Web allows the consumer to have fun.	6.8	46.6	45.2
Customer Service		14.2	67.6	16.4
• responsiveness	merchants provide the necessary information in a form that allows the consumer to conduct a prepurchase search, make a selection, place an order, make a payment, take a delivery, and receive support after the sale.	10.5	66.2	21.5
• reliability	merchants can be counted on to deliver on their promises.	10.0	68.5	19.6
• tangibility	goods and services are displayed in a visually appealing way.	3.7	71.2	24.2

Continued

	Items composing the factor			
• empathy	merchants understand and accommodate their individualized needs, such as providing universal access to services, linguistic or currency translation, and audio rather than text-based interaction.	2.3	28.3	68.9
Consumer Risk				
• economic risk	using the Web to shop will lead to monetary losses through poor purchase decisions.	6.8	41.6	51.1
• social risk	shopping on the Web will be perceived as imprudent or socially unacceptable.	5.9	50.7	43.4
• performance risk	goods and services bought on the Web will not meet consumers' expectations.	42.9	54.3	1.8
• personal risk	the process of shopping will result in harmful personal consequences to the consumer.	.5	43.8	55.7
• privacy risk	the process of shopping on the Web puts the consumers' privacy in jeopardy.	4.5	27.2	68.1
		2.3	32.0	64.4
Outcomes				
• Attitude toward Internet shopping	I like the idea of shopping on the Internet; the idea of shopping on the Internet is appealing; using the Internet to shop is a good idea.	11.0	26.9	61.2
• Intention to shop	I intend to shop on the Internet frequently. I plan to do more and more of my shopping on the Internet; I use the Internet to collect information about goods and services; I intend to buy goods and services over the Internet.	16.0	67.4	16.4

NOTE: In some instances, the percentages do not total 100 because of missing responses.

Table 9.3. Regression Results from the Structured Questionnaire

	Beta	F	Significance
Attitude toward Internet shopping			
Product value factor	.344	3.914	.000
Shopping experience factor	.398	5.598	.000
Customer service factor	.042	.430	.667
Consumer risk factor	−2.850	3.591	.001
Intention to shop on the Internet within the next 6 months			
Product value factor	.264	3.358	.001
Shopping experience factor	.179	2.821	.005
Customer service factor	.176	2.020	.045
Consumer risk factor	−.068	.961	.338

Although risk was cited as a barrier to shopping on the World Wide Web by study participants, it was not as important as the other factors known to affect patronage behavior in traditional retail and direct marketing channels— product value, shopping experience, and customer service—particularly for intention to shop. Risk dimensions consisted of personal risk (personal harm from the loss of credit card information), privacy risk (loss of privacy), performance risk (a product or service fails to meet expectations), economic risk (a poor purchase decision), and social risk (disapproval of others). Personal risk was the most significant determinant of overall risk. Age and educational level of the respondents impacted perceived risk significantly (B = −.184, p = .04; B = .183, p = .02, respectively). Younger participants reported lower risk perceptions, whereas participants having more years of education reported higher risk perceptions. In the focus group sessions, participants raised credit card concerns, although several participants took the view that actual risk was overstated.

The think-aloud protocols from the pilot study highlighted security as an issu· but only at a certain point in the buying process. During browsing, some ⁀ound it annoying that they were constantly reminded that the site was ⁀on't care about security right now." However, when one of the ⁀ho had never shopped on the Internet actually purchased a product ⁀was comforted by the message that the site was secure: "secured ⁀ng, okay, all right, this is where I want to be."

⁀ consistent with a recent Malaysian shopping survey (see ⁀z/survey) reported in *New Strait Times* (May 13, 1996), ⁀f interesting products to buy was a more common ⁀ percent of the respondents) than security concerns

(16 percent of the respondents). Most respondents in that survey who had actually purchased a product or service had used a credit card.

Overall, when people are not prompted for issues related to security, they do not think of those risks as often as issues of product value, customer service, and shopping experience (a result from the open-ended questionnaire). However, when prompted to think of the credit card concern, most participants acknowledged that it is an issue for them (a result from the structured questionnaire). Other research reinforces the finding that security issues are not stopping people from browsing and even from buying on-line. This is also echoed in a recent discussion of privacy on the Internet that suggests "while consumers are keen on privacy in the abstract, they are usually willing to trade it for some kind of economic benefit" (Hagel et al. 1996, p. 62).

Myth 2: Internet Shopping Appeals Only to Young Male Computer Nerds and Yuppies

Web retailers are encouraged to target "college educated white males in their early thirties, earning higher than average incomes and employed in the computer, education, and other professional fields" (Quelch and Klein 1996, p. 61). Further, Hoffman, Kalsbeek, and Novak (1996) found that those who actually buy on the Web use the Internet at least once a week and are frequent Web users.

The fact that women are a minority on the Web, consisting of only 20 to 30 percent of the user base (Hoffman, Kalsbeek, and Novak 1996; Fram and Grady 1995), even though they are the prime decision makers about household purchases, has led some to question the commercial viability of the Web (Burstein and Kline 1995; Fram and Grady 1995). At the same time, recent reports suggest a steadily growing female Internet population. "Fueled by growing Internet usage among women, the outlook for selling goods and services over the Internet, from supermarket staples to high-end specialty gifts, appears more likely every day . . . the number of women users is growing twice as fast as the number of male users" (*Discount Store News*, May 6, 1996, p. 17). Gattuso (1996) reported that although only 17 percent of women on-line are buying, they account for 31 percent of the existing on-line purchases.

Aside from gender, which was deliberately skewed to females, our sample of shoppers closely matched the demographic profile of Internet users reported by O'Reilly and Associates (1995). Although our sample was 85 percent female, 134 respondents expressed positive attitudes toward Internet shopping, 59 were neutral, and 24 were negative. Study participants were, however, more cautious in their intention to shop. Only 36 were positive that they would be shopping on the Internet in the next six months; 147 were neutral, and 35 were negative. Many participants suggested that they were more likely to use the Internet to obtain information about products and services than to purchase them. In summary, although the study participants were nothing like the stereotypical 20-year-old computer nerd, they nonetheless developed positive attitudes toward Internet shopping.

We regressed the set of demographic variables, including age, education level, household income, years of employment, and gender on attitude toward shopping on the Web and intention to shop on the Web. The results showed that age and gender impacted attitude toward Internet shopping, although these variables accounted for only four percent of the variance in attitude. Similar results were observed when the demographic variables were related to perceptions of product value, shopping experience, service quality, and risk. The only significant results obtained in these four regressions were years of employment on service quality and education level and age on risk. In all four regression analyses the demographic variables explained less than five percent of the variance in the shopping factors. This suggests that individuals' views about Internet shopping are not necessarily predictable directly from general demographic characteristics.

Myth 3: The Biggest Potential Advantage of Internet Shopping is Time Saved and Convenience

Convenience is often found to be the most important determinant of retail store patronage as well as of many forms of direct marketing, such as catalog shopping and TV shopping. Women have been found to value convenience even more than males with respect to catalog patronage (Eastlick and Feinberg 1994).

Our results from the open-ended questionnaire also indicate that convenience was, indeed, the single most salient shopping factor for our sample and the most frequent reason consumers would shop on the Internet. Shoppers emphasized the reduced physical effort, time saved, and greater convenience that the Internet could afford.

However, whereas 187 of the 220 study participants mentioned reduced effort, 106 of the 220 also complained that it still took too many steps to find a specific item. Hence, although virtually everyone noted the convenience of Web shopping, they also believed that it was not effortless enough. Some found the Web hard to navigate, and almost everyone was disappointed with the outcomes of their goal-directed shopping. The participants were disappointed that they were not able to easily compare prices across retailers. Many viewed Web shopping as more cumbersome than catalog shopping. The following think-aloud protocol highlights some of the frustrations. One shopper had typed in "leather belt" into a search engine and expected with one click to see a number of alternative leather belts: "Let's see if I can find a leather belt; four matches, ok; footballs, no, that's not leather belts, but they are leather footballs; Harley Davidson simulated leather backpacks, no; leather writing pads, no; men's wallets, nope; all I want is a belt. Okay, so it doesn't want to give me belts, ok, we go into Sharper

Image. Sharper Image will have belts. Welcome, great gifts, this month's special (the shopper is reading), what's this month's special, easy to get distracted . . . the great Internet does not sell a single leather belt."

The structured questionnaire revealed that the positive attitude toward Internet shopping seemed to be attributable to enjoyment of the experience as much as it was to time savings and convenience. Almost half of the sample felt that shopping on the Internet was like play, whereas only about a quarter perceived any significant time or effort savings. Hence, the results reinforced that the shopping experience was highly important and salient. However, it was not so much the reduction in effort as it was the playful nature of the Internet that influenced participants' perceptions of the shopping experience.

Myth 4: The Internet Consumer has Access to a Broad Selection of Lower-priced Goods and Services

The extant literature extols the benefits that will accrue to consumers from the Internet. Benjamin and Wigand (1995) suggested that "the consumer will have access to a broad selection of lower-priced goods" (p. 62) providing "maximum choice at lower price" (p. 70). Champy et al. (1996) thought that "marketplace power shifts to consumers" (Champy et al. 1996). Quelch and Klein (1996) predicted that "the Internet will lead to increased standardization of prices across borders or, at least, narrower price spreads across country markets."

With respect to the breadth of selection, our results from the open-ended questionnaire suggest that participants were largely positive about product variety on the Web but were deeply disappointed with the lack of product variety at any particular site. About a third of the shoppers expressed disappointment with the small number of products typically found among a particular merchant's offerings and the limited information available about products. Participants were disappointed that many organizations' sites featured fewer offerings and much less information about products than did their printed catalogs.

In our open-ended questionnaire, other product-value factors, price and quality, were less frequently mentioned than variety. About 20 percent of the participants mentioned that they expected to see lower prices on the Web. The comments about quality were less pointed than about price, suggesting that some consumers might have difficulty judging product quality on the Web. Merchants rarely provided assurances of the quality of their offerings.

Results from the structured questionnaire reinforced the finding that variety contributed to positive attitudes toward Web shopping and that the lack of discounts and lower prices contributed to the disappointment with Web shopping. Of all product-value factors—price, quality, and variety—price seemed to be the most important product-value-related determinant of participants' attitude toward Internet shopping and their intention to shop in the future. The talk-aloud protocols and the focus group results similarly reinforced this finding with such comments as "I don't think there are any good deals here. Why should I shop here?"

To summarize, product-value factors were the most important predictor of intention to shop. This suggests that for the cash register to ring on the Web, consumers will expect to see a broad array of goods competitively priced (Fram and Grady 1995). No "fun" technology will eliminate this need for functional benefits to the consumer.

Myth 5: Web Storefronts Offer High-quality, Personalized Encounters

According to Bitran and Lojo (1994, p. 385), the quality of service "depends not only on offering products that meet customers' needs and delivering them efficiently, but also on creating an atmosphere and overall experience that is satisfying." Hoffman and Novak (1996) argued that the Internet storefronts provide greater consumer control and are more accessible, flexible, and sense-stimulating than traditional retail stores.

Responses to the open-ended questionnaire indicated that the study participants believed that merchants were not attuned to their needs and expectations. They were dismayed by the difficulties in trying to do goal-directed shopping and locate specific products such as athletic shoes or specific merchants such as Bloomingdales. Consumers were also frustrated by numerous broken or inactive links. Also, they thought the store directories were misleading, making them expect one thing but providing another. The participants frequently got lost in the aisles of the malls. A common feeling was, "I would already be on my way if I were in a real mall."

Even the participants who stumbled across items that were novel and interesting, much the same way that they do when window shopping, found that many sites provided limited support for the buying process. Merchants had not considered the needs of consumers for information about policies related to returns, shipping charges, product guarantees, and the like. In some instances, to place an order the customer was expected to remember product codes, calculate taxes, and add in shipping costs—all of the things that focus group participants believed computers should do for them.

Study participants were also disappointed with product presentations and the inability to try or touch the merchandise: "You can't touch things, so it's not the same as shopping." They also thought that the product descriptions fell short of those in catalogs, although one of the advantages of the Web is supposed to be the "vast information on products" (Lustigman 1995).

Even though study participants acknowledged that the Internet allowed them to shop at their own pace and offered them convenient, 24-hour shopping, they felt that "the wait to get into the different shops on the Internet is too long." Similarly, they were concerned about how hard it might be to get after-sales service for goods and services bought on the Internet. This concern is reinforced in the popular press: "Tales abound of luckless cybernauts whose flowers ordered on-line never reached the intended recipient, instigating a nightmare of endless phone calls to tech support to finally learn that a server was down the day the order was placed" (*Information Week*, August 5, 1996, p. 40).

According to the structured questionnaire results, customer service did not affect the study participants' attitude toward shopping although it did influence their intention to shop. Thus, the lack of information on company policies with respect to pricing, returns, delivery times, and guarantees did not affect the participants' attitude toward Internet shopping but did temper their enthusiasm for completing a commercial transaction on the Web.

In summary, our data suggest that study participants found customer service to be largely nonexistent on the Web. Service issues will be important if Web merchants want to turn browsers into customers.

Myth 6: The Web is a Retail Channel Very Different from Other Direct Marketing Channels

Hoffman and Novak (1996) described the Web as a "phenomenal marketing opportunity" that radically changes the characteristics of direct marketing. The Web changes direct marketing and selling from passive to interactive, from a single medium to multimedia, from a one-to-many to many-to-many communication model, and from a segmented customer base to personalized direct marketing. Lustigman (1995, p. 36) similarly noted that "establishing an on-line site also makes it easier to personalize the shopping experience."

Our results from the open-ended and structured questionnaires suggest that although the Internet channel is different, it is not that different in the way that merchants currently use it. As one study participant said, "MegaMall is nothing but a big billboard to advertise." Sites today are static and passive and do not provide customized encounters to individual consumers or to the same customer community.

All this is not to say that the Web does not offer new retailing opportunities and capabilities beyond traditional channels. However, leveraging those capabilities requires merchants to think of the customer creatively. This type of creativity is absent in many retail Web sites. For example, few sites use effective price-comparison mechanisms or integrated selling as part of other value-added activities, or even augment the traditional product with value-added service offerings such as information, news, services, or subscriptions. The few success stories on the Web remind us that, "The companies whose sales have started to blossom on the Web generally present some characteristic there that can't be found in the normal shopping experience" (*San Diego Daily,* May 28, 1996, p. 1).

Myth 7: Nobody Knows You are a Dog on the Internet

As one *New Yorker* cartoon caption states, "On the Internet, nobody knows you are a dog." By now, this phrase has become an established truism (*Financial Times,* March 14, 1996). Quelch and Klein (1996) depicted the Internet as particularly revolutionary for small and start-up firms because "small companies will be able to compete more easily in the global marketspace" (p. 60). Do consumers care who they are buying from?

Our open-ended and structured questionnaire results suggest that reliability and overall reputation are very important to consumers shopping on the Web. Study participants were drawn to merchants with familiar names. This might be perhaps because merchants made little effort to convince consumers of their reliability and overall reputation. The focus group sessions further revealed that participants were skeptical of stores they had never heard of, particularly those perceived to be operated by individuals. Focus group participants also inquired about who regulates and monitors Web stores and whether a better business bureau existed.

Although several study participants commented favorably on the international shopping opportunities in their answers to the open-ended questionnaire, the focus groups revealed considerable skepticism about them. Also, the sites did not inform the participants of the process of buying from overseas, as the following think-aloud protocol suggests: "I wonder how you order from Euromall if you like something; how [they handle] currency and prices, and how long it takes if you order something to get it." In one focus group session, several participants stated that they would give preference to a "locally run" Web store. They also suggested the importance of knowing the geographical location of the physical store: "I would not order from a store that does not provide an address and a telephone number."

In this sense our results run counter to the writings of the popular press that a small merchant can reach a global customer base on the Internet (e.g., Heenan 1995). For example, 40 percent of the customer base of the successful Internet Shopping Network is reported to be from overseas (Hapgood 1996). A well-established Internet book shop, Amazon.com, Inc., has no physical store. In brief, study participants enjoyed browsing through virtual sites run from overseas locations, but they indicated a preference for buying from familiar and local sites that also had a physical presence.

CONCLUSION

Table 9.4 summarizes the myths and some of the emerging results from our research. It is important to note that at this time the results are tentative at best.

Table 9.4.   Emerging Empirical "Facts" about the Myths

Myth	Emerging Empirical "Facts"
Myth 1: The biggest obstacle to Internet shopping is the lack of security.	Risk is an inhibitor, but removing it will not be sufficient. Perceived value, positive shopping experiences, and good customer service are at least as important as minimized risk.
Myth 2: Internet shopping appeals only to young male computer nerds and yuppies.	Women who are affluent, technically literate, and interested in shopping can be favorably disposed toward shopping on the Internet.
Myth 3: The biggest potential advantage of Internet shopping is time saved and convenience.	Enjoyment of the experience appears to be as important as time saved and convenience, all of which are important for positive attitudes and intention to shop on the Web.
Myth 4: The Internet consumer has access to a broad selection of lower-priced goods and services.	Although shoppers are impressed with the number of different retailers on-line, they are disappointed with the depth of the product lines being offered. Shoppers do not find prices particularly competitive.
Myth 5: Web storefronts offer high-quality, personalized encounters.	Customer service information is nonexistent on the Web. For example, Web merchants do not provide information on quality assurances of their offerings, deliveries, and after-sales service. There is little attempt to develop on-line sustainable relationships with the consumer.
Myth 6: The Web is a retail channel very different from other direct selling channels.	Although the Web is different, merchants do not exploit those differences to their advantage.
Myth 7: Nobody knows you are a dog on the Internet.	Shoppers are concerned with the reliability and reputation of Web merchants, and because of a lack of such information on the Web, they are drawn to stores with familiar names and brands.

In our study, most of the 220 primary household shoppers, of whom 85 percent were women, developed positive attitudes toward Internet shopping. Sixty-three percent reported having a positive shopping experience after spending some 50 minutes browsing on the Web. Sixteen percent expected to shop on the Internet within the next six months. These shoppers were not the typical male computer nerds in their twenties or early thirties often associated with the Web and Internet shopping. Rather, these shoppers were primarily women from affluent areas who were educated, technologically literate, and interested in shopping in general.

Although risk, particularly relating to stolen credit card information, was a major concern to shoppers, it appeared that it will not prevent shoppers from buying if they can find something of interest. Finding a specific product was, however, effortful. Study participants found shopping on the Internet to be fun and frustrating at the same time.

To get women in large numbers to shop on the Internet, merchants need to focus on the traditional factors known to affect consumer behavior: product value, shopping experience, and customer service. One source reminds us that "female on-line shoppers seek out sites that offer many of the elements they prefer while shopping in-store, such as selection, good value, good visuals, quick purchasing and one-stop shopping" (*Discount Store News,* May 6, 1996, p. 17).

Also, reputation is critical in Internet shopping. Although merchants can initially carry their reputation from traditional channels to the virtual channel, such a reputation can be quickly lost. For example, Wal-Mart's recent launch of its Internet retail site was plagued by technical problems that left the one million consumers attempting to access it on its first day frustrated and unimpressed (*Computerworld* 1996).

Merchants will also need to take advantage of the unique characteristics of the Web: the interactive, multimedia, many-to-many communication model, and personalized direct marketing. This does not, however, mean that better designed sites necessarily use the latest technology. Instead, they use the Web's unique characteristics to support the way their customers shop. The consumer does not view Web shopping from a *technology* perspective but from a *shopping* perspective that incorporates product, price, convenience, service, and reputation.

NOTE

1. We use the terms "Internet" and "World Wide Web" ("WWW," "Web") interchangeably and as synonyms in this chapter.

10

Privacy, Surveillance,
and Cookies

Larry R. Leibrock

Some of the most important Internet issues that marketers and, indeed, society at large will have to face in the near future are those of Internet privacy and surveillance. A major reason for these issues is the "cookie." A cookie is an information packet that possesses both benefits and costs for Internet service providers as well as users (e.g., marketers and consumers). However, despite their context, privacy and surveillance are not technology issues; ultimately they are societal issues that must be publicly addressed and debated.

WHAT IS A COOKIE?

A cookie is an electronic "token," piece of data, or record transmitted by a Web server to a client computer. Technically it involves an intersystem process that results from the HTTP daemon; the server actually sends a transaction—an electronic signal—to a client computer over the Internet and expects a return transaction.

Currently the prevailing technology for server-client exchange is implemented on a session by session basis, with a session consisting of a series of transactions (interactions) that extend from the time a user logs on a particular server and interacts with that server until the user logs off. Generally about 20 cookies (tokens or transactions) occur per session, with each cookie being approximately four kilobytes in magnitude.

What happens to those 20 cookies after the session? One of two things happen. They may just go away when the user logs off, in which case they are called "nonpersistent." More likely, however, they are archived. In such a case they are written to the server and the client computer and called "persistent." Thus they become resident on the hard drive of the user's computer. Think of a cookie as an analog to caller ID, except that it is more than caller ID because it can also capture a wide variety of data.

The cookie process collects data that the user normally provides as he or she is interacting with a particular server. In some cases it provides data about data (the latter are then referred to as "meta-data"). The cookie process may not always describe the transaction itself; it may describe, for example, the search paths followed when a user interacts with a particular server.

Generally, cookies are exchanged by most current graphic browsers, including Mosaic, Netscape, and Explorer, and most client computers can receive and store 300 cookies. What is in the cookies? Cookies typically store the user's name or ID as the person logged onto the particular server, the visited site and prior visitation patterns, and something that is called user preferences. For example, if a user does not want the cookie to be downloaded on his or her computer, the cookie collects that information.

From a technical point of view cookies can be compared to a server's log. A server's log captures all interactions that any client computer has with that particular server. These interactions are written into a log file that resides on the server. Relating cookies and server logs is not a problem and can be done fairly easily. Although the cookie file and the server log are technically two distinct files, there is no reason they cannot be compared and collated.

There is a tool available called a "page refresh," which periodically loads a page automatically. The refresher notion implies that cookies actually alter the page of information. As such, the cookie is essentially setting tags or semaphores and changing the page based on the interaction. For example, when the page nonshow graphic is set, that information is passed directly to the server. This means that somewhere there are records of every page that a user has visited. These records can easily be shared among servers so that a particular server could know what page(s) a user has visited before the server was ever visited by the user.

The server log stores all data in terms of search patterns that occurred on that server. So if a user visited sites to learn how to make bombs, data on the search pattern are available. Someone could pull up that archive and find out that the user conducted a search to make bombs. Note that the files containing this information are readable files (they are ASCII text files). Thus even someone who is not a computer "geek" can easily determine the exact pages that were searched.

These readable files are intended only for the server's administrator; they reside under a root or directory that only the administrator has permission to access. But that does not mean the files cannot be read by someone other than the administrator. Cookie files are not encrypted. They are plain text files.

Try this exercise. Power up your home computer and open your browser. If you are running Windows 95, in the directory where your browser is kept you will find a file called cookies.txt. Open it and you can track the sites that you have visited in the last couple of days.

The purpose of the exercise is to reinforce two points: (1) the cookie file is an unencrypted file in your directory, and (2) no one asked your consent or permission to put it there. Browsers currently do not permit exclusion. A user can open his or her browser and see an alert that lets him or her know that a cookie is being sent from the server to the user's computer. But regardless of whether the user checks the alert, the cookie process still functions. From a technical point of view, there is currently no guaranteed way to prohibit cookie interactions with a client computer.

Coping with Cookies

Until recently servers typically did not expressly show what cookies they were implementing. If a user connected to a server on the Internet and elected to have any kind of interaction with the server, the server had no requirement to show the user if it was in fact implementing cookies. Now, however, the most popular browsers have an alert button that, when activated, indicates a server is attempting to implement cookies. By activating the alert, a user is made aware of the cookie process but cannot prevent it.

Several strategies have been proposed to cope with the cookie process. Because it is difficult for anyone except the cookie originator to delete cookies, strategies have focused on developing proxy servers to filter out cookies or software that can "eat" cookies following a site interaction. Unfortunately for those concerned about privacy invasion, at the present time no strategy is foolproof.

SOME IMPLICATIONS

By themselves cookies are neither good nor bad. But what are some of the implications of cookie technology? Currently the technology is moving much faster than the law. Therefore, the Internet is like a vast (endless) unpoliced frontier that is "governed" only by an unwritten user code of etiquette, a code that is rapidly changing and increasingly being disregarded.

From a marketing point of view cookie technology offers some interesting benefits. Of course, there are also some attendant costs associated with cookie technology. For example, there is a company, which will remain anonymous, that allegedly is capturing and selling users' names without their permission. Is this practice analogous to the practice of constructing data bases from subscription lists, or is it an invasion of privacy and therefore unethical or even illegal?

Three Marketing Uses

Cookies are being used fairly aggressively in many Internet advertising sites and in target marketing applications. More specifically, cookies currently are being used in three different ways. A common use is to add functionality and simplicity to a Web site by using cookies to facilitate site access and interaction. For example, *The New York Times* (www.nytimes.com) Web site uses cookie technology in such a way that users can store their names and passwords so that future interactions are facilitated. This use also facilitates virtual shopping because it permits the maintenance of shopping lists or shopping baskets between shopping trips.

Cookies are also used to track a user's travel within a Web site. This allows the site provider to learn what visitors are interested in and if they are having any problems navigating the site. For example, by tracking site navigation a site administrator can learn how many links are typically required to reach a specific page. If the number is deemed excessive, easier ways to reach the page can be devised. Interse (www.interse.com), a commercial ad tracking company, uses cookies to track users' movements through the Web sites that it monitors for clients to determine the effectiveness of site offerings. Firefly Network (www.firefly.com; see Chapter 2) uses cookie technology to track users when they visit a Web site, follow the pages they view, and then direct the user to particular areas of the site or deliver targeted advertising banners. Similarly, Focalink (www.focalink.com) employs cookie technology to ensure that a visitor to a particular Web site is not repeatedly exposed to the same advertisement.

The third, and most appealing, use of cookies is to tailor a Web site to each visitor's needs or interests. This use facilitates relationship marketing because information content is determined by the visitor. PointCast Network (PCN) provides an excellent example of customizing information for each individual user on the basis of cookie exchanges.[1]

Although the benefits that can accrue to marketers from the three uses are readily apparent, relying on cookies too much can lead to problems. For example, all three uses assume that consumers use only one computer for their browsing. To the extent that different computers are used, or several individuals use the same computer, the cookie process does not function very effectively from a marketing perspective.

The Privacy Issue

Cookie technology is clearly scalable and extendable to many things. About a year and a half ago, Microsoft began offering its service network, MSN. When a user dialed in to join the network, Microsoft scanned the user's hard drive using cookie technology in the sense of saying, "Tell me what applications you are running on this computer." The applications data were then brought over to Microsoft. At first blush the idea sounds good, because doing so could potentially allow Microsoft to better serve the user. The problem, though, is that Microsoft never asked for the user's consent to find out what types of applications he or she was using. Should Microsoft be able to look at a user's files without obtaining the user's permission? If repair people come to your house to check something, they need to have your consent to enter your house. If the repair people do not have your permission, they are trespassing, literally violating the law. Is not scanning a computer's hard drive without the owner's permission trespassing? As an aside, Bill Gates, Microsoft's chairman and CEO, has repeatedly stressed in recent interviews (e.g., Levy 1996) that his company will now only pursue such interactions with the express permission of users.

Now a lawyer might claim that the operating system users purchase for their computers is not really theirs—the users simply license the system. Well, lawyers can claim whatever they want to, but from a privacy perspective, scanning a hard drive is essentially encroaching on someone's knowledge space or work space. That space needs to be protected, at least through informed consent.

At the same time, there are also some ways to positively apply cookie technology. For those of us who have teenage children, cookies can be used to keep track of sites that we don't want our children to visit. And there have been implementations of cookie technology with some special systems. For example, you could let your son have the "keys to the modem" with the assurance that he won't visit *Playboy*. This use of cookies might possess major social benefits.

There is an ongoing discussion in the Web community about something called personal information exchange. An MIT-based consortium is attempting to address conditions under which cookies will be permitted and the kinds of personal information that can be exchanged. Microsoft's new version of NT has something called a wallet. The wallet is essentially a special place on your hard drive that only you can look at, although you can give another computer or a browser the right to look at it following verification. The wallet uses public key encryption to control who has access to it.

The issue of verification is closely linked to those of privacy and surveillance. For electronic commerce to occur with any magnitude, users must know with virtual certainty with whom they are interacting. Cookie technology allows electronic authentication of who users say they are. Some of the new operating systems, such as Apple version 7.2 and NT 4.0, permit digital signatures. Verification will become more and more common in a marketing environment; without it, an intimate business transaction is not possible (nor is relationship marketing). Secure client-server interaction is an issue that must be resolved, and quickly.

Privacy is not guaranteed or technically verifiable in the present Web environment. You cannot verify that a system is secure. You can only verify that a system is not secure. Consequently, you cannot ensure that information you send or receive over the Internet will be released only to people you designate.

Cookie data are going to be warehoused and used by mass marketers. It is just a matter of time until marketers start collecting and analyzing data to examine Internet and Web usage, user characteristics, and buying patterns. In fact, it is just a matter of time until cookies will be automatically relayed to server disk logs and warehoused for future use. Moreover, the idea of a network scanner—a process that listens for cookies across the network—will probably be implemented in the not-too-distant future to capture data without the knowledge of either the sender or the receiver. Think of the scanner as a kind of a traffic cop, one that surreptitiously monitors your Internet activity.

CONCLUSION

Internet privacy and surveillance transcend the cookie process. Some of the functions that cookies permit, such as site tracking and tailoring, can be accomplished by other means (e.g., registration). Consequently, eventually a categorization or classification scheme is required that reflects the levels of personal information consumers will be willing to share. Privacy is not "all or nothing." It is conditional. Thus, it will be necessary to define a hierarchy of secured information. Wildstrom (1996) cited an organization, eTrust (www.etrust.org), that has been established to develop a classification scheme for commercial Web sites. According to eTrust's scheme, every commerce-based Web site would have a logo indicating whether it collected no data, collected data for its own use only, or collected data for third-party use. Individuals accessing a site with the eTrust logo would then be able to make an informed decision as to whether they want to interact with the site. Going beyond the eTrust scheme, it would seem to be ethical practice to attach a privacy icon to every Web page, regardless of whether it is commercial or noncommercial.

To be effective, classification schemes must ultimately be mandated by society and controlled by operating systems, not by servers or client computers, and must not just exist for a few applications. Security enablers will have to be installed in operating systems if privacy is to be assured. But this will only come about after public debate. The technology required to enable privacy is trivial. Privacy and surveillance on the Internet must be addressed through open public policy debates, not backroom technophiles. Because of their impact on society, technologies such as cookies will most likely be subject to governmental regulations. Representative Markey's bills to address Internet privacy and the public indignation over the on-line P-TRAK data base are only the first salvos in what will likely be a major confrontation.

NOTE

1. The down side of PCN, though, is that it does such things as unilaterally and automatically install a screen saver on a user's PC. Although the screen saver is relatively easy to remove, the point is that there was no attempt by PCN to obtain the user's informed consent prior to installing it.

11

Electronic Marketing: Future Possibilities

Joseph F. Hair, Jr. and William W. Keep

Predicting the impact of technology on marketing is a daunting task. By the time this chapter is typed, much less when this book is published, new technologies will have emerged that ultimately will impact marketing, particularly electronic marketing, in ways we simply cannot now imagine, no matter how creative or future oriented we are. To not attempt such predictions, however, is to effectively acknowledge failure. As we set forth our predictions, we will do our best to avoid some of the more famous erroneous predictions and statements lacking in foresight, such as

> The phonograph is of no commercial value.
> —THOMAS EDISON, 1880

> Everything that can be invented has been invented.
> —CHARLES DUEL, DIRECTOR, U.S. PATENT OFFICE, 1899

> There is no likelihood that man can ever tap the power of the atom.
> —ROBERT MILLIKEN, NOBEL PRIZE WINNER IN PHYSICS, 1923

> Who the hell wants to hear actors talk?
> —HARRY WARNER, 1927

> I think there is a world market for about five computers.
> —THOMAS J. WATSON, CHAIRMAN, IBM, 1943

> There is no reason for any individual to have a computer in their home.
> —KEN OLSON, PRESIDENT, DIGITAL EQUIPMENT CORP., 1977

Although technology has always influenced marketing, its impact has never been greater, nor has the rate of technology-driven change ever been faster, than it is today. One does not need a crystal ball to see that the future of marketing, as well as the survival of many of its current players, will be dictated by when and to what extent technology is embraced.

This chapter is an outgrowth of brainstorming sessions held near the end of the University of Texas symposium "Electronic Marketing and the Consumer," and thus we owe a debt of gratitude to symposium participants for their input. We hope we have correctly incorporated their thoughts, and we apologize if we have not. In addition to incorporating participant input, we have relied on a number of sources, including Davidow (1996), Karolefski (1995), Levine (1996), Lieback (1996), Raphel (1996), and Zuckerman (1996).

We have organized our predictions around ten major headings. Although each heading highlights a generalized implication of predicted changes, the changes are not independent. Rather, they are, in fact, quite interrelated. For example, a single new technology may engender changes in the way buyers collect information, manufacturers track customized products, and sellers provide customer service. These changes suggest, therefore, the range of possible implications as marketers assimilate the opportunities afforded them through electronic marketing.

Following each heading are comments explaining and supporting the predicted changes. We have not attempted to sequence the headings in their order of importance or impact because relative importance is debatable. Needless to say, however, some changes are likely to have a greater impact than others.

TEN PREDICTIONS

Improved Market Information for Sellers

New technology will facilitate an expansion of the rapidly growing database marketing trend. This expansion will also be fueled by two other developments: more extensive marketing research efforts, which will enable better understanding of consumer behavior, and the coordination of old and new media, which will enhance an organization's ability to communicate with consumers. The ultimate result of this trend will be true one-to-one marketing.

The implementation of new technology merges with marketers' continuing efforts to collect, analyze, and interpret data. In the future marketers will perform database functions at near real-time speed. Along with instantaneous exchange of information, there will be immediate on-line assessment of the effectiveness of marketing strategies, particularly in promotions and pricing, to identify their effectiveness across unique and ever-smaller consumer segments. The ability to rapidly recognize and respond to marketing trends will be critical to maintaining a competitive advantage.

In a world where scanners are ubiquitous, "smart cards" provide basic customer information at point of purchase, and customer-specific electronic interactions create historical records, sellers will make marketing decisions based on individual or household demographics, historical product/service choices, responses to promotions, and brand loyalties. Increasingly, behavioral data will indicate consumer preferences and, perhaps more importantly, the media, message and timing of promotions that stimulate responses. The basic process of analyzing market information and developing appropriate marketing strategies will be similar to those utilized in the past. But the process will be significantly more complicated as a result of the amount of available market information and the challenge of developing customer-specific strategies. Marketers who master this more complicated environment will be rewarded with customer loyalty based on increased customer satisfaction.

Improved Market Information for Buyers

Information search processes for buyers will also be enhanced. Individual buyers will have more information available than they can even imagine. Initially, as is the case with today's Internet search engines, a product/service search will produce so many matches that the searcher will be inclined to give up. The ultimate task for electronic marketing will be to design expert systems to help consumers sift through and find the critical pieces of information— probably less than five percent of the available information. As these systems evolve, electronic marketing will become an informative and efficient process for the buyer.

Locating products and services according to shopper-defined criteria will be the first interactive step. Currently, electronic shoppers buy from electronic sources offering low-risk products, products for which the shopper already has sufficient information, such as prerecorded CDs, books, towels and linens, and computer hardware and software. Electronic food shopping, already in limited use, appears on the near horizon as consumers seek time flexibility while obtaining their favorite brands. Food shopping lends itself to electronic marketing because of the average consumer's familiarity with food products and the tendency toward repeat purchases.

Soon electronic shoppers, however, will search for more than just product availability. Electronic shoppers will view products in three dimensions; obtain detailed information on product make-up, care, and usage; ask questions; and in some cases actually sample the product electronically. Products and services that can be digitized, such as newspapers, magazines, books, and music, can be presented in small samples before the shopper makes a purchase decision. Shoppers will also increasingly customize their purchases. Electronically configuring component products like computers and stereos on-line is already possible. As technology reduces manufacturing costs, more integrated products such as apparel and furniture will also be subject to customization. Control and customization will be the natural result of increased consumer information, delivered on demand.

Increased Interactivity Between Buyers and Sellers

The level of interactivity between buyers and sellers will increase dramatically. Product/service development today under the best circumstances is based on focus group interviews and surveys. In the future, much more extensive customer input will be possible, with continuous input from idea generation to actual product launch, and even through product adoption. In short, products and services will be configured to each customer's priorities, leading to significantly increased customer power in the marketplace.

In place of today's strategy of target marketing, consumers will increasingly come to companies for their product/service needs, and they will remain with those companies that respond quickly and effectively. Through timely electronic inquiries customers will make their wants known and will evaluate companies' ability to comply. Electronically savvy consumers will obtain information not only on products and services, but also on fill rates and response times as well. Marketing services will be measured in fractions of seconds, and consumer expectations will increase accordingly.

Sellers will also benefit by sending electronic messages to potential customers. Customized responses based on previous buyer behavior will clarify communications and reduce defections. Hundreds of thousands of electronic "cold calls" will be conducted in seconds. Some sellers have already established electronic "chat rooms," providing a social environment for customers as well as an important source of market information. Individualized messages to facilitate current and future purchases will develop as individual customer profiles expand through increased interaction.

Enhanced Interconnectivity Between Buyers and Sellers

Increased interactivity between buyers and sellers is facilitated by enhanced interconnectivity capabilities. Real-time buyer-seller contact in which information is obtained and used almost simultaneously by both sides through instantaneous feedback will become the norm. Moreover, exchange of information will be enhanced dramatically through improved creative and production technologies. Electronic workstations in companies and further penetration of PCs in households will enable widespread customization of products and services along with reduced costs and increased flexibility. Key to this ability thus far has been the rapid spread of desktop publishing, ink jet customization and coloring systems, and automated insertion and binding capabilities that enable an organization to attract consumers' attention and persuade them to purchase. As this technology moves into the electronic marketing arena, marketers will be able to customize communications with potential customers quickly and in a format desired by those customers, making the interconnection more meaningful and more effective.

Enhanced interconnectivity also can mean more and better methods of communications. Internet connections through computers and televisions, facsimile machines, pagers, express mail, and satellite-based communications complement more traditional methods of conventional mail service, telemarketing, and face-to-face selling. As a result, buyers contact sellers, and sellers can respond from virtually any time zone and location. Consumers can view and purchase products over the Internet during a lunch break at work or when logged on at home through their favorite Internet access service. Future applications may even allow consumers to purchase items when watching their favorite television program or movie. Under one scenario, consumers watching a television show or movie will be able to purchase the swim suit worn during the beach scene by their favorite actor or obtain leasing information on a car driven in the chase scene—while they continue to watch the show. Motivated by consumer demands, buyers further back in the channel of distribution will be equally demanding as they contact their suppliers to check on orders from the shop floor, as they travel on airplanes, or even as they play golf.

As any experienced marketer knows, the buyer's ability to contact the seller at any time through a variety of media is a mixed blessing. On the one hand, sellers will be able to contact customers and potential customers using various communication platforms. Customer feedback will increase, and seller response times will decrease accordingly. On the other hand, faster response times and greater customization require greater organizational flexibility. If markets are arenas within which buyers and sellers meet, enhanced interconnectivity presents the possibility of creating markets at any time in any location.

Emergence of New Market Intermediaries

With the dramatic increase in information, we will experience the emergence of new market intermediaries. One obvious intermediary will be information warehouses. Although these warehouses will begin by providing storage capabilities, they will evolve into entities that integrate and process massive amounts of data and then sell the data to organizations to enhance their marketing efforts. A parallel effort will be the emergence of intelligent software agents and hardware to facilitate search, evaluation, and understanding of data. Perhaps the first application of this technology will be by intermediaries that help searchers sift through the ever-increasing amount of information available on the Internet.

Searching for information and product/service sources will not, however, resemble the current matching process. New search engines will rely on artificial intelligence that goes well beyond the current notion of key words. For example, a search using the words "casual apparel" will reveal products related to a casual lifestyle without the word "casual" appearing in a title or description. The search engine will "know" that products associated with certain activities are considered to be casual. These changes will be made possible by increasing computer power and an in-depth understanding of linguistics. Just as in the past, when advertising agencies provided expertise in noninteractive communications, new intermediaries will analyze and respond to the dialog between retailers and consumers.

Market intermediaries will do more than search for and analyze information. They will also address the fragmentation of formerly integrated selling and buying functions. For example, some electronic marketers selling at the retail level will maintain no inventories and minimal physical facilities. Their function will be to match consumers with available products. Once the sale has been made, the intermediary will then electronically place the order with a supplier who will ship directly to the consumer. This specialty technology-based service is essentially that of a broker having no physical inventory or store atmosphere, but also having no person-to-person contact with the customer. The function of the broker is not new, but the specialty area will gain importance at the retail level as the selling function is separated from other retail functions.

Expanded and More Technology-based Channels of Physical Distribution

Physical distribution through electronic channels will become widespread. Electronic channels will distribute any kind of product or service that can be converted to a digital format and transmitted either through fiber optic cable or satellites. Products flowing through electronic channels will include movies; music; newspapers; magazines and books; money; tickets for airlines; stage plays and concerts or any other form of entertainment; and market research information. Thus, products that can be digitized will be available in various formats from a variety of sources.

Smart cards will allow consumers to carry information and electronic cash in a manner that will speed purchases and transfer information to the seller. Prestored information, for example, will expedite airline ticket purchases, car rentals, and food service. Service distribution channels will be reconfigured to respond to better and more immediate demand information. As a new channel of distribution, the electronic highway will span geographic boundaries, more closely coordinating products and services with demand. Even education will be electronically distributed as universities and other educational institutions at all levels (including primary, secondary, and vocational) increasingly offer distance learning courses and students obtain lessons from CD-ROM and Internet sources.

Many products, of course, will still require the more traditional physical distribution channel, complete with warehouses, trucks, and some manual labor. Technological improvements, however, will continue to shorten delivery times and improve service levels. Future developments will include the expanded use of bar codes that speed physical inspection and facilitate the automation of receiving, storing, picking, and shipping. Smart chips that carry large amounts of information will be attached to products and components. Such information will assist in the customization of products as they move through the production process and facilitate tracking. Smart chips will also contain information on who purchased the product, when the product was purchased, the promised time of delivery, and any special delivery instructions.

As consumer dollar volumes of electronic purchases grow, new delivery channels will develop. The available options will increase to the degree that the purchase transaction is separated from immediate product acquisition. Possibilities range from consumers picking up prepurchased products from distribution centers where the products are stored according to purchase order, temperature storing requirements, and pick-up times, to home delivery services. These options already exist in groceries and food services and will spread to other products as consumers increasingly demand them.

Additional Technology-based Consumer Services

Time management difficulties will continue as customers seek more control over their lives, both personal and professional. This will be particularly true at the retail level as baby boomers move into their 50s and search for ways to simplify their lives. Obvious services like bill paying, time and activity organizers, callback reminders, "To Do" lists, trip schedulers, and so forth will emerge first. But others, such as routine food purchases or recommendations on product/service purchases similar to those existing on the Firefly Web site on the Internet, will not be far behind.

From a marketing perspective, digitized information facilitates the delivery of consumer services. Unlike telephone messages, surveys, and written correspondence, electronic messages can be sorted, categorized, analyzed, and stored with remarkable speed. This increased speed benefits consumers with faster turnaround times and lower costs. New "push" or "webcasting" software will allow prerequested information to be delivered to consumers as it becomes available. Rather than receiving information such as stock prices and baseball scores at regular intervals, new services will send information only when triggered by criteria established by the user.

The increase in electronic communication methods will move many channel interchanges to electronic formats. Although improved information may be the most obvious form of interchange, technology-based services will range from home security to automatically upgrading computer software via the Internet as upgrades become available. Consumers buying from an on-line supermarket will select and print recipes at home while an order for the necessary ingredients is automatically placed with the firm. Vendors in the marketing channel will analyze relevant market and firm-specific information on a continuous basis, proactively anticipating their customers' needs.

More Worldwide Sourcing

National boundaries will fall even faster than they have in recent years. Technology will enable individuals and groups to bypass existing sources of products and services and choose those that most closely meet their needs. Competition will be facilitated not only by the Internet, but by other technologies such as ISDN (Integrated Services Digital Network), HDTV (high-definition television), satellite transmission, 900 telephone service, CD-ROM, and interactive voice response. Some traditional channel intermediaries will disappear, whereas those that survive will be most in tune with customer needs and desires.

Several obstacles will slow, but not stop this process. For example, although English currently is the standard global language, resistance will remain from ethnocentric countries and from those where education levels are low. Moreover, there will also be problems for products requiring visual and sensory information. Problems associated with visual aspects will evaporate with improved technology, such as HDTV, but sensory aspects like taste and smell will be more challenging.

Retail history reveals the impact that nonstore selling can have on shopping behavior. During the rapid growth of mail order catalogs almost one hundred years ago, worried retailers admonished shoppers to spend their dollars at local retail stores. Although catalogs obviously did not displace retail stores, they did successfully establish geographically dispersed markets by offering products and services, many of which were not available locally, at competitive prices. We can expect similar changes as customers are linked electronically to retailers throughout the world. Current technology allows electronic retailers to facilitate and customize an electronic shopping experience by analyzing the customer's most recent electronic shopping activities. This form of customization is less costly and more individualized than the "targeted" printed messages and catalogs developed by direct marketing firms.

Increased Emphasis on Building Customer Loyalty

In the future, building and maintaining customer loyalty will be more difficult, but more important. As alternative sources of products and services increase geometrically, relationship marketing skills will become even more important in enhancing customer loyalty. True partnering between buyers and sellers will be necessary, and not just the lip-service partnering so prevalent today. Moreover, the current battle between national and private brands will become more complex. Retailers with strong private brands such as The Limited, The Gap, L.L. Bean, and Lands' End will use electronic marketing to maintain and build their current customer base. These efforts will be countered by the use of strong national brands such as DKNY, Ralph Lauren, Nautica, and

Liz Claiborne to attract customers into "new" virtual stores. Leveraging an established corporate brand, whether owned by a retailer or a manufacturer, will become an effective mechanism for small competitors attempting to enter the marketplace.

Understanding and responding to customers has always been the key to building customer loyalty. Electronic marketing will effectively shorten the distance between the customer and primary decision maker in the firm. Although decision makers will deal with customer data aggregated at some level, marketing strategies will become increasingly individualized. Historical data bases will provide behavioral information allowing for customer-specific marketing. Retailers and customers alike will accumulate detailed information on consistency of performance to better evaluate the value of their business relationship. Electronic retailers will use data bases to customize product service offerings, and promotion and pricing strategies will be triggered by individual customer behavior. Consumers will receive individualized marketing communications that do not require individualized attention.

Safeguards Designed to Provide Information Security and Buyer/Seller Confidentiality

Privacy issues relating to electronic marketing stem from two sources: the increasing ability of firms to collect, analyze, store, and transfer customer-specific behavioral information, and the electronic "tracks" left by consumers as they correspond, search, and shop via the Internet. Maintaining the privacy of consumer data has been an issue for direct marketing firms for some time. New technology, however, provides increasing capabilities to capture and store large amounts of behavioral data, and therefore necessitates even more emphasis on resolving the privacy issue so that it is a win-win situation for both the buyer and seller.

Firms will not only have demographic and psychographic profiles of their customers, they will also be able to determine the extent to which actual behavior corresponds with anticipated behavior. The more complete the customer file, the more accurately the firm can predict future purchases. Customer information can be (1) used to tailor products and services to increase customer satisfaction, (2) used to develop customer-specific promotion and pricing strategies that optimize response rates, (3) sold to other organizations that will use the information to generate their own unsolicited, and perhaps unwanted, marketing programs, and/or (4) stolen or copied and sold to virtually anyone without the knowledge or consent of the consumer. It is the last two possibilities that cause the most concern among marketers and consumers.

The Internet also presents a new privacy issue—the ability to follow electronic movement and correspondence. Electronic tracks called "cookies" (see Chapter 10) can lead interested parties along the electronic paths taken by a single user. When visiting an Internet site a user's computer can be searched by the server at the Internet site for previous Internet activity. A record can be made and used or sold. In addition, e-mail addresses taken from electronic correspondence can be captured, used, and/or sold, generating unwanted electronic junk mail. Correspondence within a marketing firm is also susceptible to being read by unintended recipients. The lack of privacy inherent in electronic activity creates a challenge for marketers interested in protecting their customers, employees, and business strategies.

Consumers' privacy and security concerns need to be carefully managed as the marketing process evolves with new technology. Because electronic transmission of data is an integral part of emerging marketing processes, privacy and security issues must be an intrinsic part of any new marketing strategy. Privacy and security policies should be planned in advance to educate consumers about how data are collected, used, and protected, so they can have some control over how information about them will be used in future marketing efforts. Marketers must begin developing these policies now to ensure that the infrastructure exists to appropriately manage these issues.

CONCLUSION

So what will be the future of electronic marketing? Let's consider some possibilities.

You place a buy order for two plush bathrobes of a certain brand to be purchased at a retail selling price of $110 or less per robe. The process begins with your preferred search engine examining offerings from manufacturers, retailers, brokers, and other electronic marketers. The search can be designated for a single sweep of the Internet or an ongoing investigation. After some time the search engine identifies two sellers, one in San Francisco and one in London. The search engine then automatically notifies both sellers that their price is being matched by a competing firm and asks for a counter offer. An order is placed with the retailer offering the lowest total price, including shipping, without your personal involvement.

Or, consider maintaining purchase records with an electronic retailer of clothing, including sizes, colors, and styles. The retailer could send a message when new merchandise is available that is comparable to the size, color, and style previously purchased. Retailers with manufacturing capabilities may simply manufacture the clothing you want after you choose from available fabrics. Similar purchases can be made for friends and family members whose size, color, and style information is likewise on file. And after you have worn your current pair of running shoes for seven months and ten days, an e-mail arrives informing you that in the past you reordered running shoes after eight months.

When your busy schedule means planning this weekend's dinner party at 11:30 P.M. Thursday night, you will do so with the confidence that you have a partner in your on-line supermarket. The supermarket software will go directly to the products you want or direct you through an interactive exercise designed to match your menu ideas with the types of foods available for the necessary number of guests. The software will identify complementary dishes, provide recipes, give nutrition information, check inventory levels, offer available manufacturer coupons, and place the order. You can choose to have the order delivered or you can pick it up at the drive-through on your way home from work Friday night. Should your plans for Friday evening change, a quick e-mail will move the merchandise from a Friday evening pick-up to a Saturday morning delivery.

To simplify your home maintenance problems you contract with a single firm to monitor the performance of virtually every electronic device in your home. Televisions, computers, integrated stereo systems, electric appliances, lighting, security, and heating and air conditioning units will all be checked from a central location before a costly maintenance visit is made.

The main challenge, of course, is predicting which technology/marketing changes will occur, and when. Some may never occur. For example, the pneumatic distribution systems outlined by Edward Bellamy (1888) never gained a foothold, and the last of the automats, automated cafeterias dispensing high-quality food through vending machines, closed some time ago. Nonetheless, electronic marketing will continue to grow because of the flexibility, information, and speed associated with electronic communications. The marketing challenge and opportunity, therefore, are found in identifying the products and services consumers will choose to purchase through the various electronic formats. Satellite-based interactive television, the Internet, CD-ROMs, video kiosks, and a host of other formats present marketers with their most important challenge: Where should they place chronically short resources? Although we cannot answer this question, we believe that, following the general philosophy of marketing, the firm that chooses well will be the one that best understands its customers.

References

Ainscough, Thomas L., and Michael G. Luckett. "The Internet for the Rest of Us: Marketing on the World Wide Web." *Journal of Consumer Marketing* 13 (Sept. 1996): 36–47.

Asimov, Isaac. "The Super Market 2077 A. D." *Progressive Grocer* 56 (June 1977): 52–3.

Babin, Barry J., William R. Darden, and Mitch Griffin. "Work and/or Fun: Measuring Hedonic and Utilitarian Shopping Value." *Journal of Consumer Research* 20 (March 1994): 644–56.

Baig, Edward. "How to Practice Safe Surfing." *Business Week* 3492 (Sept. 9, 1996): 120–1.

Baker, Michael J. *Companion Encyclopedia of Marketing.* London, England: Routledge, 1995, p. 626.

Baskin, Carolyn. "From the Locker Room to the Living Room." *PC World* 13 (Nov. 1995): 72.

Bellamy, Edward. *Looking Backward, 2000–1887.* Boston, MA: Ticknor and Company, 1888.

Benjamin, Robert, and Rolf Wigand. "Electronic Markets and Virtual Value Chains on the Information Superhighway." *Sloan Management Review* 36 (Winter 1995): 62–72.

Bennett, Peter D. *Dictionary of Marketing Terms,* 2nd ed. Lincolnwood, IL: NTC Business Books, 1995.

Berthon, Pierre, Leyland F. Pitt, and Richard T. Watson. "The World Wide Web as an Advertising Medium." *Journal of Advertising Research* 36 (Jan./Feb. 1996): 43–54.

Bitran, Gabriel, and Maureen Lojo. "A Framework for Analyzing the Quality of the Customer Interface." *European Management Journal* 11 (Dec. 1993): 385–96.

Blattberg, Robert C., and John Deighton. "Interactive Marketing: Exploiting the Age of Addressability." *Sloan Management Review 33* (Fall 1991): 5–14.

Bollier, David. "The Future of Electronic Commerce, A Report on The Fourth Annual Aspen Institute Roundtable on Information Technology." The Aspen Institute, Aspen, CO (http://www.aspeninst.org) (1995).

Borsuk, Mark. "Third Wave Wipeout: Infotech's Impact on Retail Space Demand." Paper presented at Institute for Real Estate Management Mid-Year Convention, June, 1996.

Boston Business Journal. "Retailers Open Online, But Will Shoppers Buy?" 15 (Dec. 22, 1995): 1.

Braun, Harvey D. "Catalog Shoppers and What Sets Them Apart." *Retail Market Analysis* 1 (1992): 6.

_____. "Just What Kind of People Buy from TV-Shopping Shows?" *Retail Market Analysis* 2 (1993): 1.

Burger, Dale. "On-line Sales to Reach $230B." *Computing Canada* 22 (Jan. 18, 1996): 17.

Burke, Raymond R. "Virtual Shopping: Breakthrough in Marketing Research." *Harvard Business Review* 74 (Mar./Apr. 1996): 120–31.

_____, Bari A. Harlam, Barbara E. Kahn, and Leonard M. Lodish. "Comparing Dynamic Consumer Choice in Real and Computer-simulated Environments." *Journal of Consumer Research* 19 (June 1992): 71–82.

Burstein, Daniel, and David Kline. *Road Warriors.* New York, NY: Dutton Books, 1995.

Business Week. "Internet Travelers Aren't Fed Up—Yet." 3490 (Aug. 26, 1996): 66.

Business Wire. "IDC Exposes the Truth about Cybershopping." May 6, 1996.

_____. "Electronic Sales Revenues Total $227M in 1Q 1996," May 13, 1996.

Canter, Laurence A., and Martha S. Siegel. *How to Make a Fortune on the Information Superhighway: Everyone's Guerrilla Guide to Marketing on the Internet and Other On-line Services.* New York, NY: HarperCollins, 1994.

Champy, James, Robert Buday, and Nitin Nohria. "The Rise of the Electronic Community." *CSC Index Insights* (Spring 1996): 1–15.

Chatterjee, Rabikar, and Sunil Gupta. "The 'Double Diffusion' Process: The Case of the World Wide Web." Paper presented at the Marketing Science Conference, Sydney, Australia, 1995.

Clodfelter, Richard, and James Overstreet. "Technological Profiles of Shopping Centers: Present and Future Use." *Journal of Shopping Center Research* (Spring/Summer 1996): 59–94.

Colman, Price. "Diller Consolidates Position with HSN Deal." *Broadcasting and Cable* 126 (Sept. 2, 1996): 48–9.

"CommerceNet/Nielsen Internet Demographics Recontact Study—March/April 1996, Executive Summary" (http://www.commerce.net/work/pilot/nielsen_96/exec.html).

"Computers." *Standard & Poor's Industry Surveys* (June 22, 1995): C64.

Computerworld. "Opening Day Jitters Hit Wal-Mart Site," 30 (Aug. 6, 1996): 6.

Dabholkar, Pratibha A. "Consumer Evaluations of New Technology-based Self-service Options: An Investigation of Alternative Models of Service Quality." *International Journal of Research in Marketing* 13 (Feb. 1996): 29–51.

Davidow, William. "Information Sage: Those Who Understand What Information Replaces Will Not Only Live Well But Prosper." *Forbes* 158 (Oct. 7, 1996): S138.

Delhagen, Kate, and Sara H. Eichler. "Women Connect." *The Forrester Report* (July 1996): 7.

Deloitte & Touche. *A Special Report on the Impact of Technology on Direct Marketing in the 1990s.* New York, NY: Direct Marketing Association, Inc., 1990.

Dholakia, Ruby Roy, Birgit Pederson, and Neset Hikmet. "Married Males and Shopping: Are They Sleeping Partners?" *International Journal of Retail and Distribution Management* 23 (No. 3, 1995): 27–33.

Discount Store News. "Internet Shopping Advances." 35 (May 6, 1996): 17.

Doody, Alton F., and William R. Davidson. "Next Revolution in Retailing." *Harvard Business Review* 45 (May/June 1967): 4–16, 20, 188.

Eastlick, Mary Ann, and Richard A. Feinberg. "Gender Differences in Mail-Catalog Patronage Motives." *Journal of Direct Marketing* 8 (Spring 1994): 37–44.

Economist. "Net Profits." (July 9th, 1994): 83–5.

English, Wilke D. "Videotex: Pandora's Box for Retailers." *Journal of Direct Marketing* 4 (Spring 1990): 7–20.

Financial Times. "The Online Challenge Flowers." (March 14, 1996): 23.

Fleischman, John. "In Classical Athens, A Market Trading in the Currency of Ideas." *Smithsonian* 24 (July 1993): 38–42, 44, 46–7.

Forman, Andrew M., and Ven Sriram. "The Depersonalization of Retailing: Its Impact on the 'Lonely' Consumer." *Journal of Retailing* 67 (Summer 1991): 226–43.

Forrest, Edward, and Richard Mizerski. *Interactive Marketing.* Chicago, IL: NTC Business Books, 1996.

Fox, Bruce. "Retailing on the Internet: Seeking Truth Beyond the Hype." *Chain Store Age Executive* 71 (Sept. 1995): 33–72.

Fram, Eugene H., and Dale B. Grady. "Internet Buyers: Will the Surfers Become Buyers?" *Direct Marketing* 58 (Oct. 1995): 63–85.

Gattuso, Gary. "Data Building Stressed by Retailers for 1996." *Direct Marketing* 58 (Feb. 1996): 7–8.

Gimein, Mark. "Paxson Stock Tests Market." *Mediaweek* 6 (Feb. 12, 1996): 8.

Glicklich, Peter A., Sanford H. Goldberg, and Howard J. Levine. "Internet Sales Pose International Tax Challenges." *Journal of Taxation* 84 (June 1996): 325–30.

Gonyea, James C., and Wayne M. Gonyea. *Selling on the Internet: How to Open an Electronic Storefront and Have Millions of Customers Come to You.* New York, NY: McGraw-Hill, 1996.

Grant, August E. "Researching the Social Environment of New Communication Technologies." In *Communication Technology Update*, August E. Grant, ed. Austin, TX: Technology Futures, Inc., 1993, pp. 339–49.

―――――, K. Kendall Guthrie, and Sandra J. Ball-Rokeach. "Television Shopping: A Media System Dependency Perspective." *Communication Research* 18 (Dec. 1991): 773–98.

―――――, Jennifer Harman Meadows, and Susan L. Handy. "The Passive Audience for Interactive Technology." *New Telecom Quarterly* 4 (Jan. 1996): 48–51.

Greco, Susan. "The Road to One-to-One Marketing." *Inc. Magazine* 17 (October 1995): 56–62.

Hagel, John III, Ennius E. Bergsma, and Sanjeev Dheer. "Placing Your Bets on Electronic Networks." *McKinsey Quarterly* (No. 2, 1996): 56–67.

Hapgood, Fred. "Foreign Entanglements." *CIO Magazine* 9 (Jan. 15, 1996): 38–43.

Harris, Kathryn. "Is Diller Scheming or Just Dreaming?" *Fortune* 132 (Dec. 25, 1995): 164.

Heenan, David A. "Global Trends: The Rise of a World-Wide Cybermarket." *Journal of Business Strategy* 16 (May/June 1995): 20–1.

Helliwell, John. "J.C. Penney to Establish TV, Phone Shop-At-Home Service." *PC Week* 4 (Sept. 1, 1987): C-1, C-4, C-41.

Herbig, Paul A., and Ralph L. Day. "Customer Acceptance: The Key to Successful Introductions of Innovations." *Marketing Intelligence and Planning* 10 (No. 1, 1992): 4–15.

Hilzenrath, David S. "Putting Prices on the Line: Bargain Hunting in Cyberspace May Not Live Up to Its Advance Billing." *Washington Post National Weekly Edition* 119 (Aug. 5–11, 1996): 21.

Hoffman, Donna L., William Kalsbeek, and Thomas P. Novak. "Internet and Web Use in the United States: Baselines for Commercial Development." Working paper, Vanderbilt University, TN: Owen Graduate School of Management, 1996.

―――――, and Thomas P. Novak. "Marketing in Hypermedia Computer-Mediated Environments: Conceptual Foundations." *Journal of Marketing* 60 (July 1996): 50–68.

Hoge, Cecil C., Jr., *The Electronic Marketing Manual: Integrating Electronic Media into Your Marketing Campaign.* New York, NY: McGraw-Hill, Inc., 1993.

Horton, Donald, and R. Richard Wohl. "Mass Communication and Para-social Interaction." *Psychiatry* 19 (Aug. 1956): 215–29.

Hyde, Linda L., Carl E. Steidtmann, and Daniel J. Sweeney. *Retailing 2000.* Columbus, OH: Management Horizons, 1990.

Information Week. "Electronic Commerce—The Web 'Ads' Up." (Aug. 5, 1996): 40.

Jarvenpaa, Sirkka L., and Peter A. Todd. "Consumer Reactions to Electronic Shopping on the World Wide Web." *Journal of Electronic Commerce* 1 (1996), forthcoming.

Judge, Paul C. "Why Firefly has Madison Avenue Buzzing." *Business Week* 3496 (Oct. 7, 1996): 100.

Kahn, Herman, and Anthony J. Wiener. *The Year 2000.* New York, NY: The Macmillan Company, 1967.

Kalakota, Ravi, and Andrew B. Whinston. *Frontiers of Electronic Commerce.* Reading, MA: Addison-Wesley Publishing Company, Inc., 1996.

Kang, Jikyeong, Youn-Kyung Kim, and Wen-Jan Tuan. "Motivational Factors of Mall Shoppers: Effects of Ethnicity and Age." *Journal of Shopping Center Research* 3 (Spring/Summer 1996): 7–32.

Karolefski, John. "Envisioning an Electronic Market." *Supermarket News* 45 (Jan. 16, 1995): S19.

Kearney, A. T. *Marketing in the Interactive Age.* New York, NY: Direct Marketing Association, Inc., 1996.

Kiley, Kathleen. "The Cyberspace Database Information Overload." *Catalog Age* 12 (Sept. 1, 1995): 56–8.

Klopfenstein, Bruce C. "Forecasting Consumer Adoption of Information Technology and Services—Lessons from Home Video Forecasting." *Journal of the American Society for Information Science* 40 (Jan. 1989): 17–26.

Koschnick, Wolfgang. *Dictionary of Marketing.* Aldershot, England: Gower, 1995, p. 173.

Kotler, Philip. *Marketing Management,* 9th ed. Englewood Cliffs, NJ: 1997.

Lanham, Richard A. *The Electronic Word: Democracy, Technology, and the Arts.* Chicago, IL: University of Chicago Press, 1993.

Levin, Gary. "Infomercial Demos Get Lift in New Survey." *Advertising Age* 65 (October 25, 1993): 3, 62.

Levine, Johathan B. "Customer, Sell Thyself." *Fast Company* 3 (June/July 1996): 148–52.

Levy, Steven. "Microsoft Century." *Newsweek* 128 (Dec. 2, 1996): 56–62.

Liebeck, Laura. "Grocery Shopping in Cyberspace: On-line Services and Retailers 'Shop' for Customers." *Discount Store News* 35 (Oct. 7, 1996): F48-49.

Lustigman, Alyssa. "Visiting the Virtual Mall." *Sporting Goods Business* 28 (June 1995): 36.

Mahajan, Vijay, and Jerry Wind. "Market Discontinuities and Strategic Planning: A Research Agenda." *Technological Forecasting and Social Change* 36 (Aug. 1989): 185–99.

McNair, Malcolm P., and Eleanor G. May. "The Next Revolution of the Retailing Wheel." *Harvard Business Review* 56 (Sept./Oct. 1978): 81–91.

McRae, Hamish. *The World in 2020.* London, England: Harper Collins, 1994.

Meadows, Jennifer Harman, Susan L. Handy, and August E. Grant. "I Like to Watch: Passive Consumption of Television Shopping as an Interactive Experience." Paper presented at the Annual Convention of the Broadcast Education Association, April, 1996.

Miller, Thomas E. "Segmenting the Internet." *American Demographics* 18 (July 1996): 48–52.

Mitchell, Vincent-Wayne. "Factors Affecting Consumer Risk Reduction: A Review of Current Evidence." *Management Research News* 16 (Nos. 9/10, 1993): 6–20.

Molenaar, Cor. *Interactive Marketing.* Aldershot, England: Gower, 1996.

Moriarty, Rowland T., and Gordon S. Swartz. "Automation to Boost Sales and Marketing." *Harvard Business Review* 67 (Jan./Feb. 1989): 100–08.

Moylan, Martin J. "US West Powers Up Potential of Electronic Yellow Pages." Knight-Ridder News Service (Sept. 3, 1996).

New Media Age. "Retailers Remain Cautious on Internet." (March 28, 1996): 11.

New Straits Times. "Survey Shows Interest in Internet Shopping." (May 13, 1996): 34.

NIMA International Fact Book 1996–97. Washington, DC: NIMA International, 1996.

O'Reilly and Associates. "Survey of Internet Usage" (http://www.ora.com/www/info/ research/users/index.html) (1995).

Quelch, John A., and Lisa R. Klein. "The Internet and International Marketing." *Sloan Management Review* 37 (Spring 1996): 60–75.

Raphel, Murray. "How Supermarkets Capture Customers with Their 'Net'." *Direct Marketing* 59 (May 1996): 14–16.

Retail Preview - Softgoods. Management Horizons 14 (Jan. 1996).

Rosenberg, Jerry M. *Dictionary of Marketing and Advertising.* New York, NY: John Wiley & Sons, Inc. 1995, p. 107.

Rosenberg, Larry J., and Elizabeth C. Hirschman. "Retailing without Stores." *Harvard Business Review* 58 (July/Aug. 1980): 103–12.

Rosenburg, Joyce M. "Malls Entice with Fun." Associated Press (Sept. 3, 1996).

Russell, Bertrand. *ICARUS or the Future of Science.* New York, NY: E. P. Dutton & Company, 1924.

San Diego Daily. "Buying on Internet Rises as Fear of Credit-Card Theft Falls." (May 28, 1996): 1.

Schneiderman, Ron. "Non-Store Shopping Growing as Consumer Habits Change." *Merchandising* 5 (Sept. 1980): 60–1.

Schwartz, Susana. "Enrollment System Aids Provident Agents." *Insurance and Technology* 21 (Feb. 1996): 16–20.

Seel, Peter. "High Definition Television and Advanced Television." In *Communication Technology Update*, 5th ed., August E. Grant, ed. Newton, MA: Focal Press, 1996, pp. 101–13.

Sheth, Jagdish N., and Rajendra S. Sisodia. "The Information Mall." *Telecommunications Policy* (July 1993): 376–89.

_____, and Rajendra S. Sisodia. "Feeling the Heat: Part I." *Marketing Management* 4 (Fall 1995): 8–23.

_____, and Rajendra S. Sisodia. "Feeling the Heat: Part II." *Marketing Management* 4 (Winter 1995): 19–33.

Skumanich, Stephanie. "Television Shopping." In *Communication Technology Update*, 4th ed., August E. Grant, ed. Newton, MA: Focal Press, 1995, pp. 63–73

Steinmetz, Charles P. "You Will Think This is a Dream." In *1999 the World of Tomorrow,* Edward Cornish, ed. Washington, D.C.: World Future Society, 1978, pp. 20–3.

Supermarket News. "Trend Watch 2000: A Special Report on How Industry Changes are Converging to Define the Future." 46 (April 29, 1996): 1.

Wallechinsky, David, Amy Wallace, and Irving Wallace. *The Book of Predictions.* New York: William Morrow and Company, 1981.

Wehling, Bob. "The Future of Marketing: What Every Marketer Should Know about Being On-line." *Vital Speeches* 62 (Jan. 1, 1996): 170.

Wildstrom, Stephen H. "Privacy and the Cookie Monster." *Business Week* 3506 (Dec. 16, 1996): 22.

Williams, Katie. "Media, Media, Media." In *Infomercial Insights.* Frank Cannella, Jr., ed. Burlington, WI: Cannella Response Television, 1995, pp. 115–23.

Williamson, Alistair D. *Field Guide to Marketing.* Boston, MA: Harvard Business School Press, 1994.

Wingfield, Nick. "Survey Finds Low Interest in Internet Shopping." *InfoWorld* 17 (June 12, 1995): 38.

Wolfe, David B. "A Behavior Model for Imparting Empathy to Relationship Marketing in Cyberspace," in *Proceedings of the Third Research Conference on Relationship Marketing: Contemporary Knowledge of Relationship Marketing,* Center for Relationship Marketing, Emory University, Atlanta, GA, 1996.

Zuckerman, Laurence. "Pushing the Envelope on Delivery of Customized Internet Data." *The New York Times* 146 (Dec. 9, 1996): C5, D5.

Index

About the Contributors

WALTER A. "TREY" BRADLEY is Senior Vice President and Chief Information Officer of Mary Kay, Inc. He joined Mary Kay, Inc., in 1994 and has since helped reshape and refocus its Information Services and Technologies (IST) organization to better meet the company's business needs. Under Mr. Bradley's direction, IST teams have launched Mary Kay *InTouch*™ for the company's sales force directors, improved annual business records, and recast the role of information management to better serve the firm. Mr. Bradley is a member of the Board of Directors of the Texas Department of Information Resources; he is also a member of the Direct Selling Association's Internet Council. Prior to joining Mary Kay, Inc., Mr. Bradley was with Price Waterhouse, United Medicorp, Inc., and Andersen Consulting. He holds a B.B.A. in Accounting from the University of Mississippi.

RAYMOND R. BURKE is E.W. Kelley Professor of Business Administration at Indiana University. He teaches marketing research in the MBA program and courses in the executive and Ph.D. programs. Dr. Burke was previously Associate Professor of Business Administration at the Harvard Business School and Assistant Professor of Marketing at the University of Pennsylvania's Wharton School. Dr. Burke's research focuses on understanding the influence of point-of-purchase factors on consumer shopping behavior. He also investigates the impact of electronic home shopping services. His virtual shopping technology is used by research firms in the United States, Canada, Europe, Asia-Pacific, and Mexico. Dr. Burke's articles have appeared in various journals, including *Harvard Business Review, Journal of Consumer Research, Journal of Marketing,* and *Marketing Science.* He is also coauthor of the book *ADSTRAT: An Advertising Decision Support System.*

RABIKAR CHATTERJEE is Associate Professor of Business Administration at the University of Pittsburgh. He received an undergraduate degree in chemical engineering and an MBA in India, where he worked in industry for eight years prior to obtaining his Ph.D. from the University of Pennsylvania. He has also served on the faculties of Purdue University and the University of Michigan. Professor Chatterjee's research interests include models of market response to new products and services, especially major innovations (such as electronic commerce), and methods for measuring and representing consumer perceptions and preferences, particularly in situations where consumers may be uncertain about the choice alternatives. His articles have been published in various journals, including *Journal of Marketing Research, Management Science,* and *Psychometrika.*

ANDREW DONOHO is principal of Donoho Design Associates in Austin, Texas. He has served as chief executive officer of two firms, D2 Software and Fusion, Inc., and is the only developer to have won *MacUser's* "Four Mouse" rating for both a software product (D2's MacSpin) and a hardware product (Fusion's Tokamac accelerator board). He is a leading thinker on Internet-related matters and a frequent consultant to Apple and other computer and software companies.

AUGUST E. "AUGIE" GRANT, Associate Professor of Radio-Television-Film at The University of Texas at Austin, is a former broadcaster who is on permanent leave from the broadcasting industry to teach and conduct research. Immediately after completing his doctorate at the University of Southern California, he joined the Department of Radio-Television-Film at The University of Texas at Austin. Although his primary interest is mass communications technology, his research and teaching reflect the convergence of communication forms through the application of new technologies. He has written numerous articles and papers about high-definition television, television audience behavior, television shopping services, theories of new media, and emerging communication technologies. He is also editor of *Communication Technology Update,* an annual review of the latest developments in more than three dozen technologies in electronic mass media, telephony, consumer electronics, computers, and satellites. Professor Grant serves as a consultant to various media organizations regarding television audience behavior and new communication technologies.

SUNIL GUPTA is a faculty member in the Marketing Department and directs the HERMES project at the University of Michigan. His research focuses on various aspects of commercial uses of the World Wide Web. Currently Dr. Gupta is working on projects aimed at understanding how the Web marketplace is likely to develop and evolve, the new types of competitive strategies needed to thrive in the on-line world, and the Internet's impact on the role of marketing research within a corporation. Professor Gupta's other research includes investigating issues of distribution channel design and efficiency, especially in newly developing economies. He is a faculty fellow of the William Davidson Institute, where he teaches about distribution channel issues faced by companies in transitional economies.

JOSEPH F. "JOE" HAIR, JR. is Alvin C. Copeland Endowed Professor of Franchising and Director, Institute for Entrepreneurial Education and Family Business Studies, College of Business Administration, Louisiana State University. He has authored 29 books and has published numerous articles in professional journals, such as *Journal of Marketing Research, Journal of the Academy of Marketing Science, Journal of Business,* and *Journal of Advertising Research.* Currently President of the Academy of Marketing Science and a Distinguished Fellow of the Southwestern Marketing Association and Southern Marketing Association, Professor Hair has been active in professional associations throughout his academic career. He has served as a marketing consultant and strategist for *Fortune 500* firms and has planned and presented executive development and management training programs in the United States and abroad.

KENNETH HILL is a senior manager at Dell Computer Corporation. He is currently responsible for the design, development, and implementation of the company's world wide Internet and Intranet services. This Dell business group was created in December 1995 and in less than six months launched an Intranet site with more than 7,000 users and an Internet site that generates 25,000 visitors a day. As one of the first 20 individuals to join Dell Computer more than 12 years ago, Hill has held several senior management positions in sales, marketing, manufacturing, and engineering. He is a frequent speaker at national conferences related to the Internet, Internet commerce, interactive marketing, and field sales force automation.

SIRKKA L. JARVENPAA is Associate Professor of Information Systems at The University of Texas at Austin. She served as a Marvin Bower Fellow at Harvard Business School during 1994. Professor Jarvenpaa received her Ph.D. in Management Information Systems from the University of Minnesota. She has published more than 50 research papers and a number of case studies. Dr. Jarvenpaa serves as the senior editor for *MIS Quarterly* and as an associate editor for *Management Science, Information Systems Research, Database, Journal of Electronic Commerce,* and *Journal of Computer-Mediated Communication.* Her research focuses on global information technology and electronic commerce.

S. KREGG JODIE is Director, Global Systems Development, at Mary Kay, Inc. He joined Mary Kay, Inc. in 1994 and has since launched Mary Kay *InTouch*™ for the company's sales force directors. He is also responsible for systems applications in 11 Mary Kay subsidiaries around the world. Mr. Jodie, a member of the American Production & Inventory Control Society (APICS) and Direct Selling Association (DSA), is certified in Production and Inventory Management (CIPM). Prior to his Mary Kay employment, he was with Andersen Consulting. He received a B.B.A. in Electrical Engineering Route to Business from The University of Texas at Austin.

WILLIAM W. KEEP is Assistant Professor in the College of Business and Economics at the University of Kentucky. He received a Bachelor of Science degree in Social Science and Economics from Michigan State University (MSU) in 1981 and a Ph.D. in Marketing from MSU in 1991. Dr. Keep teaches retail/distribution management at the University of Kentucky; his research interests include retailing, marketing strategies, and marketing history. He has published papers on retail image, shopping center and mail-order shopping, and retail diversification in such journals as *Journal of Macromarketing, Educational and Psychological Measurement, Journal of Retailing and Consumer Services, Journal of Marketing Channels, Industrial Marketing Management,* and *Journal of Managerial Issues.* He has recently completed research on shopping behavior funded by the International Council of Shopping Centers Education Foundation. His nonacademic experience includes two years with a retail trade association, three years with an electric wholesale firm, and experience in the public sector in both state and federal government.

LARRY R. LEIBROCK is a program manager for Hewlett Packard. Currently he is "on leave" to The University of Texas at Austin as Chief Technology Officer for the Graduate School of Business. After receiving his undergraduate degree, Dr. Leibrock served in the United States Army for eight years (presently he is a Lt. Colonel in the U.S. Army Reserves). He then entered the private sector, working for such firms as Electronic Data Systems, Sperry, Execucom, and Cimpoint prior to joining Hewlett Packard in 1989, where he specialized in Federal and NATO information security and network operations. In 1994 he received his Ph.D. from the University of Texas in Information Sciences.

WALTER MAYBERRY is one of the founders of Sequent Computer Systems. He currently is an Internet entrepreneur and investor.

JOHN M. MCCANN is Professor in the Fuqua School of Business at Duke University. Professor McCann holds a Ph.D. from Purdue University and has taught at Cornell University and the University of California at Berkeley. Previously he worked in new product development at General Electric and IBM and was employed as a managing consultant at Data Resources, Inc. Dr. McCann's current teaching interests include a series of offerings titled Courses in Managerial Informatics; he is also developing a new course titled Marketing in a

Globally Internet-worked World. He founded and directed the Marketing Workbench Laboratory, a research center at the Fuqua School dedicated to researching methods for using marketing information. This laboratory was sponsored by IBM and 25 large consumer packaged-goods manufacturers, retailers, and vendors. The laboratory's research program produced more than 20 knowledge-based systems, which are described in two books: *Expert Systems for a Scanner Data Environment* and *Databases and Knowledge Systems in Merchandising*. Professor McCann's articles have appeared in *Marketing Science, Management Science, Journal of Marketing Research, Journal of Consumer Research, Organizational Behavior and Human Performance, Journal of the Academy of Marketing Science,* and *Naval Logistics Quarterly,* among others.

ROBERT A. PETERSON holds the John T. Stuart III Centennial Chair in Business Administration and the Charles Hurwitz Fellowship at the IC^2 Institute, The University of Texas at Austin. Professor Peterson is a past chairman of the Department of Marketing Administration at The University of Texas at Austin and past editor of *Journal of Marketing Research* and *Journal of the Academy of Marketing Science.* He has authored or coauthored in excess of 150 books and articles; his articles have appeared in nearly four dozen journals. Professor Peterson has received numerous awards and honors. He is listed in such standard references as *Who's Who in America,* and in 1988 he received the Outstanding Marketing Educator Award from the Academy of Marketing Science. In 1991 he was a recipient of the Circle of Honor Award from the Direct Selling Education Foundation. He is a fellow and past president of the Southwestern Marketing Association, a former vice president of the American Marketing Association, and has served on the governing boards of the Academy of Marketing Science and the Decision Sciences Institute. Currently he chairs the Board of Governors of the Academy of Marketing Science.

FRED PHILLIPS is Professor of Management and Head of the Department of Management in Science and Technology at the Oregon Graduate Institute. He is also an affiliate staff scientist at Battelle-Pacific Northwest Laboratories. Until 1995 he was at The University of Texas at Austin, where he held the titles of Director of Research and Academic Programs and the Judson Neff Centennial Fellow at the IC^2 Institute, and where he served as Senior Lecturer on the faculties of Marketing, Economics, and Asian Studies. Formerly a vice president at MRCA Information Services, where he designed the industry's first interactive computer inquiry system for data-based consumer research, Dr. Phillips attended Tokyo Institute of Technology and received his Ph.D. from The University of Texas at Austin in Mathematics and Management Science. He has held teaching and research positions at the Universities of Aston and Birmingham in England, General Motors Research Laboratories, and St. Edward's University. He is the author or coauthor of many publications in operations research and marketing. Dr. Phillips is a founder and member of the Advisory Board of the Austin

(Texas) Software Council, advises several software companies, and teaches a course in software commercialization at the Oregon Graduate Institute.

KAREN SHAPIRO is Vice President and Internet Channel Manager at Bank of America in San Francisco. She is responsible for the Bank's Internet strategy and presence. Dr. Shapiro and her team work with all departments of the corporation that have a business need to be on the Internet. During her 15 years at Bank of America, she developed and managed a school to train upscale bankers and implemented end-user computer support programs. Previously Dr. Shapiro served as a consultant to the Corporation for Public Broadcasting, the National Endowment for the Arts, the National Institute for Education, and KQED-TV, San Francisco's public television station. Dr. Shapiro began her career in the late 1960s as co-founder of the underground TV theater, Channel One. Material from several Channel One programs was coalesced into a film that became a comedy cult classic, "The Groove Tube." Dr. Shapiro's bachelor's degree is from Columbia University, and she earned a Ph.D. from Stanford University, where she taught several courses on the structure of mass media industries, audience behavior, and the construction of TV commercials. Dr. Shapiro has been actively involved in the multimedia community in San Francisco for the past eight years, serving as Vice President of the International Interactive Communications Society in 1992; in 1993 she was elected to the founding board of the Multimedia Development Group.

JAGDISH N. SHETH is Charles Kellstadt Professor of Marketing in the Gouizeta Business School, Emory University. Formerly he was Robert Brooker Professor of Marketing at the University of Southern California and Walter Stellner Distinguished Professor of Marketing at the University of Illinois. He has also served on the faculties of Columbia University and the Massachusetts Institute of Technology. Dr. Sheth has published 26 books and more than 200 articles in marketing and other business disciplines. One of his books, *The Theory of Buyer Behavior* (with John A. Howard), is a classic in the field of consumer behavior and is one of the most cited works in marketing. He has received numerous awards for his work, including the 1992 P.D. Converse Award for outstanding contributions to theory in marketing from the American Marketing Association. He has also been named an Outstanding Marketing Educator by the Academy of Marketing Science and has received the Outstanding Educator Award from Sales and Marketing Executives International. Professor Sheth has worked for numerous companies in the United States, Europe, and Asia, both as a consultant and a seminar leader. His clients include AT&T, Bell Canada, Ford, Motorola, Northern Telecom, 3M, Whirlpool, and General Motors.

RAJENDRA S. SISODIA is Associate Professor of Business at George Mason University. Before joining GMU, he was Assistant Professor of

Marketing at Boston University. Dr. Sisodia has a Ph.D. from Columbia University. His research, teaching, and consulting expertise spans the areas of marketing strategy, marketing productivity, business impacts of information technology, Asia-Pacific business practices, and the impact of the information highway on marketing. Dr. Sisodia has published more than 40 articles in journals such as *Harvard Business Review, Journal of Business Strategy, Marketing Letters, Marketing Management, Marketing Research,* and *Journal of Services Marketing.* He has also authored about two dozen cases, primarily on strategic and marketing issues in the telecommunications industry, as well as a number of telecommunications industry and company analyses. He has served as a consultant to numerous companies, including IBM, Price Waterhouse, AT&T, MCI, Sprint, Bellcore, Perot Systems, Telecom Italia, BellSouth, and Northern Telecom.

DAVID SMITH, Vice President of New Media at KVO Advertising and PR in Portland, Oregon, is responsible for overseeing the strategic planning and implementation of clients' programs using a variety of multimedia techniques, including the World Wide Web, electronic mail, and CD-ROM. KVO's new media clients include Hitachi America, . CheckFree Corporation, First Technology Federal Credit Union, Mentor Graphics, Wall Data Corporation, and Tektronix. The New Media group helps KVO clients expand their business opportunities using the Internet and other computer-based communications. At KVO, Mr. Smith has also served as Associate Creative Director and Head Copywriter. Before joining KVO he worked in technical trade journalism and electrical engineering. He holds both bachelor's and master's degrees in Electrical Engineering from Cornell University.

PETER A. TODD is Associate Professor in the School of Business at Queen's University, where he chairs the Ph.D. program. He received his Ph.D. in Management Information Systems from the University of British Columbia. Dr. Todd has published articles in a variety of MIS journals, including *MIS Quarterly* and *Information Systems Research.* His primary research interests include the adoption and diffusion of information technology, decision support and behavioral decision making, and human-computer interaction.